Black Belt Scalawag

Black Belt

Scalawag

Charles Hays and the

Southern Republicans in

the Era of Reconstruction

William Warren Rogers, Jr.

The University of Georgia Press

Athens & London

© 1993 by the University of Georgia Press
Athens, Georgia 30602
All rights reserved
Designed by Erin Kirk
Set in 10 on 13 Janson Text by Tseng Information Systems, Inc.
Printed and bound by Thomson-Shore, Inc.
The paper in this book meets the guidelines for
permanence and durability of the Committee on
Production Guidelines for Book Longevity of the
Council on Library Resources.

Printed in the United States of America

97 96 95 94 93   C   5 4 3 2 1

Library of Congress Cataloging in Publication Data
Rogers, William Warren
    Black Belt Scalawag : Charles Hays and the Southern
    Republicans in the Era of Reconstruction / William Warren
    Rogers, Jr.
        p.   cm.
    Includes bibliographical references and index.
    ISBN 0–8203–1513–3 (alk. paper)
    1. Hays, Charles, 1834–1879. 2. Legislators — United States —
    Biography. 3. United States. Congress. House — Biography.
    4. Reconstruction — Alabama. 5. Alabama — Politics and
    government — 1865–1950. I. Title.
    E664.H415R64 1993
    328.73′092 — dc20
    [B]   92–25885
                                                        CIP

British Library Cataloging in Publication Data available

Photograph of Charles Hays on frontispiece by Mathew Brady.
Courtesy of Roberta Hays Lowndes.

To my father and mother

Contents

Preface

       Charles Hays seemed an unlikely convert to the Republican party during Reconstruction. Born into the Black Belt aristocracy of Alabama in 1834, he was raised in a prominent, slaveholding, Democratic family and was working slaves on his own plantation lands when the Civil War broke out. He resisted secession until Abraham Lincoln's election to the presidency and then took his place in the ranks of the Confederacy. The Civil War's outcome preserved the Union and assured the abolishment of slavery, but the advent of Reconstruction only provoked further bitter political strife. First in Alabama, and then on the national scene, Hays participated in the fratricidal politics of the times. In 1867 he defied Southern political orthodoxy and joined the Republican party. For the next ten years he was one of its most visible figures in Alabama, the leader of what amounted to a political army in the west-central part of the state. Its members, almost all former slaves, elected Hays repeatedly to office. He served as a delegate to the Alabama constitutional convention of 1867, sat in the state senate, and was elected to four terms in the U.S. House of Representatives. No other Southern Republican spent as much time in Congress during Reconstruction. And certainly no other Republican, at least in Alabama, was so vilified.

    Hays was a controversial figure in an era of unprecedented political tension and bitterness. Although Gen. Robert E. Lee's surrender at Appomattox Court House had settled the issue of the Union's divisibility, other questions remained. When and under what circumstances would the former Confederate states return to the Union? What was the status of the

four million former slaves? The Union was pieced back together before
the fate of the freedmen was determined. The former slaves' place in society, described by historians John and LaWanda Cox as the "critical issue"
of Reconstruction, would take much longer to resolve.[1]

The Republican party set the ultimate agenda for Reconstruction. That
party gained complete control of Congress in 1866 and of the presi-
dency two years later. Carried out under Republican auspices, "Radical Reconstruction" represented, as Eric Foner has recently noted, "a
radical departure, a stunning and unprecedented experiment in interracial democracy." Republican-sponsored legislation—most significantly
the First Military Reconstruction Act and the Fourteenth and Fifteenth
Amendments to the Constitution—seemed to portend democracy in the
South and full citizenship for the freedmen.[2]

The triumph of the congressional Republicans over President Andrew
Johnson forced major adjustments in the South. Although the details
varied, the pattern of Southern Reconstruction politics followed the same
weave. State Republican parties formed and claimed political power. Ar-
rivals from the North, pejoratively referred to as "carpetbaggers," and
Southern whites, derisively known as "scalawags," led the parties. The
freedmen comprised the foot soldiers. Republican-crafted constitutions
were ratified, Republican governors were inaugurated, and Republican-
dominated legislatures were convened—the political guard had changed.

As the party of Lincoln gained political ascendancy and the lines of Reconstruction crystallized, opposition among white Southerners formed. In
Alabama as elsewhere, a white majority attempted to undermine the newly
laid Republican foundation, which was based precariously on the national
party's commitment to the freedmen. What followed on a state level in
each of the eleven former Confederate states was a period of political turmoil. Democrats routinely faulted their adversaries for financial extravagance, corruption, usurpation of state authority, and military rule. But
from the outset the race question dominated debate. Differing perceptions
of the freedmen's place in society ultimately defined Reconstruction politics. On that question, the true measuring stick of Republicanism, Charles
Hays and his fellow party members were condemned as Radicals.

The specter of "black equality" justified the use of violence for some.
Central to this study, and of Reconstruction studies generally, is the theme
of political intimidation. The Ku Klux Klan, the White League, and other
night riders terrorized Republicans across the South well into the 1870s.

The Alabama Black Belt that Charles Hays knew illuminates the mentality, extent, and tragedy of the entire Reconstruction South.

Although violence contributed to the Republicans' fall from power in the South, so did party infighting, corruption, and the resiliency of the traditional white Democratic power base. The Democrats seized control of the state government in Alabama in 1874. "Redemption" was becoming a political reality in every Southern state, and the Republican party entered a period of sharp decline. Hays's postwar political career spanned the rise and fall of the Republican party in Alabama.

Traditional historiographical sources have afforded Charles Hays brief and unflattering attention. Walter Lynwood Fleming provided the first scholarly assessment of Hays's career in *Civil War and Reconstruction in Alabama* (1905). Fleming portrayed Hays as "the most notorious of the Reconstruction representatives."[3] The maligned scalawag's standing had not improved several decades later. Writing in 1940, John Witherspoon DuBose, author of *Alabama's Tragic Decade*, labeled Hays "the most active and turbulent of the scalawags."[4]

Fleming studied under William Archibald Dunning of Columbia University, a scholar who inspired an entire school of post–Civil War thought and writing. Reconstruction, the Dunning interpretation went, was a dark time of Republican misrule and corruption. Scheming carpetbaggers and scalawags used blacks as political pawns and helped themselves to the spoils of office. The aberration that was Radical Reconstruction went forward in each Southern state. In the 1870s legitimate government was restored and the costly sham of rule by miscreants concluded when Democrats scourged the Republicans from their temples in Jackson, Atlanta, Montgomery, and the other Southern state capitals.

Although the pioneer Dunning studies have real value, the work of more recent generations of historians, which has been aided greatly by the utilization of new source material, generally presents a more objective, revisionist view of Reconstruction. Revisionist state studies have provided a sympathetic perspective on Republican regimes, and several Republican party members have been rehabilitated in the process. Accounts such as William Harris's *The Day of the Carpetbagger* and Elizabeth Nathans's *Losing the Peace* outline events from a revisionist point of view in Mississippi and Georgia. On the subject of Reconstruction in Alabama Sarah Woolfolk Wiggins has made a fine start in *The Scalawag in Alabama Politics*, but no broad revision of the work of the Dunning school has been undertaken.[5]

But while the revisionist state studies have definitely begun to refurbish the reputation of the maligned scalawag, a closer look at this class of men and their motivations requires biographical treatment. There has been precious little of that. As early as 1963 Allen Trelease drew attention to the problem in an article entitled "Who Were the Scalawags?" "Next to no attention" had been paid to Southern Republicans, he observed, and the class remained "an unknown quantity." In several articles David Donald, William Harris, and Otto Olson have since attempted to come to terms with the scalawag class, yet the answer to Trelease's question remains uncertain.[6] The paucity of reliable sources partly explains this neglect. Collections of manuscripts are scarce, and so are Republican newspapers (only two in Alabama are of assistance).

Arguably the best biography of a Southern Republican is Lillian A. Pereyra's book on James Lusk Alcorn. In 1869 Alcorn became Mississippi's first Republican governor, and later he served in the U.S. Senate. As Pereyra points out, Republicanism for Alcorn was less about freedmen's rights than about economic development and reunion. In that way he represents a certain scalawag prototype. Alcorn and most Southern Republicans were moderates who worried that embracing Radicalism risked alienating whites whose conversion was essential to establishing Republicanism in the South. Their support for something resembling racial equality, an idea perhaps philosophically incompatible with other long-held beliefs, or perhaps simply politically unwise, was grudging and opportunistic. Eric Foner has confirmed this pattern recently in his *Reconstruction: America's Unfinished Revolution.*[7]

Charles Hays's biography reads differently. Although he shared the pragmatic concerns of other Southern Republicans, Hays's words and actions reveal a genuine compassion for the freedmen. In Republican newspapers, testimony collected by congressional investigative committees, and the pages of the *Congressional Globe* and *Record* he emerges as a man of conviction. Another measure of his empathy is revealed by the extreme invective directed at the Black Belt scalawag by Democrats.

True Radicalism was rare. The number of monographs on Southern Republicans is extremely limited. No study of a Radical exists. I have attempted here to address that void.

Acknowledgments

I am greatly indebted to many individuals for their help in completing this study. Michael Fitzpatrick, Wayne Flynt, Tennant McWilliams, Jerrell Shofner, and Robert David Ward read the manuscript and offered useful advice. Sam Webb and Lawrence Powell also have my thanks. I owe a special debt to Sarah Woolfolk Wiggins at the University of Alabama. An authority on Alabama Reconstruction, she suggested an approach and a framework in which to place Charles Hays. Other colleagues, including Mike Denham, John Inscoe, Ric Kabat, Paul Pruitt, and Ben Wall, have provided much appreciated encouragement. From Eutaw, Patta Steele unraveled some complicated transactions and expressed unfailing interest.

Much of the research was completed at the Alabama Department of Archives and History, in Montgomery. Staff members there, especially Joe Caver, Diane Jackson, and Keeta Kendall, were tremendously helpful. In Montgomery, Mr. and Mrs. Nimrod Frazier and the late Sarah Martin were gracious hosts. Bill Irwin, a transplanted Alabamian, provided direction at the William R. Perkins Library at Duke University; John White did the same at the Southern Historical Collection at the University of North Carolina. At Florida State University the staff of the Documents, Maps, and Micromaterial Department in the Ralph Strozier Library have been helpful and cooperative, as have the staffs at the National Archives and the Library of Congress. As fate would have it, I had the use of bound volumes of the *Congressional Record* donated by Hays at the University of

Alabama. I certainly appreciate the help and kindness of Joyce LaMonte and the entire special collections staff at the Amelia Gorgas Library in Tuscaloosa.

Obtaining materials often required going through interlibrary loan channels: Phyllis Holenburg, Barbara Strickland, and Priscilla Rankin have been exceedingly diligent. Also diligent were several typists: Miriam Rogers, Helen Ellis, Betty Wedgeworth, and Debbie Lilly. Gainesville College has been generous with various research grants, for which I am indebted to Steve Gurr and Amy Reeder. I would also like to thank Michael Senecal, who copyedited the manuscript.

Two people have been of inestimable benefit. Roberta Hays Lowndes, the granddaughter of Charles Hays, has welcomed me at her home in Decatur, Georgia, on numerous occasions. She has provided personal knowledge, correspondence, and photographs, and has added greatly to whatever merit this study may have. William Warren Rogers generously gave me the topic that he had started. He read various drafts and offered needed criticism as well as encouragement. I hope the end result begins to offer some repayment.

Black Belt Scalawag

1 An Aristocratic Background

Charles and Hannah Sommerville Hays joined the steady stream of Scots-Irish immigrants to America sometime in the latter half of the eighteenth century. They settled in the Chester District of South Carolina. Little outside of a genealogical order is known of their life there. A child, George, was born to them on November 12, 1779. Two more children, Charles and Mary, followed. The elder Charles Hays made a modest living by farming. When he died in about 1820, his family owned little. His oldest son sold what they did have. Assuming responsibility for the family, George Hays moved to Alabama with his mother and sister. Charles seems to have moved farther west.

Alabama was just opening up, and thousands of settlers from more established Southern states made the raw but potentially rewarding frontier their destination. George Hays settled in Greene County, prior to the Treaty of Fort Jackson in 1815 the domain of the Choctaw and Creek Indians. The county had been named for Revolutionary War hero Nathaniel Greene and was created in 1819 when Alabama became a state. Greene County lay in the heart of what would become known as the Alabama Black Belt, an area of rich dark soil stretching west from Montgomery (the future state capital) toward Mississippi that would soon support an extensive concentration of cotton plantations and slave laborers. Both the fertile loamy soil and a river system facilitating commerce attracted settlers to Greene County. The Tombigbee River, originating in Mississippi, flowed southeastwardly and defined the county's western boundary. The Black Warrior River wound serpentine-like through the county (and later became its eastern border). Following the Indian removal, settlers with surnames such as Meriwether, Steele, McKee, McAlpine, and Campbell streamed into the area. The early residents established themselves around such settlements as Boligee, Clinton, Forkland, Havana, Newbern, Mesopotamia, Pleasant Ridge, Springfield, and the first county seat, Erie.

Many of the settlers brought slaves with them, and others bought them after arriving. Whatever the circumstances of its introduction, forced black labor soon became central to prosperity of the county: the number of blacks increased quickly and early in the 1830s surpassed the white population. The racial imbalance continued to widen during the antebellum period. The 1850 census revealed that 9,265 whites lived in Greene as compared to 22,176 blacks.[1]

Not among the first, yet residing there before a large influx of settlers reached the county, George Hays purchased rich tracts of land in the "Fork," formed by the convergence of the Black Warrior and Tombigbee rivers in the southwestern reaches of Greene. He selected an elevated site near the community of Boligee to build the modest home that became known as Hays Mount and was living there at least by 1822, when he began serving as Boligee's justice of the peace.

George Hays never regretted leaving South Carolina. Greene County was typical Black Belt country, and the Black Belt—the American southwest in the 1820s and 1830s—was experiencing a veritable explosion of growth. For an enterprising man—and Hays was certainly that—opportunity was great. Various crops—corn, rye, wheat—flourished in this agricultural kingdom, yet the arable Black Belt soil was perfectly suited for the cultivation of the lucrative "Georgia green" strain of cotton, and all crops bowed to it. Always with diligence, if often wastefully, farmers and planters in Greene cultivated large amounts of the crop. Cotton commanded generally high prices, and, though planters claimed higher profits than the yeomanry, all classes were remunerated. Throughout the antebellum period Greene ranked among the highest cotton producing counties in Alabama. Hays quickly turned the indigenous advantages of the place to his own advantage.

If Hays did not own slaves when he arrived, he soon acquired them. From Thomas Patterson, a Greene County resident, Hays in 1828 purchased Moses (age seventeen), Harry (seventeen), and James (twenty-two) for $1,200. Several years later he paid slightly over $700 for three more young black males. There were many such transactions for which no records exist. Owning a work force of more than one hundred slaves by 1830, Hays had become an archetypal cotton planter, part of an aristocratic plantation class developing in one of the richest counties in the state.

Labor on his plantation lands differed little from the local pattern. Preparing the soil and planting took precedence as winter yielded to spring, and in late summer the work increased as harvesting began. Hays's slaves picked, ginned, and then hauled the cotton to a Tombigbee River landing where, loaded onto boats, the bales were transported to Mobile. Prosperity allowed (and soil erosion required) that planters constantly add to their land holdings. Hays transacted considerable business at St. Stephens, the Washington County land office that served much of central and south Alabama. The planter's name also appeared frequently in the grantee column of the Greene County deed books. Cultivating more acres required more labor as well, and by the late 1830s Hays owned more than 175 slaves.

Hays's extraordinary business acumen seems to have been matched by his generosity. He donated land near Boligee on which a church, Bethsalem Presbyterian, was built in the 1830s. He also sent supplies to Ireland and arranged for the passage of relatives victimized by the potato famine there. Many Hays beneficiaries from Ireland established themselves on lands in the Fork.[2]

The business-minded planter did not marry until he was fifty-six. On Christmas Eve 1832 he wed twenty-one-year-old Anne Miller Beville, the only child of Woodville Woodliff and Judith Wilson Beville. The Bevilles had moved to Greene County from Virginia and boasted a distinguished Huguenot lineage. Granting that a romantic attraction existed, the marriage between Hays and Anne Miller Beville did not lack an element of convenience. Hays wanted heirs. Apparently both recognized that their age difference might be a problem. Before becoming Mrs. George Hays, Anne Miller agreed to a contract limiting her share of the estate. The couple's first child, Charles, was born on February 2, 1834, at Hays Mount. Two girls, Mary (born in 1836) and George Anne (born in 1838), followed.

Only Charles would retain any memory of his father. Faced with deteriorating health, George Hays drafted a will in July 1838. On July 30 he died of an unknown illness. As the detailed will provided, Hays was dressed for burial "in suit of fine black cloth ruffle . . . black satin vest, black silk socks and pumps" and interred in a spot he had selected near Hays Mount.

The main beneficiary of his will was Anne Miller. The generous settle-

ment considerably enlarged on the marriage contract, which the will pronounced "null and void." Anne Miller received Hays Mount, quarterly
payments amounting to fifteen hundred dollars annually, and three house
servants: Eliza, Sarah, and Mary Bouden. The services of Dick, the gar-
dener, and Brister, who handled the carriages and horses, also accrued to
her. Hays's will reveals a devoted father as well as husband. He split his
extensive land holdings among Charles, Mary, and George Anne and also
divided his field slaves equally among the three. With obvious paternal
affection he specified that Charles receive his gold watch and rigging. He
also asked that both Mary and George Anne be provided carriages when
they turned fifteen and that on their next birthday both be given a chance
to select five hundred dollars worth of jewelry. Hays included some care-
ful advice for the executors concerning the girls: "Be very cautious about
whose company they go in, as there will be many attempts made to entrap
them for their fortune. Keep them from knowing men who are engaged
in no business." Finally, Hays specified that each should be provided a
"finished education" at schools "distinguished for their moral as well as
intellectual character."[3]

Widowed at the age of twenty-seven, Anne Miller Hays married John
Warburton Womack on December 27, 1839. Womack had not long resided
in Greene County, having spent most of his life in Butler County, Alabama. As editor of the *Greenville Whig* and as a state legislator, Womack
had been a leading Butler County citizen. Why and when he moved to
Greene County is not known, but once there he made friends and a fine
reputation. Womack owned slaves and land, but he depended on his law
practice for a living. He thought highly of the temperance cause, led a
sober life, but also enjoyed pleasurable pursuits. Writing his brother in
Butler County a month before he married Anne Miller, Womack related
his experiences at a Black Belt springs resort. He claimed, "I am now a beau
of the 'first water' — and captain of the banjo at this place."[4] Acquaintances
liked Womack, respected his abilities, and, as a contemporary assured, he
was "a boon companion, the center of the circle." Anne Miller appreciated
position and wealth. Womack offered both. All indications point to a suc-
cessful marriage. Charles, only five when his father died, quickly gained
several half sisters and brothers. Anne Miller Hays Womack gave birth to
Winston Lowndes (1840), Sidney (1842), Martha (1843), Pauline Caroline
(1845), and Octavia (1847).[5]

Only the outlines of Charles Hays's youth are known. He was raised in

Eutaw. The town had absorbed the tiny community of Mesopotamia and in 1839 replaced Erie as the Greene County seat. The growing Womack family required a large home, and a sprawling two-story wooden house on Mesopotamia Street suited them well. It was there that "Charley," as he was called, passed his boyhood. His education began at a local school directed by two brothers, A. A. and B. A. Archibald. Church was also mandatory. Womack was a staunch Methodist and capable of being puritanical. Charley was ten years old when Womack wrote that "not one of my children has ever tasted a drop of toddy—nor seen anybody else do it—nor shall they under my roof."[6] Leaving the Archibalds' tutelage, Charley enrolled at Greene Springs School (west of Eutaw near Havana) at about the age of twelve. Headmaster Henry Tutwiler offered a broad curriculum including ancient history, geography and languages, natural philosophy, mathematics, English, and a cryptic subject called "Mental and Moral Science." Besides instilling knowledge, Tutwiler determined to insure the "formation of and preservation of correct moral habits." Weekly compositions and daily recitations were feared only slightly less than the written and oral examinations that concluded each term. The headmaster's well-known aversion to corporal punishment provided only limited compensation.[7] "There is probably no school in the State, if in the South," averred a local newspaper editor, "where young men can be better prepared for the high classes in College."[8]

Womack's aversion to alcohol did not make a lasting impression on his stepson, who would enjoy bourbon all his life. Womack's love of politics, however, carried over completely: both stepfather and son found the political game continually absorbing. Originally a Whig, Womack had once chastised Andrew Jackson in a celebrated public letter. By the 1840s he had converted to the Democratic party and by late in that decade was prominent enough to receive mention as a gubernatorial candidate. Local Whigs and Democrats carried on animated debates, and Womack assumed a leading role in them. With good reason Hays would recall his pre-war identification with the Democratic party as stemming literally "from childhood up."[9]

At seventeen Hays left Eutaw to attend the University of Georgia (Franklin College) in Athens. Womack had some bearing on that decision, having attended the university himself. Hays took his place alongside twenty-one other freshman men in the fall of 1851. Owen's *Anabasis, Sallust*, and a *Review of Arithmetic* required his immediate attention. Church attendance and punctuality at a morning recitation in theology were also required. Classical studies—including Homer's *Iliad* and Horace's *Odes*—occupied him in his second and third freshman terms. No account of his academic record exists, but evidently Hays finished his freshman year and the first term of his sophomore year successfully before withdrawing, for reasons unknown. Faculty minutes recorded in February 1853 reveal that "A desmission [*sic*] was ordered to be sent out to Chas. Hays of the present Sophomore Class who left in good standing at the close of the last term."

After withdrawing from Georgia, Hays transferred to the University of Virginia in Charlottesville. Although the term had already begun, he was allowed to enroll in March. He elected to take courses in natural philosophy and chemistry and paid a fee of $30 for each of his areas of study. He obtained lodging at the Johnson Boarding House. Yet Hays did not stay at Virginia long.[10]

Controversy back home may have interrupted Hays's education. The management of his father's estate had not gone well. After George Hays's death in 1838 responsibility for the estate had devolved to William P. Gould as executor. One of Greene County's earliest residents, Gould was a planter and George Hays's friend and neighbor. Unfortunately, continual losses on the Hays estate strained and then broke the relationship between the Gould and Hays-Womack families. In 1845 the children of George Hays brought suit against Gould in the local chancery court, charging negligence and mismanagement. John Womack represented the plaintiffs and won the case. After Gould's removal the question of his financial compensation became the subject of adjudication. In 1851, the year Charles Hays went to college, the case was argued before the state supreme court. Although Gould's supervision had, as one justice admitted, been "unfortunate to the interest of the estate," the justices ruled that he was due compensation. The bench did not fix the amount, however, and the case was remanded to the chancery court.[11] As Gould wrote in his diary, "We have now arrived at a new epoch in the Seven years [*sic*] war with the Hays Estate."[12] The drawn-out struggle continued. Both sides called witnesses to establish their positions during 1852 and 1853. Ultimately Gould was awarded by the chancery court very little of the $6,000 he claimed, and the case was finally argued in 1854 before the state supreme court, whose justices upheld the chancery court settlement. An outraged Gould remained convinced that he was a victim of "legal robbery."[13]

Whether or not there was a relationship between Hays's decision to leave the University of Virginia and the adjudication can only be guessed. But Hays did leave Charlottesville, never to return. One year after the settlement, in 1855, he turned twenty-one and came into his inheritance. Despite the estate reverses, he immediately became a wealthy man. The course of his life seemed set. Hays could settle into the career his father and stepfather had envisioned for him.

Throughout his life Hays would demonstrate a penchant for the unconventional. But the next few years were relatively uncomplicated. Between 1855 and 1861 he remained in Greene County. He built a home in Boligee, ten miles south of Eutaw in the Fork, naming the modest residence "Sebastapol" in honor of the Russian Crimean outpost. At Sebastapol Hays began to build his personal library. Womack had sought to instill in all his children and stepchildren "the habit of thought and reflection," and as he became more mature Hays applied Womack's teaching. Without benefit of a complete college education, the mature Hays often quoted Byron to his wife and Shakespeare to political audiences, demonstrating his considerable talent for self-instruction.[14]

If Hays embraced "the habit of thought and reflection," he also exhibited a positively Jeffersonian love of the land. Under generally favorable conditions—tractable labor, superior soil, and usually high cotton prices—he successfully managed his plantation holdings, buying and selling land frequently and clearly prospering. In a series of land dealings two transactions stand out. In June 1856 the young planter sold a large but undisclosed amount of land to William McAlpine for $4,356. Two months later he bought Hays Mount (about 1,000 acres) from John and Anne Miller Womack. By 1860 he had over 2,000 acres of land in cultivation and was working nearly a hundred slaves. The efforts of his work force that year produced 6,000 bushels of corn and 220 bales of cotton. Bequeathed money, land, and slaves, Hays had built on his inheritance and owned an estate valued at $112,500. He was not yet thirty years old.[15]

Well before then, however, the debate over slavery threatened his world and the life of the South. The divisive question had killed one party (the Whig) and given birth to another (the Republican). Since taking on greater national importance following the Mexican War, the slavery expansion issue strained the bonds of the Union. In Greene County, where slavery defined social and economic life, John Womack became a forceful and eloquent defender of the peculiar institution. Tolerating little dissent, he accused the *Philadelphia Saturday Evening Post* of "secretly instilling abolitionist sentiments" and summarily canceled his subscription in 1855 when that journal printed a particularly offending article.

Nor could Hays ignore the mounting criticism of slavery. His position was both conventional and predictable: blacks were inferior and must be managed, and abolitionism threatened to undermine the entire framework of society. Hays would later speak disparagingly of the "chains of slavery," but now he exhibited no special empathy for blacks. In fact, if later critics are to be believed, he beat his chattel. To alter the master-slave arrangement was to question the natural order and invite utter chaos. Given Hays's background, he could hardly have thought otherwise. He agreed with Womack, who wrote in 1855, "God himself condemned the African race to that condition." [16]

As Hays feared, the debate over slavery, rather than subsiding, intensified in the late 1850s. By the 1860 presidential election the emotional question threatened to split the Union. Uniting under the Republican banner antislavery forces nominated Abraham Lincoln and drafted a platform opposing slavery's extension beyond its present boundaries. The right of owners to take their chattel into the territories divided the Democratic party into two irreconcilable camps. A Southern wing, led by Robert Barnwell Rhett, William Lowndes Yancey, and other "fire-eaters," insisted on full, federal protection of slavery in all territories. Northern Democrats favored the position articulated by Sen. Stephen A. Douglas of Illinois. A "popular sovereignty" exponent, Douglas believed that the citizens of each territory should decide the issue themselves. A significant number of Southerners accepted his argument.

Womack certainly did. He rejected the "Yanceyites" as extremists and defended the "Little Giant" in an open letter to the *Eutaw Independent Observer* in 1859. He wrote that to insist on slavery where the majority dissented represented "the extremest folly." The significance of the upcoming Charleston Democratic-party convention did not escape the fifty-nine-year-old barrister. "We are now standing on a narrow promontory," he declared, adding that "the hour is too solemn to debate the enactment of laws to protect slavery in the territories. . . ." [17] At the Charleston convention both Womack and Hays, who attended in unofficial capacities, supported Douglas and hoped for compromise. Years later Hays recalled his concern that "the disorganization of the Democratic party would bring about the dissolution of the Union." [18]

Developments in Charleston and what followed fulfilled his and Womack's worst fears. After the Democrats refused to satisfy the Southern extremists, the twenty-seven Alabama delegates ceremoniously departed on May 2 (under orders from the state Democratic party). Delegates from several other Southern states joined them the next day. The remaining Democrats failed to unite on a candidate and agreed to reconvene in Baltimore, Maryland, later in June.

The differences that divided the pro- and anti-Douglas factions in Alabama were not resolved during the interim. Meeting separately, the disputing camps further defined their respective positions at Montgomery on the same day, June 4. Those inclined to accept Douglas met at Commercial Hall on Montgomery's busiest thoroughfare, Dexter Avenue. The occasion also provided Hays's political baptism. He and four other delegates represented Greene County.

Later that month, in Baltimore, all hopes of forging a united Democratic coalition were dashed. The slavery question proved insoluble. Those dissatisfied with anything less than the positive support of slavery in the territories withdrew to Baltimore and nominated John C. Breckinridge, a Kentucky slaveowner and senator. Meanwhile, Northern and Southern Democrats amenable to popular sovereignty tapped Stephen Douglas.

Most Southerners left the regular Democratic party in 1860. Many supported Breckinridge, and others deserted for Tennessean John Bell, the nominee of the Constitutional Union ticket. The position of Hays and Womack—that Douglas was acceptable and the only Democrat who could defeat Lincoln—was shared by a comparative few. In the election Breckinridge easily carried Alabama and ten other slave states, but Lincoln triumphed in all the free states and emerged victorious. The Illinois politician's elevation to the White House was greeted with near universal outrage in the South. South Carolina promptly left the Union on December 20, 1860.

Many in Alabama were also seriously considering that course. In the Black Belt, where secession sentiment was strongest, even Womack succumbed. The embittered Democrat drafted a lengthy open letter recommending secession in early December 1860. Equivocation, he now believed, invited further economic exploitation by the North and the demise of slavery. With the admission of free states imminent, Womack reasoned, slavery's foes could eventually force emancipation. He could think of no reason for Alabama to remain in the Union and many for leaving a country dominated by "open and avowed enemies" who "hate and despise us and our institutions" and are "planning our destruction." [19]

Few argued with him in Greene County. If various issues caused strain and contributed to the sectional break, the slavery debate was most elemental. Questioning the peculiar institution in Greene, where a large number of citizens owned slaves, and where more cotton was raised in 1860 than in any other county in Alabama, provoked a predictable response. Following a visit to Eutaw from Boligee after the November election, William Gould anxiously noted the "intense excitement" and judged "Immediate Secession [*sic*] rampant." He recorded in his diary that citizens brazenly "talked loudly of guns and trumpets," as the "speediest and most effectual means of shivering to atoms the hated and abominable Union." [20]

Assenting to public opinion and a legislative ordinance, Gov. Andrew B. Moore called a state convention. Alabamians went to the polls on Christmas Eve 1860 and elected a body of delegates that convened at Montgomery on January 7, 1861. Following debate between the secessionists, who favored immediate withdrawal, and the cooperationists, who favored further deliberations, the secession ordinance passed on January 11 by a vote of 61 to 39, and Alabama became the fourth state to join the Confederate States of America. Mississippi and Florida had exited just days earlier. Georgia, Louisiana, and Texas soon followed Alabama, and after the April 12 firing on Fort Sumter, Virginia, Arkansas, North Carolina, and Tennessee also joined the Confederacy.

Hays had viewed the breakup of the Union with more trepidation than most Alabamians. His service as a delegate to the Douglas convention in Montgomery evinced a certain political temperance and caution. Having supported Douglas, he had opposed the extreme rhetoric of militant Southern voices. Yet he also resented abolitionism. As a Southerner he felt for his native region a strong kinship and a sense of loyalty (an attachment that survived the vilification of Reconstruction). And as a slaveholder, Hays felt personally threatened. Following Lincoln's election Womack believed "duty, honor, interest, safety, all require that Alabama should withdraw from the Union." [21] Hays had agreed with Womack in the past, and there is every reason to assume that he continued to be influenced by him. That he had entertained doubts concerning secession was largely irrelevant in spring 1861. Hays would serve the Confederacy.

Hays's service record defies precise documentation. He joined the staff of Lt. Col. (later Brig. Gen.) Marcus Joseph Wright sometime in 1861. Wright had recently married Hays's half-sister Pauline Caroline. Hays gained a preferred position as inspector general or aide-de-camp in the Army of the Tennessee. Comparatively few soldiers went to war with a servant. Two accompanied Hays. He was present at the Battle of Belmont in Missouri in November 1861, but he was back in Greene County soon thereafter, and he spent more than one extended period of the war at home. But it would be erroneous to state, as one individual did, that Hays "never heard a bullet whistle." He never shirked what he considered his duty. In April 1862 Hays was in Mississippi at Shiloh. Later that year, in September, he was present at the Battle of Chickamauga in Tennessee. After Chickamauga he was promoted to the rank of major.

In August 1863 John Womack died. Without Womack, who had conducted Hays's plantation business in his absence, Hays felt compelled to return home for good. The original Conscription Act of April 1862 granted an exemption to overseers on plantations with twenty or more slaves. Citing responsibilities on his plantations, Hays asked for and received a dispensation from military duty and went home to Sebastapol.[22]

Everything was not business. Hays passed a great deal of time in nearby Tuscaloosa. The attraction was Margaret Cornelia Minerva Ormond. Nicknamed "Queen" as a child, she was the daughter of John James and Minerva Jenkins Banks Ormond. Ormond was a native of Bristol, England, who had moved to Virginia and then to Alabama in 1827. The Ormonds had settled in Tuscaloosa in about 1835 and built an imposing two-story brick Georgian-style home. John Ormond sat as a justice on the Alabama supreme court from 1837 to 1848; coincidentally, he had written an opinion awarding a greater share of the Hays estate to Anne Womack following the death of George Hays. Queen's social status at least matched that of Hays. The war worked no insurmountable hardship on their romance. Hays frequently made the thirty-mile carriage trip from his Sebastapol home to Tuscaloosa, and on one visit in 1863 he asked Queen to marry him. She consented.

The ceremony united two of the most distinguished families in west Alabama. Although the pale of war hung over the wedding, the event was the social occasion of the season. The couple was married on December 21, 1863, at Christ Episcopal Church in Tuscaloosa. The twenty-one-year-old brunette bride wore a lace and ivory brocade satin dress of the Empress Josephine period. At twenty-eight, standing by her, Hays looked much as he would the rest of his life. Of average height, with deep brown eyes and dark hair, he wore a beard highlighted by flashes of red. An uninvited rival congratulated Queen for having "married into the best of people" and to such "a nice young man as Major Hays."[23]

Margaret Cornelia
Ormond "Queen" Hays
(photograph by
Mathew Brady; cour-
tesy of Roberta Hays
Lowndes).

The war necessitated that the couple be separated for much of the next sixteen months. Hays returned to duty early in 1864. Correspondence between the two during that period reveals a close and romantic relationship. In May Hays wrote Queen, "I cannot endure this separation much longer." Adding to his anxiety was the knowledge that he would soon be a father. Queen was in Tuscaloosa where she could receive the best care. Hays wished her relations well, and jokingly concluded, "Say to them I shall expect them to take care of you and the *Baby Boy*."[24] Half a year later, in November, Hays replied to a "beautiful and consoling" letter from his wife. Writing from Georgia, he asked, "When will I be permitted to return to the arms of my beloved wife?" By that time Queen was eight months pregnant. Hays ignored the fact that his privileged position had gained him more furlough time than most. Distance from Queen even moved him to some pedestrian philosophizing. "The man who is married and is compelled by circumstances to absent himself from his wife," he observed, "is indeed unhappy." He recounted to Queen the hardships of camp life.

The previous night's rain had soaked what passed for blankets, but even the best of circumstances would not have satisfied him, for "I am absent from you and on that account cannot expect to be happy." He did report an enjoyable reunion with some former University of Georgia classmates. Atlanta had fallen several months earlier, and Hays realized that the life of the Confederacy was growing short. He wrote wistfully of "peace" and pessimistically of the "miserable demoralized command" to which he belonged. His servant, Willis, was equally ready for the war to end. "Willis has exerted himself to pleasure me and is a more handy and a better servant than I ever thought him," Hays wrote. "He however wants to get back," Hays continued, "for fear of getting to [*sic*] close to the Yankees." News that he had become a father soon arrived. Queen gave birth to Mary Hairston on November 21, 1864.[25]

Hays felt more relief than disappointment at the close of the war four months later in April 1865. Yet his loyalty to the South during the conflict cannot be doubted. He took part in several campaigns involving the Army of the Tennessee. As late as May 1864, when disaffection had set in across the Confederacy, Hays wrote hopefully to Queen that "our independence is certain and speedy."[26] He later spoke as a true proponent of the Lost Cause, criticizing a political foe for "skulking behind a pitiful printing press" while he did "what little I could for my country."[27] Speaking during Reconstruction from the floor of the U.S. House of Representatives, Hays would say, "I went and I tried to do my duty there to the best of my ability."[28] In fact, Hays's military career was not distinguished, but it was nothing to be ashamed of. He came home to his family in 1865.

2

The Fall of the Son

The Civil War ended on April 9, 1865, at Appomattox Court House, Virginia, when Ulysses S. Grant extended terms of surrender to Robert E. Lee. Five days later John Wilkes Booth assassinated President Lincoln. Lincoln's successor, Andrew Johnson, inherited the critical task of restoring the Union. Favoring a quick restoration, the new executive quickly established provisional governments in every Southern state. In a proclamation issued in May, in which he set requirements for readmission to the Union, Johnson demanded that each state ratify the Thirteenth Amendment freeing the slaves, repeal its ordinance of secession, and repudiate its war debt. It was not what Johnson included, but what was excluded from the May proclamation that stunned the Radical wing of the Republican party. The president did not base the settlement on any recognition of citizenship status for the freedmen. He did not envision such a scenario.

In Alabama, Lewis E. Parsons began his tenure as provisional governor in June. He had supported Stephen Douglas for president in 1860, opposed secession, and practiced law in Talladega during the war. In the other former Confederate states Johnson would entrust men with similar credentials with the South's future. The Alabama provisional state legislature quickly carried out Johnson's minimal instructions. The other ten Southern states also fulfilled the prerequisite conditions. Even so, when the Thirty-ninth U.S. Congress met in December 1865, a Republican majority blocked the Southern states' return.

The reasoning of the Republican congressmen varied. Southerners had tactlessly elected former high-ranking Confederates to their ranks. Several state legislatures had been less than forthcoming in repudiating the ordinances of secession. The legislatures had also established Black Codes. These laws, applying only to freedmen, seemed to indicate that whites were intent on complete subordination of the former slaves. Under the circumstances, Congress created the Joint Committee on Reconstruction to assess the Southern situation. Readmission would have to wait.[1] In Alabama, Parsons headed the provisional government from June to December 1865 when Robert M. Patton assumed control. Highest on Patton's immediate agenda was bringing order to the prevailing economic chaos. The loss of capital invested in slaves had had tremendous economic repercussions. Plummeting land values shook the faith and dimmed the hopes of most white Alabamians. Thousands of acres lay fallow and would stay so indefinitely, partly because of the reluctance of freedmen to work. Money was scarce and basic commodities were in short supply. The collection of a federal cotton tax added to the misery.

Involving itself in the troubled economic milieu was the Bureau of Freedmen, Refugees, and Abandoned Lands. Created by Congress in March 1865, the Freedmen's Bureau, as the organization was commonly known, aided the destitute of both races. The bureau's most important function concerned the overseeing of contractual arrangements between white landlords and black tenants. In Reconstruction Alabama, as elsewhere, the Freedmen's Bureau also became a powerful political force.

That the former slaves would no longer work the land was a reality so shocking that it defied comprehension. A few makeshift and isolated labor agreements were concluded in the South during 1865, but landowners were discouraged. Weather exacerbated the situation. Oppressive heat scorched corn and other crops, and drought conditions prevailed from mid April to September. The lack of reliable labor, falling real estate values, inclement weather, and postwar economic dislocation combined to frustrate initial revitalization efforts.

Reestablishing himself under the new circumstances was Hays's major preoccupation. In spite of his faith in his ability to overcome his problems, he would never fully recover from the economic damage of the war. Yet Hays displayed a certain resiliency. Work at the Sebastapol and the Hays Mount places had continued all through the war, and at war's end the Greene County planter made labor arrangements with freedmen, the large majority of whom had been his slaves. Even so, he could not escape the prevailing adversity. Hays was working over one hundred slaves on his lands in 1860. That investment, totally lost, represented at least half of his capital assets. And although he did not lose an acre of land as a result of the war, his holdings were worth no more than one-half of what they formerly commanded. Compounding his difficulties, in September 1865 about fifty bales of his cotton were destroyed when his gin house burned. Small wonder that Hays would later recall the situation following the war as one of "chaos and confusion."[2]

Hays had no difficulty in obtaining a pardon from President Johnson. One of Johnson's first presidential actions had been to offer the vast majority of former Confederates amnesty if they swore an oath of allegiance to the Union. Fourteen classes of Southerners were exempted from the general pardon and were required to apply individually to the president. Among those Johnson did not include in the general pardon were former Confederates who possessed $20,000 worth of taxable property in 1861. The president blamed secession on the "slaveocracy" and required that its members apply to him individually for amnesty.

Hays had owned well over $20,000 of property, and he arranged with several persons to draft letters of recommendation in July. Those who wrote in Hays's behalf included Col. C. C. Thomas, commander of the 95th Indiana Infantry stationed in the vicinity; William P. Webb, a prominent Greene County lawyer; and John A. Winston, who had served two terms as Alabama governor before the war. Each man attested to Hays's character and loyalty. Hays wrote directly to President Johnson on August 1. Aware of the president's general disapproval of the planter class, he identified himself as a "farmer." Recounting his opposition to secession, reluctance to enter the ranks, and, once enlisted, his limited military role, Hays built a strong case for himself. He alluded to the "so-called Confederate States," branded the attempt to independence "insurrectionary," and pledged "emphatically" his support to the U.S. government.

Hays's words did not square exactly with his present economic status or with his Confederate career. But considering the letter's nature—a plea for consideration—Hays's license with the truth is not surprising. If the application were favorably received, Hays would regain his political privileges and be spared possible impending penalties.

The petitioner's comments regarding the future were more sincere. Addressing the president in the third person, Hays pledged "to spend the remainder of his life as a good and faithful citizen of the United States."[3]

The pardon request indicated his larger desire to put sectional differences behind, or, as he maintained, to "bury the dead past" and "throw off the shackles of sectional feelings."[4] Hays's openminded compliance and outlook impressed Colonel Thomas. The Union officer's letter noted the Alabamian's exemplary "deportment" and declared that he "was willing and anxious" to accept change. It should be noted that the fact that Hays cooperated with the Freedmen's Bureau and with military authorities was not especially noteworthy; so did other citizens.[5] A certain receptiveness to change on Hays's part hardly constituted a political conversion (the Republican party did not even exist in Alabama yet). But the lenient President Johnson granted his pardon on September 12, 1865.

Economic conditions improved little in Greene County in 1866. Because the freedmen owned no property, and since landowners were almost helpless without their labor, cooperative work arrangements evolved. The former slaves worked for fixed wages or for part of the crop. Hays and his fellow landowners arranged with blacks to work, but the crops parched through the spring and summer due to lack of rain. Generous estimates put the cotton yield at one-fourth that of 1860. Even when the rains started, editor William O. Monroe of the *Eutaw Whig and Observer* lamented, "They come too late." For the Hayses, brightening their despair, came the birth at Sebastapol of their second child, Anne Miller, named for her grandmother, on September 23, 1866.[6]

Meanwhile, following Johnson's frustrated efforts to ease the Southern states' return, relations between the president and congressional Republicans seriously deteriorated in 1866. Presidential vetoes of the Freedmen's Bureau Extension Bill and the Civil Rights Bill (later overridden) pointed to basic differences. Johnson gained support among Northern Democrats but lost all favor with the Republican majority. Fundamental to the problem was a differing perception of the freedmen's status. An outspoken and growing number of Republicans had committed themselves to extending to the freedmen basic citizenship rights. The Fourteenth Amendment provided the most precise reflection of that concern. Defining citizenship as extending to all Americans regardless of race, and guaranteeing "due process" and "equal protection" of the law to all citizens, the amendment lay at the heart of Republican ideology. Also central to establishing the freedmen as citizens was extending them the right to vote. Under the amendment, a state that denied male citizens suffrage would have its representation in Congress decreased. Equally controversial, section three of the amendment barred from public office persons who had taken an oath to defend the constitution and violated it by serving the Confederacy.

Although not specifically stated, ratification of the Fourteenth Amendment seemed to promise readmission. The Tennessee legislature complied and rejoined the Union, but Tennessee was the exception. Encouraged by Johnson's defiance, every other Southern state rejected the amendment between October 1866 and January of the next year. The collective provisions of the amendment—and none more than section three—caused extreme resentment. Despite the efforts of Governor Patton, the Alabama legislature defeated the amendment twice.

Obstruction in the South could not halt what George Clemenceau, a young French visitor, referred to as the "revolution which has been carried out."[7] He anticipated something resembling parity for the freedmen. In Congress, the "Radical Republicans," joined by more moderate party members alienated by Johnson's obstinance, provided the impetus for the fundamental changes Clemenceau predicted. The Radicals' numbers increased following the 1866 midterm elections. In most cases Republicans who endorsed the pending Fourteenth Amendment defeated Democratic candidates who rejected it.

The implications of the 1866 election soon became clear. A large Republican working majority in Congress seized control of Reconstruction when the Thirty-ninth Congress convened early in 1867. In March Congress passed over Johnson's veto the First Military Reconstruction Act. Acting on the assumption that no legal government existed in the South, Congress divided the ten Southern states remaining outside the Union into five military districts. A major general administered each district, and troops assumed stations in the South. Existing provisional or civil governments such as the Patton administration in Alabama remained in place, but each was subordinate to the military regime.

The First Reconstruction Act also established a format for readmission to the Union. Its terms required eligible individuals in each state to register and vote to hold a constitutional convention. Only blacks and whites capable of taking the so-called test oath could participate in the election. The oath denied the vote to officeholders who had previously sworn to uphold the Constitution and then aided the Confederacy. If voters approved the constitutional convention, delegates must then frame a new constitution that permanently enfranchised the freedmen and submit the constitution to the voters for ratification. Finally, readmission was made contingent upon the state legislature's ratification of the Fourteenth Amendment. The measure defined, and—by requiring the truly most radical concession of Reconstruction, black suffrage—expanded the Republican agenda in the South. What white Southerners contemptuously referred to as "Radical Reconstruction" now began.

Alabama, Florida, and Georgia composed the Third Military District, and Gen. John Pope, its commander, established his headquarters in Atlanta in March 1867. Congress soon answered another question: how Reconstruction was to be set in motion. The Supplemental Reconstruction Act of March 23 empowered the military commanders to register voters and hold elections.

Among members of the emerging Alabama Republican party—composed of Northern expatriates, native whites, and the overwhelming majority of the freedmen—the course seemed clear. Over three hundred black and white delegates met at Montgomery on June 4–5, 1867, and formally chartered the state Republican party. They endorsed congressional Reconstruction and the Fourteenth Amendment and condemned civil and political discrimination. Central to the political indoctrination of black Republicans in Alabama and throughout the South was the Union League. Set up locally throughout the South, the Union League acted as a wing of the Republican party.

Alabama whites were divided over what course to pursue. A significant group accepted the congressional strictures because they felt they had no other realistic choice. Readmission was preferable to continued limbo and military rule. Other whites, repulsed by Radicalism, would have nothing to do with congressional Reconstruction. They warned against cooperation and drew horrific images of black suffrage, former slaves in political office, and "Africanization." Both this division and the general apathy prevalent among Alabama whites were apparent when Conservatives held their convention in early September in Montgomery. Delegates from only thirteen counties attended, and the convention took no position on the upcoming constitutional convention referendum. But it hardly mattered. Reconstruction would go forward. General Pope had begun the process of returning a soundly Republican Alabama to the Union by dividing the state into forty-two voting districts.[8]

As in other states, well-defined issues separated Republicans and Demo-

crats in Alabama during the years of Reconstruction. Differing philoso-
phies concerning blacks and their place in society represented the most
fundamental division. With some perspective, a white Alabamian would
state in the mid 1870s, "The only issue that I have ever been able to see
there is that of the whites against the blacks." Although he oversimplified,
the race question did define Reconstruction politics.[9]

   In the Black Belt, where freedmen easily outnumbered whites, the Republican party immediately became powerful. What occurred in Greene
County occurred in many other Alabama counties as well. A few white
organizers, both native and nonnative, began preaching the Republican
gospel. Union League chapters were formed, and blacks, impressed by
the league's ceremony and secrecy and moved by the rhetoric (and sometimes false promises) of Republican prophets, eagerly sought political baptism. From the first faint stirrings grew a political army. Blacks from
Union, Greensboro, Boligee, Eutaw, and various crossroads and settlements composed the party's ranks in Greene. Consecration occurred in
August. Greene County Republicans held their organizational meeting
at the Greek Revival courthouse in Eutaw on August 24, 1867. William
Miller assumed the role of chairman. Since moving from South Carolina
to Alabama in 1836, Miller had prospered as a businessman and was one
of the largest property holders in the county. The Unionist had been by
his own admission "publically and privately opposed to the war from first
to last." John A. Yordy was appointed secretary. Yordy, a former captain
in the Union army, acted as a Freedmen's Bureau agent. Greene County
Republicans adopted a resolution favoring congressional Reconstruction
and elected two delegates to the constitutional convention. One was a
freedman named Benjamin Alexander. The other was Charles Hays.[10]

   It seems inconsistent at best that a Black Belt planter who had worked
more than a hundred slaves and fought for the Confederacy would switch
to the Republicans. But Hays fundamentally accepted the new order envisioned by congressional Republicans. That fact distanced him greatly
from most of his fellow whites, who in the words of one Freedman's Bureau official considered "the Negro as a connecting link between the white
man and Baboon."[11] Hays's empathy for the freedmen was apparent. He
would speak of what was "right and just" and the cause of the "oppressed"
and "downtrodden." While he considered social equality unfeasible, he
considered the extension of political and economic opportunities to the
freedmen a fundamental goal, necessary and in his mind morally correct.

As he had watched events play out in 1866–67, Hays had grown increasingly disillusioned with the Democrats. He regretted the state legislature's rejection of the Fourteenth Amendment. He later recalled dispairingly "the reign of an Andrew Johnson governor" (Robert Patton) and a rebellious "Andrew Johnson General Assembly" that had refused to ratify the amendment. He also realized that Southern resistance would only prolong the period of limbo outside the Union and risked the establishment of more radical and punitive terms for reentry. Alabama had been out of the Union seven years, and acceptance of real change promised the state's return. But nothing less than acceptance would work, and the Democratic power structure either did not comprehend or refused to accept that reality.

Undoubtedly Hays came to his decision after much anxiety, introspection, and doubt. But the decision had been made by the time of that hot August day in Eutaw. He thanked the Republicans for their confidence and promised faithful service. The Republican party had found an unlikely spokesman. So had the freedmen. Confused and destitute, searching for dignity and equitable treatment, the former slaves would look to Charles Hays for direction.[12]

Hays assumed a prominent role in local Republican politics during the summer and fall of 1867. As a leading member of the local Union League, he helped mobilize Greene County blacks in the months before the constitutional convention referendum. He delivered speeches and rallied blacks to Republicanism. At Clinton, a small Greene County community, Hays was especially effective. He reported in September that following the oratory there, "we used them up . . . badly." Conservatives in Greene County mounted some opposition initially but then totally capitulated. A group representing the county Democratic party visited Hays at his home on September 17. An understanding was reached: Hays agreed not to deliver any more speeches, and the Conservatives promised not to oppose the local nominees to the constitutional convention. With obvious satisfaction, Hays wrote fellow Republican Charles W. Pierce the next day, "I look upon the canvass as closed in Greene" and explained that the Republican nominees could "run around the track without opposition." What this meant for the Republican party was obvious. And there were benefits for Hays: he was in the enviable position of facing no opposition in his bid as a congressional convention delegate.[13]

Pierce, a Union veteran and native of New York, served as the ranking officer at the subdistrict Freedmen's Bureau headquarters in nearby

Demopolis. Hays advised him to disband any black military organizations in the interest of peace, but he also asked that troops be sent to Eutaw on election day in case of disorder. In the meantime the voter registration continued. As the October election neared, Pierce wrote Hays, "Without exception so far as I can learn all will vote the Republican ticket . . . whose platform and principles they fully endorse." Blacks attended rallies and even delivered speeches, but these activities did not fully prepare Greene County whites for what they witnessed during the first week of October: former slaves casting ballots at the polls in Eutaw.

A large majority of Alabama blacks, and whites in fewer numbers, approved the constitutional convention. Since the Democrats did not offer any candidates, all of the elected delegates were Republicans. Hays and four others were elected from the Twenty-second District (Greene and Hale counties). Alabamians had registered and held a referendum quicker than any other state. The constitutional convention, scheduled to meet the next month in Montgomery, offered the earliest test for the Republican-inspired democratic experiment.[14]

Montgomery was cosmopolitan compared to the Greene County hinterland. The second-largest city in Alabama (after Mobile), it claimed about 12,000 inhabitants. Situated near the headwaters of the Alabama River, Montgomery had briefly served as the capital of the Confederacy and had hosted the presidential inauguration of Jefferson Davis. A widely traveled Englishman, visiting in 1868, noted its handsome residences, tree-lined streets, and rose- and oleander-filled gardens, and described Montgomery as "one of the prettiest towns I have seen." Various boardinghouses and three hotels — the National, Central, and Exchange — accommodated visitors. The massive columned capitol overlooking the city from a hilltop stood at the head of Dexter Avenue.[15]

Most of the approximately one hundred delegates who assembled for the constitutional convention in Montgomery were Alabamians, but a sizable minority were of Northern birth, and a smaller number, about twenty, were black. Almost all were politically inexperienced. William W. Screws, staunch Democrat and editor of the *Montgomery Advertiser*, noted that the convention had "few members ever heard of outside their counties." [16]

Convening in the Senate chamber room of the capitol, the delegates deliberated between November 5 and December 6. Controversy characterized the twenty-eight-day gathering. That the freedmen would be enfranchised was academic. Which classes of whites would be allowed to vote was much less certain, and debate over that issue dominated proceedings. Factions quickly formed. Daniel H. Bingham, a north Alabama Unionist, led a radical group that included Datus E. Coon, a former Union army brigadier general; John C. Keffer, a Pennsylvanian recently appointed chairman of the Republican State Executive Committee; and, from Massachusetts, John Silsby, former proprietor of the Republican newspaper the *Mobile Nationalist*. These radicals believed that casting a wide proscriptive net was necessary to maintain the Republican party in power and to safeguard the rights of the freedmen. They felt that to advance political rights to those of dubious loyalty risked recent gains. An aversion to such proscriptive measures united others. "While I accord, and will vote, equal civil and political rights to the colored man," promised Joseph H. Speed, "I am unwilling to disfranchise white men." Speed and Henry C. Semple, both former Confederates and Alabama citizens, were the chief spokesmen for a smaller coalition promoting inclusion.[17]

Some indication of the delegates' opinions was revealed by a resolution offered by Semple on November 9. His proposal provided for universal male suffrage once Alabama returned to the Union. Twenty-two delegates supported Semple's plan. More did not. A caustic Democrat, editor Joseph Hodgson of the *Montgomery Mail*, noted the solidification of political lines, distinguishing between a "Conservative Rump" and a "Radical Rump."[18]

Two days later (November 11), the Committee on Elective Franchise reported. Unable to agree, committee members submitted majority and minority reports. The majority report recommended that Alabama's citizens take an oath acknowledging the "political and civil equality of all men" and that all those who did not vote in the constitutional referendum be disenfranchised. (The First Military Reconstruction Act required that a majority of all registered voters ratify each state constitution. That opponents of the constitution would register with no intention of voting for or against the document, thereby preventing the mandatory majority of votes from being cast, was an open secret.) The minority report signatories endorsed universal suffrage and urged the convention to respect the late president Lincoln's principle of "charity toward all and malice toward none."[19]

Hays took no part in the debate over this or any other issue. Yet, he clearly objected to political punishment. Enfranchising blacks, but arbitrarily denying a class of whites the vote, he believed fundamentally wrong. Hays also feared the political fallout from such a move. Proscription would embitter native citizens whom the young Republican party desperately needed to attract. His position, given his Southern and Confederate background, was reasonable and to be expected. He was one of twenty-two delegates to vote with the Conservative Rump to sustain Semple's attempt to head off disfranchisement. Of the numerous Northern newspaper correspondents covering the first constitutional convention, one, a *New York Herald* reporter, connected Hays to "a small band of moderate and rational delegates."[20]

Despite the efforts of the Semple-Speed faction, Bingham and other radicals incorporated most of the majority report into the constitution. Most controversial was a provision preventing citizens from voting who had been excluded from holding office by the Reconstruction Acts and the pending Fourteenth Amendment. That class included officeholders who had taken an oath before the war to uphold the U.S. Constitution and violated it by aiding the Confederacy. The proscription controversy often overshadowed the methodical construction of a constitution bearing an unmistakable Republican imprint. The establishment of a Bureau of Industrial Resources reflected the Republican party's attempt to attract capital and develop state resources. Public education was also a party priority, and framers created a Board of Education to direct an endowed public-school system. All executive offices were made elective. As the Fourteenth Amendment was still pending, the delegates in a symbolic move also defined state citizenship to include blacks.

On December 5 the convention voted 67 to 9 in favor of accepting the constitution. Almost one-fourth of the delegates were absent or abstained, and, several days later, thirteen white delegates, eight of whom had voted against the document, signed a public letter of protest. Among them were Semple, Speed, and other moderate delegates with whom Hays was in agreement.

Hays had generally opposed partisanship and the Bingham faction. Yet he recognized the inherent improvements offered by the document. Besides, he expected the disabling provisions to be repealed (a clause allowing the legislature to remove the voting restrictions was incorporated into the constitution). Nothing could be done unless state government was legitimated and Alabama readmitted to the Union. Despite his reservations, Hays signed the constitution.

Ratification of the constitution still remained to be accomplished. Although opposition to the convention had been limited, opposition to the document itself was overwhelming. The ratification campaign stimulated the revival of the Democratic-Conservative party in Alabama. Acting largely on the advice of former governor Lewis Parsons, the State Democratic Executive Committee pursued a policy of "active non-participation." As expected, whites registered with no intention of voting for or against the constitution, hoping to deny the mandatory majority needed for ratification by boycotting the election.

The convention had formed a Republican caucus and nominated a state ticket just before recessing. William H. Smith, a Randolph County Unionist, received the gubernatorial nomination. At the caucus and in the weeks ahead, other Republicans announced for various offices. Hays's inactivity at the convention could have been construed as stemming from a personal disillusionment with politics, the Republican party, or both. Nothing could have been further from the truth. He was eager to pursue a political career, and declared for the Twenty-second District (Greene and Pickens counties) seat in the state senate in December.[21]

The peculiar circumstances of the campaign—he had no opposition and the election would not stand if the constitution failed—dictated Hays's strategy. He impressed on the freedmen that voting for the constitution was in their interest, reiterating the themes of Union and the Republican party using reason, promises, and oratorical flourishes (quoting Shakespeare and the Bible). Hays rallied blacks to his candidacy by articulating Republican guarantees of citizenship and opportunity. A rueful opponent later conceded that Hays "made the black man believe he was their special friend,"[22] and another estimated that "he could go out there and blow a horn" and rally 2,500 black voters.[23] A phalanx-like coalition had begun to take form.

Overall, between February 1 and February 5, 1868, almost 71,000 Alabamians voted for ratification. But a majority of registered voters did not participate in the election, apparently defeating the constitution. Gen. George G. Meade, who had replaced Pope as Third District commander, suggested to President Johnson that the convention reassemble and draft a more acceptable document. Meade's suggestion went unheeded. Because of the situation in Alabama, congressional Republicans framed the Fourth Reconstruction Act. The measure, which became law without President Johnson's signature on March 11, 1868, stipulated that only a majority of the votes actually cast in a constitutional referendum was necessary for ratification. Applied ex post facto, the last of the Reconstruction Acts validated the February election and provided for absolute Republican hegemony in Alabama.[24]

The organization of a state government awaited the convening of the
legislature in July. With readmission certain, political debate crystallized.
Whites generally equated Republicanism with black equality, disenfranchisement, the recent enemy, and imposed authority. The constitution,
considered by many to have been fairly defeated, provided another source
of alienation. A large white majority considered themselves victims of an
illegal government bent on degrading whites and elevating blacks. Republicans assailed the opposition as treasonous and backward-looking. The
unprecedented circumstances made for extreme partisanship. As one Alabama Republican observed, "Whigs and Democrats used to abuse each
other very fiercely in speeches and newspapers but such things scarcely
ever affected our social relations." Party affiliation took on added dimensions in Reconstruction Alabama. Elaborating, he explained, "I notice what
I never noticed before, that the estimate of a man is more controlled by
his politics than by anything else." [25]

Perhaps no Republican in Alabama during the next decade would under-
stand that statement better than Charles Hays. As a Republican, he fell
immediately into disrepute among white Greene Countians. The family's
high standing made his alleged apostasy more shocking. The Hays name
became one of reproach. Invoking the esteemed memory of George Hays,
an observer regretted "the fall of the son." [26] In the hill counties of Alabama, where Unionists had thrived and often became Republicans after
the war, political toleration existed. But in the Black Belt heartland there
was very little of that among the white population. White society in the
county where Hays had been raised and claimed friends rejected him. The
extent of the personal ostracism is uncertain, but evidence suggests that
few hid their antipathy. As Hays himself stated, any white in the Black
Belt "in favor of the policy of Congress and of the Reconstruction Acts is
regarded as an enemy of the country." [27]

Hays quickly became the object of scurrilous and hyperbolic attacks. An
indictment of his conduct, taking the form of a public letter to the *Tuscaloosa Independent Monitor*, appeared as the constitutional convention closed.
Its author, signing himself, "I know em," believed that Hays's recent Republican conversion could best be understood in the context of his past. Of
"low Celtic origin," Hays had inherited land (ill-got) and slaves (whom he
abused). Hays's detractor dismissed his Civil War service in opportunistic
terms, claiming that Hays had lingered at home before capitalizing on his
brother-in-law's officer status and gaining a position analogous to a "camp-

follower." Even so, vanity required that he stick "a star on each shoulder" and style himself "major." Calculation and self-interest continued to guide him after the war, continued the critic. Hays's attraction to Republicanism was transparent. A combination of necessity (Hays needed blacks to work his lands) and an inflated sense of his own importance (though he could not be elected "overseer of a neighborhood road") explained his apostasy.[28]

Hays became accustomed to such attacks. Rarely did he reply. An abiding belief in the correctness of his position provided him with a measure of personal peace. In 1867, two years removed from the war, as the South finally began to move toward regaining its former place in the Union, Hays was confident about his course. He faulted Johnson. The president had opposed the Civil Rights Bill, the Fourteenth Amendment, and the First Military Reconstruction Act on the grounds they represented an unconstitutional federal usurpation of power. Behind that rationalization was a not-so-muted attempt to establish the freedmen as second-class citizens. Hays blamed Democrats for not recognizing that "the past is gone." The "past" that he spoke of was less a finite period of time than a mindset. His willingness to accept the freedmen's new standing, combined with his fellow whites' unwillingness, formed the crux of an irresolvable disagreement.[29]

3

Apostasy Confirmed

Charles Hays stayed busy in the late winter and spring of 1868 before the state senate met in July. One event involved an addition to the family. At Sebastapol, Queen gave birth to John James Ormond on February 15, 1868. At last Hays could claim a son. Supervising his plantation operations, as always, also required his attention. Although Hays owned assets and land, he was in desperate need of cash. In 1868 he began a pattern of borrowing money. Then and in the future, William Miller provided Hays with the funds he needed. The Republican probate judge loaned Hays $5,000 in February 1868. Without the money, the circuit clerk recorded, "it would have been impossible for him to have gone & make [sic] a crop." Hays mortgaged four wagons, thirty-six mules, farming equipment, and his cotton and corn crops. The next month he sold parts of the Sebastapol and Hays Mount places to Miller. His affluent friend paid $9,600 for more than 2,600 prime acres in the Fork. Cornelia Ormond Hays's name appeared on the bill of sale. Increasingly, Queen would underwrite her husband. Hays, and almost all planters, had seen their capital worth decline sharply after 1865. The loss of capital invested in slaves and the resulting decline in land values were severe setbacks. Cotton prices had fallen precipitously between 1865 and 1867, and prospects improved little in the ensuing few years.[1]

Compounding Hays's problems was a deteriorating political situation. In the weeks prior to the February constitutional referendum, Greene County whites had used both conventional and unconventional means to turn blacks away from the Republican party. Freedmen's Bureau agent

John Yordy claimed that vigilantes created "*a reighn [sic] of terror complete.*" The situation did not calm down after the election. In March a group of young men administered a beating in Eutaw to Joseph Hill, a white Republican preacher who operated a school for freedmen. After a controversial military trial, an army commission court sentenced the seven guilty parties to terms at Fort Jefferson federal prison, two hundred miles west of Key West in the Dry Tortugas region. The defendants gained statewide martyrdom as victims of "bayonet rule" and "radical justice." Later that month, on the night of March 20, incendiaries burned the Eutaw courthouse to the ground (the building housed information linking whites to political crimes). In his monthly reports to authorities in Montgomery, Charles Pierce, commander of the Freedmen's Bureau subdistrict in nearby Demopolis, described the beating of Hill and outlined other serious problems. The various reports indicate a sharply escalating violent trend. Pierce mentioned in his March report the appearance of the Ku Klux Klan in Greene County.[2]

The violently anti-Republican Klan had spread from Tennessee throughout the South by 1868. Opposition to Republicanism, as elsewhere, quickly degenerated into terrorism in Alabama. Klansmen (often disguised) whipped, hanged, shot, and intimidated Republicans (usually black) in the name of white supremacy. Night riding was primarily employed for political purposes, but landlords also used terror as a weapon against reluctant laborers.[3] General Meade soon responded from his Atlanta headquarters. He issued a general order on April 4, 1868, aimed at curbing violence in the Third District, and the next day he wrote President Johnson of "unmistakable signs of disorder in this State and Alabama from secret organizations, such as have disturbed Tennessee."[4]

The Black Belt would be the scene of some of the most notorious political crimes during the Reconstruction years ahead. An active Klan formed in Greene. As elsewhere, young and embittered Confederates comprised its membership. Older and better-placed individuals in the community usually did not directly participate, but their failure to condemn the crimes encouraged the lawless among them. Sometimes groups of individuals acted under the aegis of the Klan, but on other occasions night riders, claiming no organizational affiliation, acted unilaterally. For Republicans the results were the same.[5] Hays believed that even the more upstanding citizens in Greene viewed the Klan as a necessary aberration and "winked at it." In bordering counties—Sumter, Tuscaloosa, and Hale—Republicans were also soon appealing frantically for protection. More of the same was expected as the election of 1868 approached.

Meeting at Chicago in May, the national Republican party nominated Ulysses S. Grant for president. House speaker Schuyler Colfax was selected as the former Union general's running mate. The party reaffirmed its commitment to the freedmen and pledged continued progress toward full Reconstruction (by then seven states had returned to the Union). Party spokesmen emphasized the theme of harmony, so well expressed by Grant's axiom, "Let us have peace." In July, in New York, the Democratic party nominated Gov. Horatio Seymour, the former governor of that state. Francis P. Blair, Jr., received the vice-presidential nomination. The Democrats openly condemned congressional Reconstruction, accusing the opposition of "military despotism" and of championing "negro supremacy."[6]

The stakes for the Republican party in the South were enormous. Although Republicans did or would soon control every Southern state government, party roots were shallow. No Republican presidential candidate had ever appeared on a Deep South ballot before 1868. The circumstances surrounding the party's meteoric rise to power were of added significance. The Republican party's creation in the former Confederacy constituted an act of political insemination. Republicanism had been imposed on the South. The party had not undergone a period of gestation and claimed no real political antecedents. Outside of the former slaves and native Unionists, Republicans lacked a natural constituency. The presidential contest would test the party's precarious foundation.

Alabama Republicans could afford to be cautiously optimistic. The Conservative boycott during the constitutional referendum and the subsequent passage of the Fourth Reconstruction Act had placed the party in complete political control of the state. In July, when the legislature convened, William Hugh Smith was installed as governor. Party members filled almost all local and state offices and all of the six congressional seats. The party even commanded some support among whites in the northern hill counties and in the piney woods to the south. Yet the true center of party strength remained the Black Belt. Between 60,000 and 70,000 of the approximately 80,000 Republican voters were former slaves, and a disproportionate number lived in that central tier of counties. Alabama was one of several Southern states where there were about as many black as white voters. With some white support, the party could maintain control.

Still, Republicans faced serious challenges. The traditional ruling elite,

William Hugh Smith,
Republican governor
of Alabama, 1868–1870
(Alabama Department of
Archives and History).

which represented a large majority of white Alabamians, was a constant threat. Also, division among state Republicans had a polarizing effect. Republican differences, obvious at the constitutional convention, would be evident also at the upcoming legislature. The circumstances of the Republican rise to authority raised further doubts. The party had seized power less than the Democrats had forfeited it by not contesting the election. And the period of Democratic disarray was over. The solidarity displayed in the constitutional referendum indicated the party's latent strength.

Under such circumstances the administration of William Hugh Smith began. Hays was one of thirty-three senators assembled in the capitol's north wing on July 13, 1868. About three times that many legislators began deliberations across the hall in the house chamber. Most of the legislators were white, but about thirty of the participants were black. Men who had moved to Alabama since the war composed the smallest contingent. Ratification of the Fourteenth Amendment provided the first significant order of business. Governor Smith's opening remarks were then read. Smith sought to reassure skeptics by claiming that the Alabama brand of Republicanism would be fiscally conservative and otherwise moderate. Among his recommendations, he urged the legislature to strike the constitutional provisions disenfranchising citizens. Directing attention from race-related questions was a strategy resorted to by moderate Republicans throughout the South, and Smith was a moderate. He devoted more attention to the importance of developing natural resources than to Reconstruction questions.[7]

The debate over voting restrictions carried over from the constitutional convention. One faction, which proved dominant, favored inclusion and the sweeping away of penalties. Other party members, often with Northern backgrounds, deferred less to the native white population's sensitivities. The most devisive question concerned proscription. Whether to reinstate the franchise and, if so, how to do so, became a point of extreme contention during the month-long session. Section three of article seven of the constitution barred thousands of Alabamians (estimates varied) from participating in the impending national election. In the senate debate opened on July 20 when John L. Pennington of Lee County asked for the formation of a joint committee to consider the governor's proposed removal of political penalties. Having established his radical credentials at the constitutional convention, Datus Coon of Dallas County challenged the idea. The former Union general considered enfranchising thousands of Alabamians — surely the great majority were Democratic voters — an untimely move. He attempted unsuccessfully to table the resolution offered by Pennington.

Although Hays had not spoken from the floor at the constitutional convention, he quickly asserted himself in the senate. He acted with the Pennington faction and assumed a leading role in the battle. Two weeks into the session, when Coon proposed that a joint committee weigh individually the credentials of the disfranchised, Hays directly confronted him. Unwilling to compromise the principle of amnesty, Hays strongly objected. He argued on July 27 that it was "high time to put down forever, all political test questions." Noting with approval "that the shackles of the slave being stricken off," Hays urged, "let us relieve our citizens of political disabilities." He excluded no one, "be they Democrats, Conservatives, or Republicans." Impressed with Hays's position, Joseph Hodgson of the *Montgomery Mail* labeled the effort "eloquent."[8] Legislators delivered "fiery speeches" as the debate continued. On August 4, Hays again rose to argue for complete amnesty. The next day the senate overwhelmingly approved a bill offered by Pennington invalidating the constitutional proscription article. Following house approval, Governor Smith signed the measure into law.[9]

Other divisive issues had in the meantime reached the floor. Massachusetts native Isaac Sibley introduced on July 22 the so-called "Ku-Klux" Bill that provided for harsh sanctions against night riders. A Militia Bill, considered several days later, would have resulted in the arming of blacks under the state's aegis. As at the constitutional convention, where a Radical-Moderate schism had developed, legislators strongly disagreed. Generally those Republicans who had opposed lifting the disenfranchising provisions supported both measures, and legislators who approved of amnesty voted for neither. Both the "Ku-Klux" and the Militia bills failed.

Hays considered both bills inflammatory and withheld his support. In Tennessee, when Gov. William Brownlow had insisted on the creation of a militia, extreme violence had resulted. Hays claimed to be "as much responsible as any man for the defeat of the Militia bill." Hays soon became an outspoken opponent of night riders. But for now, hoping that the legislation would not be necessary, he withheld his endorsement of the "Ku-Klux" Bill.

Even more controversial was the voting question. Governor Smith had pointed out that the assembly had to provide legislation enabling voters to register. In early August, as the session neared an end, Mobile County senator Frederick G. Bromberg introduced the Presidential Electors Bill. Instead of holding a general election in November, Bromberg proposed that the state legislature cast Alabama's eight electoral votes. Bromberg, Sibley, Coon, and other recognized Radicals claimed that Democratic fraud and probable violence justified taking the unconventional step. Objecting to the scheme as undemocratic and divisive, twelve senators, including Hays, mounted strong opposition. An equal number supported Bromberg. Senate president Andrew J. Applegate (an Ohio native) cast the deciding vote favorably on August 7, and the house concurred. Governor Smith did not. Decrying the measure as "wrong in principle," Smith vetoed the Presidential Electors Bill. The veto set up the final act of the extraordinary session. The Coon-Sibley camp frustrated attempts to pass a voter registration law before adjournment. As matters stood, Alabamians lacked the legal means to vote in the national election when the legislature broke up on August 12.[10]

Hays had played a significant role during the month-long session. Opposition to the Ku Klux Klan, Militia, and Presidential Electors bills indicated the Greene County senator's moderation and his determination not to increase political tensions. A memorial that he framed confirmed his restrained outlook. Hays cited Alabama's acknowledgement of the end of slavery and the perpetuity of the Union. Giving Radical language a different twist, he proposed that Congress lift the political disabilities of all citizens regardless of "race, color or previous condition." [11]

Extreme criticism of the legislature and individual legislators was standard fare in Montgomery's daily newspapers, the *Advertiser*, the *Mail*, and the *Picayune*. It was significant that a Democratic press predisposed against the "menagerie" did not denounce Hays. The omission was not an oversight. Hays's opposition to Radical-sponsored legislation had gained him favor among Conservatives. *Montgomery Mail* editor Hodgson pointed to the senator's "abuse towards the Radicals." [12] As the legislature adjourned, the *Advertiser* noted that Hays, William B. Jones, and others critical of the Radical contingent planned to speak in opposition at a public meeting. Hays apparently agreed to speak and then reconsidered. Some observers felt Hays's return to the Democratic party was imminent. How seriously he thought of doing so is not known. But his moderation and his expressed dislike for Sibley, Coon, and other senators probably reflected more than Hays intended. The *Montgomery Picayune* commended Hays for supporting "the white men of the South." [13] The inference that he was prepared to abandon the freedmen assumed too much.

Hays was back in Greene County at least by August 21. Writing to Governor Smith from Eutaw that day, he advised him against issuing a proclamation providing for an election. Various sources speculated that Smith might do so in light of the situation. Hays believed that marshalling the Republican vote in Greene would "result in riots of the worst character." An election risked violence, and "it is all that the Union men of this county can do to stay here." He cited the anxieties of peace-loving Democrats as well as Republicans. Despite his personal feelings, Hays did not want to be held up publicly as opposed to an election. Writing in "the strictest confidence," he requested that Smith not publish his letter.[14]

Hays did not exaggerate the situation. Reaction among Greene County whites to recent political events ranged from reluctant acceptance to outright defiance. During Hays's absence in Montgomery, relations between the few white Republicans and the Democratic population had further deteriorated. Changing the political guard at Eutaw had proved something less than a formality when Probate Judge William C. Oliver refused to surrender his office in July. Like other Conservatives, Oliver believed the constitution had been legally defeated and that he still retained his right to office. In July, Probate Judge-elect William Miller wrote Governor Smith about the situation and added, "The spirit of Rebellion [*sic*] is as strong now as it was." He referred the governor to Hays (sitting in the legislature) for corroboration.[15] Late in July, escorted by soldiers, Miller finally assumed office. More trouble lay ahead. The Republican probate judge found a threatening Klan notice tacked to his office door two weeks later.

John Yordy of the Freedmen's Bureau also endured mistreatment. He was refused lodging at a Eutaw hotel in August. Following the incident, R. A. Wilson, a Freedmen's Bureau official in Demopolis, and James B. Clarke, Eutaw's town chancellor, exchanged hostile letters. Clarke responded to Wilson's threat to station black troops in Eutaw by refusing to take responsibility if whites slaughtered Yordy, fellow Radicals, and the troops. By September, the sheriff had resigned, no one would serve, and, according to Yordy, there was "hallooing [*sic*], cursing on the streets, and shooting . . . every night."[16]

Among those articulating the opposition and greatly contributing to animosity was the *Eutaw Whig and Observer*'s editor, Joseph W. Taylor, who had quickly established a reputation for extremism. He and Hays were committed enemies. To Hays's way of thinking, Taylor was the worst kind of Democrat: unreconstructed and influential. Taylor's incendiary remarks added to the boiling, emotionally charged atmosphere. The supporting cast of leading Eutaw Democrats included lawyers James Clarke, John J. Jolly, and John G. Pierce.[17] Each of these men resented Hays. They were natural adversaries.

More perplexing was Hays's relationship with William Jones. Jones lived at Demopolis, in Marengo County, which bordered Greene County to the south. He had owned slaves, supported John Bell for president in 1860, and served the Confederacy briefly. His conversion to Republicanism was no less shocking locally than Hays's had been. Jones knew Hays well. They had sat (and voted) together in the state senate. Even more than Hays, Jones had been outspoken in his disagreements with senate Radicals. Hays had hinted at returning to the Democratic party—Jones would actually do so in the summer of 1868 after the burden of Republicanism in Marengo County had become overbearing. "When a gentleman's social relations are assailed, when his family are compelled to ask enjoyments only at home," a distressed Jones wrote Governor Smith from Demopolis in August, "it is no more than right something should be done to remedy such unfortunate evils." He continued in a similar tone for three pages, rationalizing that "no one unless a political fool could stand such." The letter stands as a classical account of what native Southern Republicans endured.[18]

One of Jones's first public acts as a Democrat was to denounce Hays in an open letter published several weeks after the legislature ended. Jones charged that Hays had recently expressed disgust in Montgomery for Coon, Sibley, and other "carpetbagging interlopers whose skins were more slimy than eels" and that he had stated his intention of returning to the Democratic party. But to John Keffer, the Republican State Executive Committee chairman, Hays had promised to proclaim his Republican loyalties on returning to Greene. A perplexed Jones asked his senate colleague, "Are you on the side of the white people [or] linking your destiny to the Carpetbaggers?"[19]

Hays did not consider the choice that cut and dry. Just days later, on September 12, Jones and Hays confronted each other at Forkland in a debate. A crowd of blacks and whites assembled in the small community located halfway between Eutaw and Demopolis, anticipating harsh words. Hays, who spoke first, welcomed the "opportunity to vindicate myself." He was more interested in clearing up misconceptions than replying specifically to Jones. Hays freely admitted that he held "different opinions from a majority of my neighbors," but he disputed those who considered him "an enemy to my race." A sense of loyalty to the Constitution, he maintained, accounted for his Republican status. The dictates of reality required recognizing the political rights recently granted to the freedmen. These guarantees, Hays emphasized, did not infringe on traditional and necessary barriers separating the races socially. These were not the words of a Radical pledged to racial equality. At the same time, Hays made clear that the freedmen's rights could not be compromised. Having earlier established that he was expected at the home of a Marengo County friend, Hays ignored calls that he remain to hear Jones, and rode off in his carriage.

Jones's reply represented less a reasoned presentation than a harangue. He recalled Hays's plan to switch parties, but money and office had changed his mind. Jones described Hays to blacks as "the worst enemy you have, because he comes to you in the disguise of a friend."[20] Among the crowd that afternoon was Francis Strother Lyon, a Marengo County lawyer. Although a Democrat and no admirer of Hays, Lyon faulted Jones for his "insulting" behavior and described him as "unmindful of the courtesies or proprieties of debate." [21] Hays had not admitted to Jones's charge of duplicity. His political loyalties were clear. The performance convinced the *Eutaw Whig and Observer* that Hays remained "as black a Radical as ever fraternized with the party." [22]

As a confirmed Republican, Hays returned to Montgomery several days later. As expected, Governor Smith had summoned a special session to pass a voter registration bill. In the absence of Datus Coon, whom *Montgomery Mail* editor Hodgson suggested "Barnum may have caged," legislators began deliberations on September 16. Among white Conservatives, Hays was held in only slightly higher esteem than Coon. Reports of his remarks at Forkland had reached Montgomery. All doubts concerning his political status were dispelled. "The cold shoulder has been justly given to him by the respectable people of the city," Hodgson wrote, and "he does not stand in society as he did at the last session of the legislature." [23]

Hays soon fell further in the Conservatives' estimation. The presidential election was less than two months away, and increasing political violence worried state Republicans. Under these circumstances the legislature authorized a joint committee to visit President Johnson and request the protection of federal troops. Hays's stature among his colleagues was obvious. He chaired the committee, composed of Senator Jerome Hinds and Representatives Thomas D. Fister, Eli F. Jennings, and Charles T. Thweatt. Governor Smith completed the delegation.

Alabama Republicans were not the first to ask for such protection. Political terrorism in the South reached a new peak during the months before the 1868 election. Violence erupted in Arkansas, South Carolina, Kentucky, Florida, and Tennessee, and in Georgia and Louisiana there was near anarchy. Despite pleas from Republicans, the Fortieth Congress had not enacted any enforcement legislation. Nor was adequate protection provided by Republican governors, who were often hamstrung by lack of resources and by political considerations. Local officials were unable, and sometimes unwilling, to enforce the law. Except for the often indifferent federal troops in the South, little stood between the Klansmen and their Republican adversaries.

Hays and his colleagues did not operate under any illusions. Johnson resented the federal presence in the South and had recently been uncooperative when approached by Tennessee Republicans. Even so, about noon on September 28, Senator Joseph S. Fowler of Tennessee escorted the Alabama delegation into the White House. After exchanging formalities with the president, Hays read legislative resolutions decrying the unrest in Alabama. The president's response somewhat surprised the delegation. He expressed concern, and what followed was described as "a pleasant conversation." The result of their meeting, and another the following day that included Secretary of War John M. Schofield, was a letter from the cabinet officer to Commander Meade. Schofield urged strict vigilance (the Second and Third military districts had been consolidated under the command of Meade and the Department of the South). The secretary of war's instructions to Meade did not propose any policy changes. He substantially reiterated a general order each department commander had received a month earlier providing for the discretionary use of troops.[24] At least professing satisfaction, Hays telegraphed the general assembly from Washington that "our mission has been accomplished." In the meantime, the legislature approved the Registration Bill, and after returning, Governor Smith signed the measure providing for a general election. The session adjourned on October 10.

Within several days General Meade issued a general order assigning troops to various areas in Alabama to supervise the election.[25] Troops supervised every national election during Reconstruction. In what one observer has described as a "counterrevolutionary atmosphere," soldiers prevented the further degeneration of the political process. Yet, as Republicans discovered, they could not provide certain protection.[26]

A brief sabbatical in Greene County offered Hays neither rest nor relief from political acrimony. He devoted much of October to campaigning through the Black Belt on behalf of the Republican ticket. U.S. senator Willard Warner accompanied him. A former resident of Ohio, Warner, a brevet major general, had moved to Alabama shortly after the war, purchased a plantation near Montgomery, and was elected by the state legislature to the Senate in 1868. He and Hays became firm allies and friends. The forty-two-year-old Ohioan did not travel far before discovering that campaigning through the Black Belt among whites passionately opposed to Republicanism was at best difficult and at worst perilous.

At Livingston, the county seat of Sumter, soon after the campaign began, the two Republicans encountered open hostility. Sumter bordered Greene to the west and closely resembled its Black Belt cousin. Just as in Greene, unrest and violence had accompanied the change in regimes, and a large black majority had voted into local office a few white Republicans. Democrats in Livingston made clear their unwillingness to hear a "carpet-

Sen. Willard Warner,
Hays's ally and Republi-
can colleague (Alabama
Department of Archives
and History).

bagger" or a "scalawag," objecting that "these men shan't speak here."
Hays knew some of the more prominent men in Livingston. Only because
of the efforts of one, Turner Reavis, a local Democrat and a respected
lawyer, were he and Warner allowed to address an audience.[27]

No such mediator emerged at Eutaw on October 22. Anticipating Republican oratory, a large crowd of blacks and a few whites crowded the
Greene County courthouse grounds. Several armed whites began harass-
ing Warner soon after he started speaking. "God-damn him, his coat-tail
is too short," one white yelled, and another ridiculed the senator's hat. A
third cried that "no damned Yankee" could speak in Eutaw. All attempts
at reason failed, the heckling became unbearable, and the Republicans
adjourned the meeting.[28]

Hays and Warner pressed on, to Marion, Greensboro, Gainesville, Fayette, and other west Alabama towns and communities. At Carrollton, the
seat of Pickens County, both men delivered uninterrupted speeches on
October 24. The *Carrollton West Alabamian*'s editor admitted that the Republicans sounded reasonable and praised Hays's "quite moderate and
conservative" legislative record.[29]

More eventful was the reception in Tuscaloosa County several days
later. Tuscaloosa, the former state capital and the present county seat,

was situated on the Black Warrior River. The town had been the scene of countless political confrontations between Republicans and Democrats. Contributing to the agitation was Edward Ryland Randolph, a bitter and uncompromising foe of Republicanism who assumed the editorial helm of the *Tuscaloosa Independent Monitor* in 1867. Randolph had helped found the local Klan chapter and had lived briefly in Greene County before the war and knew Hays. Whatever their past relationship, the turmoil of Reconstruction redefined it. Hays became one of the ascerbic editor's most enduring targets.

On October 28, at about noon, the Greene County senator began his speech in a second-floor courthouse room. Two or three hundred freedmen and about twenty or thirty whites, including Randolph, were in the audience. Hays quickly got to the point: a vote for Ulysses Grant was a vote for peace. Casting a ballot for the Seymour-Blair ticket risked a resumption of the sectional conflict. It required little provocation on Hays's part to upset some obviously intoxicated whites, who began taunting him and making it almost impossible for him to continue. The situation soon worsened, and when a pistol shot rang out from downstairs, chaos reigned temporarily. Following the return of order, Warner was asked to speak, but he declined out of deference to Hays, and the meeting broke up. Randolph gloated in his account (complete with illustrations) of the retreat of the "so-called white men." Warner and Hays concluded their eventful swing through the Black Belt several days later, just before the election.[30]

Grant ran well in all sections of the country and easily defeated Horatio Seymour. He carried nine of the eleven former Confederate states. His defeat in Georgia and Louisiana was directly attributed to the crimes of nightriders. In Alabama, where twelve companies of infantry supervised the election, Grant received 76,414 votes to Seymour's 72,477.

The Union general triumphed in Alabama because of his strong showing in the Black Belt. In counties like Greene, where freedmen far outnumbered whites, Grant received three times as many votes as Seymour. Hays was partly responsible for the large black turnout. Aware of the senator's contribution, editor John G. Stokes of the *Montgomery Alabama State Journal* praised Hays for working "untiringly and with zeal" and for epitomizing those "who have stood out against the storms of obloquy and abuse."[31]

Several days later, in early November, the state legislature met in Montgomery. Returning to the theme of economic development, Governor

Smith stated in his opening remarks that "capitalists abroad are anxiously seeking information respecting the latent resources of Alabama." Surveys of the Coosa, Cahaba, and Black Warrior rivers were badly needed, and Smith urged that they be undertaken. Hays listened in agreement. Yet he was more interested in Smith's comments about the recent political violence. The governor called attention to a pattern of disturbances. Without mentioning the Ku Klux Klan, Smith asked that a committee be formed to investigate the situation.

In part, Smith was reacting to the shocking murder of M. T. Crossland. Several days earlier the Tuscaloosa County Republican senator and two companions had been ambushed not far outside of Tuscaloosa, and Crossland was killed by a shotgun blast. Although various theories were advanced concerning his death, the most logical assumed he had been murdered because of his Republican loyalties.[32]

Hays stayed extremely busy during the two-month session, introducing and steering through legislative channels measures both local and state in design. Due to his efforts the period of collecting taxes in Greene was extended. More important, Hays authored a bill providing for the strict observance of a constitutional article earmarking one-fifth of annual state revenues for education. As a member of the Internal Improvements Committee, Hays backed the governor's development plans, applauding the approval of the Coosa River survey plan and regretting the defeat of the Cahaba River plan. Anxious that the projected Black Warrior study go forward, Hays drafted a congressional memorial requesting federal funds.

Consideration of a common carrier bill pointed to Hays's deepening commitment to colorblind principles of fairness. Laws guaranteeing equal access to public accommodations were passed by several Republican-controlled Southern legislatures. Early attempts to do so in Alabama failed. During the first session a measure establishing integrated accommodations on steamboats, railroads, and other public conveyances had passed the house but had stalled in the senate. A similar proposal now suffered the same fate. That was not Hays's fault. On December 16, in an unrecorded "long speech," Hays futilely promoted the common carrier bill.[33]

Bringing to justice political outlaws concerned Hays even more. The subject of enforcement legislation gained wide attention. The Joint Committee on Outrages (formed at Smith's request soon after the legislature met) submitted its conclusions following the Thanksgiving recess. Committee members had taken testimony establishing the existence of an active

and conspiratorial white brotherhood. The committee proposed three statutes. Prospects of passing some enforcement legislation had improved
since the failure of the Ku Klux Klan Bill during the first session. Gubernatorial pressure, recent presidential election violence, the Crossland murder, and the committee findings contributed to a sense of urgency.

For several days, in late November and early December, the subject
totally dominated discussion. Democratic reaction was predictable and
sometimes innovative. The *Montgomery Advertiser* ridiculed "imaginary
Ku Klux Klans," and the *Mail* warned facetiously of "these strange and
dreaded creatures that carry their heads under their arms" and "live in the
crevices of the rocks." [34] The legislature enacted two laws. One established
severe penalties for masked outlaws, absolved anyone of fault who killed
these disguised criminals, and threatened law enforcement officials with
punishment for failing to pursue such offenders diligently. A second statute
leveled a $5,000 fine on citizens in counties where mobs or disguised out-
laws committed political murders; surviving relatives would receive the
money. Governor Smith signed both before the legislature broke up on
the last day of the year. [35]

Hays felt such coercion was necessary. Certainly his recent experiences
while campaigning indicated the need for protection. And profoundly
affecting him was the murder of M. T. Crossland. The Tuscaloosa County
senator's death was more than a distant crime to condemn in the ab-
stract. Hays and Crossland had been friends. Taking the execution-style
fate of Crossland for what it was—a political assassination—Hays denounced the perpetrators. Hays initially impressed those he met as genial.
A better acquaintanceship with him revealed a certain volatility. As an observer commented, the Crossland murder was "well-calculated to rouse
Senator Hays's venom." [36] Hays had drafted a resolution denouncing the
"cold-blooded" murder and the "organized band of assassins." [37] Later, as
a congressman, he would shift his focus to the entire South and demand
enforcement legislation. For the present the theater was Alabama.

By the end of 1868 Hays had resolved a personal dilemma. He had originally left the Democratic party because Conservatives seemed wedded
to the past and oblivious of the war's mandate. Little had changed since
he made that decision. His former party remained pledged to white supremacy, and—equally offensive to Hays—unresigned to the authority of
the federal government. Hays considered the Seymour-Blair platform an
uncompromising manifesto that only rebels, not loyal citizens, could em-

brace. Yet the extremism of some Radicals had caused him to vacillate briefly. But the course of men such as Datus Coon and Isaac Sibley was ultimately less upsetting to Hays than that of the unrepentant and unreconstructed Conservatives. And Hays could work inside the Republican party to temper certain elements. He hoped to exert a moderating influence. When *Eutaw Whig and Observer* editor Joseph Taylor accused Hays of inciting unrest among the freedmen, Hays replied, "I defy him to point to a single act of mine since I have been in public office which was extreme, vindictive, or bitter."[38] The Republican pointed out that he had counseled peace and opposed measures that threatened tranquility. In the same public letter Hays pointed to his love for Alabama. His words had little effect. The incongruity of Hays's personal background and his recently adopted political loyalties continued to confound and anger whites. Hays's enemies invariably attributed his Republicanism to self-aggrandizement and opportunism. They were not completely wrong. Hays was neither selfless nor disingenuous. He had already turned his attention to higher office.

4

A Southern Republican
Goes to Washington

One day into the new year 1869, Hays wrote Charles Dustan, a Republican friend, "I envy your being in New York but know that you will make a good thing of it and occasionally drink a good bottle of wine and eat a good dinner in remembrance of your poor persecuted scalawag and carpetbag friends." He mentioned the Fourth District Republican nominating convention in June and his hopes of receiving the nomination to run for the U.S. Congress. Although he did not expect opposition, Hays concluded, "I hope you will be [there] to assist a needy friend."[1] By June, Dustan would long since have returned home to Marengo County.

Bearing on Hays's decision to seek the congressional seat was an opportunity. Late in 1868, Charles Pierce, the incumbent Republican congressman from the Fourth District, accepted a position as assessor of internal revenue of the First District. A special congressional election was set for Tuesday, August 3, 1869. Hays immediately declared his candidacy.

Many Black Belt Republicans believed that Hays was the most logical nominee. Early in 1869 an unidentified Republican commented, "he deserves it and I hope he may get it."[2] Undoubtedly the unidentified Republican based his endorsement on Hays's state senate record and his record of service to the party. Hays enjoyed powerful Republican support across the Fourth District. James A. Abrahams backed him in neighboring Sumter County. More than sixty years old, Abrahams had been a planter, store owner, and, since May 1867, Sumter's probate judge. In Hale County, separated to the east from Greene County by the Black Warrior River, Hays claimed the allegiance of William T. Blackford, a Greensboro doctor who had forfeited local respect among whites by serving as the Hale County probate judge. Pierce Burton also favored Hays's candidacy. After the war ended he had moved to Marengo County from Massachusetts, and he served as a Freedmen's Bureau agent, sat with Hays in the constitutional convention, and in 1869 began editing the *Demopolis Southern Republican*. In Choctaw County, further to the south, Hays depended on Joshua Morse, a former highly reputed member of society who created a "storm of opposition at home" by joining the Republican party.[3]

Hays's political prospects were also firmly anchored in Greene County. William Miller provided his friend political as well as financial aid. Miller had accepted the lucrative position of collector of customs in Mobile, but his successor in the Greene County probate judge's office, Attoway R. Davis, a native Alabamian, was also an ardent Republican. So was Samuel W. Cockrell. Forced to maneuver on one leg since Malvern Hill, the former Confederate colonel and local lawyer had shocked friends by joining the Republican camp. Also active locally were John Coleman, Hays's former overseer; Samuel B. Browne, a local lawyer and for a time a tax assessor; and Lowndes Womack, Hays's half-brother. Among the more articulate and active blacks supporting Hays were Kimbrough Jeffries, Nimrod Snoddy, Lloyd Leftwich, and Benjamin Alexander.

In Greene and throughout the Fourth District, Hays carefully cultivated his support. That his name was immediately mentioned for Congress when Pierce announced his resignation was no coincidence. He had written other prominent Republicans besides Charles Dustan. Among some, he had reason to expect help. He apparently had previously endorsed their office bonds. (Many Southern Republicans could not meet their bonds.) An ambitious man like Hays did not hesitate to use what leverage he possessed.

If Hays were nominated, the demographic balance in the Fourth Congressional District favored his election. The fourteen-county district was carved largely from the Black Belt. Three or four times as many freedmen as whites lived in Greene, Hale, Marengo, Perry, and Sumter counties, and blacks held a slight numerical advantage in Choctaw County as well. In Pickens and Tuscaloosa counties, whites comprised a narrow majority, and elsewhere, in Autauga, Bibb, Baker (renamed Chilton in 1874), Fayette, Sanford (renamed Lamar in 1877), and Shelby counties, a large white majority existed, but these counties in the district's eastern and northern extremities were less populated than the Black Belt. More than 128,000 freedmen lived in the Fourth District, as compared to 76,000 whites. With

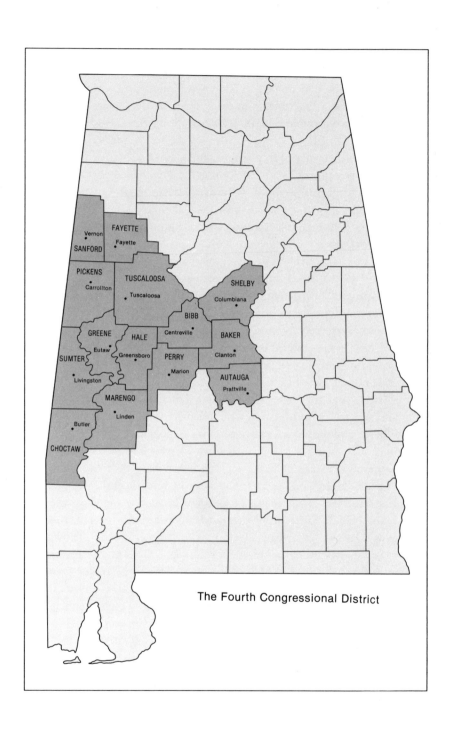

The Fourth Congressional District

Charles W. Dustan, Hays's opponent in the 1869 congressional election (Alabama Department of Archives and History).

reason, one party member referred to the district as the "Gibraltar of Republicanism."[4]

Securing a congressional nomination required a majority vote of the delegates at the district convention, which was scheduled to take place on June 16, in Marion, the county seat of Perry. Meeting earlier, Republicans in each county chose representatives and sometimes endorsed a candidate. Representation was determined proportionately by the number of Republican votes cast countywide during the 1868 presidential election.

Hale County Republicans convened on May 15 and pledged Hays their support. Republicans in Greene County met a week later at Hays Mount. That site, the original Hays family homestead, often had served as the setting for Republican rallies. Six delegates pledged to Hays were named: three blacks and three whites. Party members in other counties did not always fall into line. Marengo County Republicans met at a freedmen's church and designated six uninstructed delegates. At Prattville, in Autauga County, a preference for Judge W. G. M. Golson was indicated.

Charles W. Dustan ultimately offered the most formidable opposition to Hays. The New York native had resided in Marengo County since retiring as a Union brigadier general after the war. As a subagent for the Treasury Department, Dustan made few friends locally collecting taxes on confiscated cotton and acting with the Republican party. He had also represented Marengo County at the constitutional convention and gradually gained some standing locally. Although the pairing seemed unlikely, he married Edith Whitfield, the daughter of a Confederate general. Her father, Nathan B. Whitfield, was a prominent Marengo County planter and the owner of Gaineswood, a noted Black Belt mansion at Demopolis. Dustan aspired to hold political office and was inquiring about various patronage positions by early 1869. As his options narrowed or disappeared altogether, the vacated congressional seat became increasingly attractive.[5]

In 1869 both Hays and Dustan were thirty-five, and as planters and members of a finite minority—white Republicans in the Black Belt—they shared common concerns. The two also shared a desire to become a congressman. Hays and Dustan had been acquainted at least since serving together at the constitutional convention. They lived in adjacent counties and visited each other socially. But that relationship was tested and then broken by the strains of politics. In May, Hays received "a very precise and caustic letter" from Dustan. He replied, "Our intercourse had always been of the most pleasing and friendly relations and you are entirely mistaken in the man if you think that I allow politics to interfere with the friendship that I have for my personal friends." Deducing Dustan's opposition, if not his exact intentions, Hays added, "If you do not think that I am the right man [for the congressional seat] go for the one you may think better suited in your judgement and I shall think none the less of you for it. But in all conscience let us be friends *personally* if not politically." After all, "If I am beaten in the convention for the nomination or if I am beaten after nomination it will not kill me." Hays continued philosophically, "I have in my life passed through much worse disasters." Less candidly he professed that he would "just as soon remain quietly at home and attend to my business which demands it as to go [to] Washington." Hays never abandoned hope of restoring his cotton lands to prosperity. But he was much more interested in politics than planting. He continued methodically to line up support during the remaining weeks before the convention. Although Dustan did not openly challenge Hays before the Marion conclave, neither did he abandon his congressional aspirations.[6]

Delegates from thirteen of the district's fourteen counties assembled at Marion on June 16. The Republicans registered formal approval of the pending Fifteenth Amendment (prohibiting disenfranchisement because of race), Grant's administration, and the national Republican party platform. Other business was not settled so easily.

Hays was the strong favorite to receive the congressional nomination. Golson offered some opposition, and Dustan commanded the covert support of several Marengo County delegates and thinly scattered loyalty elsewhere. A resolution offered by John W. Dereen, a Marengo County ally of Dustan, tested Hays's strength. He proposed requiring two-thirds of the delegates to approve any choice for the nomination. Those committed to or leaning toward Hays defeated that obvious attempt to block his nomination.

Another contentious issue involved the amnesty question. The Fourteenth Amendment's political disabilities remained in place despite criticism from both parties. Anyone who had before the war taken an oath to support the Constitution and then violated the oath by aiding the Confederacy was forced to apply individually to Congress for a pardon. Concerning that question, Judge P. E. O'Connor, another Dustan supporter from Marengo County, moved for adoption of a resolution endorsing the removal of political disabilities and the abolition of test oaths. A majority opposed moving from the national Republican platform's position. The national Republican party did not mention the word *amnesty* (the Democratic platform did) and left the question of voting to each state. O'Connor's proposal was tabled.

Any sense of suspense regarding who would be the nominee ended with the defeat of Dereen's resolution. Joshua Morse of Choctaw County placed Hays's name in nomination. Golson's name was offered but immediately withdrawn, and Hays was nominated by acclamation. Two delegates, probably Dereen and O'Connor, offered token resistance.

Events in Marion culminated a remarkable political ascent for Charles Hays. In two years he had established himself as a leading state Republican politician. A certain amount of money, social stature, political luck, and ability had paved the path. In a short and emotional acceptance speech, the nominee said, "I think this is one of the happiest days of my life." Thanking the delegates for their confidence, he promised, "I will in the future, as in the past, support the great principles of freedom and equal rights maintained by the Republican party." Having moved with Machiavellian purpose to secure the nomination, Hays now attempted a political maneuver requiring even more finesse. He hoped to build a bipartisan consensus: his appeal for Republicans to close ranks included entreaties to the Democrats. The congressional nominee of the Fourth District offered political foes "the olive branch of peace."[7]

The few Republican journals responded to Hays's nomination with endorsements of his character and credentials. Editor John Stokes of the *Montgomery Alabama State Journal* described him as a distinguished party servant and "a gentleman of culture, learning, influence and wealth." Pierce Burton echoed the praise in the *Demopolis Southern Republican*. More surprising was the position of the *Montgomery Advertiser*. Editor William Screws had known Hays when he sat in the state senate. His impression was not altogether unfavorable. Screws reasoned that as a native, a political moderate, and a man of property, Hays was at least preferable to his carpetbagger predecessor.[8]

Indecisiveness characterized the efforts of Fourth District Democrats before their party district convention in Marion on June 23. Some observers speculated that the Conservatives would not offer any candidate. The disabilities imposed by the much resented Fourteenth Amendment excluded some. A more crucial consideration was the large Republican majority in the district. Alarmed by party inactivity in the Fourth, editor Hodgson of the *Montgomery Mail* decried the despondency and urged Conservatives to coalesce and overcome the Republican plurality of 4,000. The admonition provoked editor Mortimer M. Cooke of the *Marion Commonwealth* to wonder how Hodgson "could have blundered as hugely in his estimate of the relative strength of the two parties in this District." Cooke offered an alternative that shocked his readers. Taking into consideration black political strength and the apparent absence of a strong white candidate, Cooke proposed running a freedman against Hays. If a Caucasian could not be found, "In God's name say we, put a negro after him."[9]

Tuscaloosa and Perry County Conservatives met and chose delegates but suggested no suitable challenger to Hays. Greene and Marengo County Democrats advised against nominating anyone. Observing the Conservatives' dilemma from Demopolis, editor Pierce Burton could not hide his smug pleasure. He wrote in the *Southern Republican* of the "weary pilgrimage" to Marion and the Democrats' "tearful task of inducing some weak-minded brother to allow himself to be offered up as a sacrifice."[10]

At the same time Burton dubiously noted the rumored candidacy of Charles Dustan. That supposition became more likely in the intervening week (June 16–23) between the Republican and Democratic conventions. Without providing any explanation seven Republican delegates to the Marion convention issued a public letter on June 18 endorsing Dustan. Among the signatories were John Dereen and P. E. O'Connor. But Dustan's candidacy was only expected, not declared. The former Union general was waiting to see what the Democrats would do.

Fourth District Democrats met in Marion on June 23. A roll call revealed the party's apathy: only twenty-eight delegates from nine of the fourteen counties answered. Those attending approved a resolution denouncing Republican rule but did little else. Agreeing it was "unwise and inexpedient" to nominate a candidate, the convention broke up without doing so.[11]

Dustan declared his candidacy as an independent Republican several days later. He almost surely would not have run if the Democrats had nominated someone. As it was Dustan expected to gain significant Conservative support. He had earlier discussed seeking the Democratic nomination with James A. Moore, a prominent Marion citizen. Moore mentioned the possibility to *Marion Commonwealth* editor Mortimer Cooke, who felt that Dustan would be better served running as an independent. Sentiment for the general existed among whites, more could be generated, and Cooke claimed, "If he runs Independent he may count [on] 3/4 of the Democratic votes here about."[12]

Thus the bizarre campaign began: a regular Republican faced an independent Republican who had the support, restricted and unrestricted, of Conservative Democrats who had no candidate of their own. Dustan's prospects improved immediately when sixteen Marengo County Conservatives issued a manifesto on his behalf. The name of Francis Strother Lyon headed the list. In his late sixties and an Alabama resident since the territorial period, Lyon was well known and respected. The influential planter had the peculiar distinction of having served in both the U.S. and Confederate Congresses. He lived in Demopolis at Bluff Hall, an impressive home on the Tombigbee River.

With the support of Lyon and the parties who signed the manifesto, Dustan had established himself as a man of integrity. According to Dustan's sponsors, Hays suffered by comparison. In fact, the manifesto's authors devoted more effort to condemning Hays than praising Dustan.

What troubled the Marengo County cabal most was the contradiction between Hays's Confederate past and his present Republican status. In pursuit of "place and power," Hays had "turned upon" his section, they felt. The manifesto authors also faulted Hays for supporting enforcement and taxation legislation in the state senate. Most precisely, the political disability question defined the difference between Hays and Dustan. The defeat of the resolution at Marion calling for the removal of political disabilities provided the basis of the sixteen Conservatives' criticism. With more partisan license than logic, the Democrats inferred Hays's reservations about amnesty and doubted his "professions of kindly feeling toward us." By contrast, Dustan's unequivocal stand against political punishment dated from the constitutional convention. And, more recently, they pointed out, he had drafted the antiproscription resolution voted down at Marion. Under the circumstances, "an open enemy in war" was preferable to a "renegade." [13]

Hays provided an immediate rebuttal in a public letter to the *Carrollton West Alabamian*. The pragmatic politician kept in mind his audience (white) and forum (a Democratic paper). His reply to those "placing me in a false light" hardly resembled a Radical polemic. Emphasizing his native ties, Hays reaffirmed his Southern loyalties and his Confederate service record extending "from the beginning to the end of the war." He denied any inconsistency between serving the Confederacy and acting with the Republican party. His controlling interest, Hays continued defensively, was restoring the relationship between Alabama and the federal government. The nominee categorically rejected proscription and directed skeptics to his voting record in the senate and his resolution petitioning Congress to remove political disabilities. If any doubts remained, Hays endorsed the resolution offered but tabled at the Marion convention.[14] His first attempt to establish a generous amnesty position had been made.

In addition to Mortimer Cooke's *Marion Commonwealth*, the editors of the *Carrollton West Alabamian*, the *Butler Choctaw Herald*, the *Demopolis Exponent*, and the *Livingston Journal* also endorsed Dustan. From Montgomery, *Advertiser* editor Screws withdrew his qualified support of Hays, denounced the Republican as a self-serving hypocrite, and commended Dustan to the electorate. Other Democratic editors refused to overlook his background. *Tuscaloosa Independent Monitor* editor Ryland Randolph noted Dustan's Northern heritage and condemned the Union general as an "unprincipled adventurer" belonging to a class of "rapacious ghouls."

Randolph did not intend his indictment of one Republican as an implicit approval of another. He attested to every word the Marengo County Democrats employed and added a few to describe the "quondam nigger-driver-now-nigger cajoler-Hays."[15]

In Hale County, editor John Harvey of the *Greensboro Alabama Beacon* framed the situation differently. The Virginia native had taken a Democratic stance at the *Beacon* since 1844 and unfailingly supported Stephen Douglas in 1860. Harvey attributed the Democratic impotence in the Fourth District to the party platform. He argued in frustration that by not agreeing to black suffrage, state Democrats "left their friends in such counties as Hale, and such Congressional districts as the Fourth, at the mercy of the Radical party." Conservatives must condone the freedmen's political rights or face defeat indefinitely. Until then, "We have not the ghost of a chance of success in any political contest." Harvey and the *Alabama Beacon* remained neutral.[16]

A debate at the Marengo County courthouse in Demopolis on July 8 offered an early test for the candidates. About three to four hundred blacks and whites gathered to hear Hays praise the Republican party and the Union and to wave "the stars and stripes magnificently." Hays was capable of eloquence, and audiences appreciated the art of oratory. But the boisterous Black Belt crowds also enjoyed give and take. An angry Hays charged that Dustan obviously placed personal ambition above party welfare. As an observer at Demopolis commented, Hays "pitched into Gen'l Dustan with a vengeance."

Taking his turn, Dustan accused Hays of packing the district convention with beholding public officials whose bonds he had signed. His own record of service to the Republican party, Dustan assured listeners, easily predated Hays's. The former general reminded freedmen how he had fought for their emancipation while his opponent struggled to preserve slavery. Dustan was not an astute politician, but he realized the political impropriety of "waving the bloody shirt" before white Southerners. Switching to a more popular subject, Dustan called for the lifting of the Fourteenth Amendment disabilities.[17]

The debate provided an exception. Usually the candidates campaigned separately with several accompanying speakers. Hays spoke in each of the district's fourteen counties. The Selma and Meridian Railroad ran east-west and expedited his travels. He also frequently took the Alabama-Chattanooga line that slashed diagonally through the Fourth District.

Carriages conveyed Hays and his entourage to points not accessible by rail. Large crowds of freedmen greeted him in Hale, Perry, Sumter, and other Black Belt counties in the Fourth District. He invariably responded by preaching the Republican gospel of equality and opportunity. Ryland Randolph claimed that Hays's speech at Tuscaloosa on July 21 was "more niggerish than any of his former efforts." [18] At other times Hays seemed more practical than principled. In predominantly white Fayette County he soft-pedaled his Republican message. "If you meet Hays," a supporter who heard the Republican nominee speak in Fayette wrote Dustan, "ask him . . . why he did not make a Negro speech up here." [19]

Hays enjoyed the advantage of being the regular party nominee. That status meant Republican officials would campaign in his behalf; more important, the party mantle conferred on him a legitimacy Dustan lacked. No one was more qualified to pass on credentials and bestow favor than the editor of the official party organ. Writing in the *Montgomery Alabama State Journal*, editor John Stokes chided that Dustan "must feel nice in his new clothes." [20] Party discipline loomed larger than usual because the regular party nominee was challenged by another wrapping himself in the party cloak. Many Fourth District Republicans agreed with William Jones. Having recently returned to the Republican party, the Marengo County politician retracted the "uncalled for" remarks that he had made about Hays the previous October at Forkland. Jones endorsed Hays because he was the designated party candidate. Expostulating in a long public letter, he warned others about supporting a man sponsored by Democrats hoping to splinter the Republican party.[21]

Establishing himself as a proponent of amnesty was Hays's burden among whites. He began by refuting in writing the allegations made by Dustan's Marengo County allies. In person, Hays moved through the towns, communities, and crossroads of the Fourth District with the same message of protest against proscription. As a correspondent at a Livingston rally in Sumter County reported, Hays "took occasion to correct the report that he was opposed to the removal of political disabilities." [22]

Dustan faced inherent problems beyond his ability to overcome. An optimistic friend felt he could defeat Hays by gaining "the whole white vote & enough of the cold [colored]." [23] But putting together such a coalition was difficult. In Marengo County, where he was well known, Dustan had favorably impressed Francis Lyon and others. It was crucial for him to gain the backing of similarly placed individuals outside his adopted home county. The independent candidate used his highly publicized opposition to proscription for leverage. At the same time he enthusiastically sought black votes. Gaining support from blacks involved promising economic help, fair treatment, and protection and, at Greensboro on July 24, accusing Hays of lacking any genuine concern for the freedmen. Appealing to both races required a delicate balancing act and a better politician than Dustan. Casting a ballot for a Union general and the late enemy presented obvious difficulties for most whites. Dustan did not facilitate matters by consistently proclaiming his Republicanism. Neither could he shake the freedmen's loyalty to Hays. Blacks insulted a Dustan speaker at a freedmen's picnic in Autauga County by calling him a Judas. The incident was isolated but symptomatic. The independent candidate reluctantly faced reality as the campaign progressed: he was convincing few blacks or whites.[24]

The belated challenge of a Democratic candidate further weakened Dustan's chances. John B. Read, a Huntsville native and University of Alabama graduate, had received an M.D. degree from the University of Louisiana at New Orleans in 1842. Since then, Read had practiced as a doctor and surgeon in Tuscaloosa. He entered the contest in mid July and issued a campaign prospectus squarely basing his candidacy on the doctrine of white supremacy. If the differences between Dustan and Hays often blurred, Read offered a distinctly different set of principles. He granted basic rights to blacks but confirmed the Democratic party as "the white man's party of this country." Historical precedents for Caucasian superiority were abundant. Read cited the histories of Africa, China, and even the Kingdom of Siam. The Southern states were no different. Postbellum developments necessitated some readjustments, but Read made it clear that he thought that Western civilization was based on white dominance.[25]

The Democratic candidate delivered his most telling blasts in the predominantly white counties of Baker, Bibb, Fayette, Sanford, Shelby, and Tuscaloosa. In Centreville, the Bibb county seat, Read opened his campaign by debating Hays on July 22. Read asked how a man who had worked slaves in his cotton fields could pose as the champion of his ex-chattel. He also accused Hays of voting for increased taxes. (The state legislature had approved a property tax.) Forced to the defensive, Hays replied that he paid more taxes than anybody in Greene County and was in complete agreement with the abolition of the peculiar institution.

Even the entry of a Democrat into the campaign did little to stoke white interest. "We can't exactly locate the Democrats in the 4th," William Screws observed from Montgomery. The *Advertiser*'s editor continued, "Some are doing nothing, some working for Dustan and some for Read and until things change, we can only bid them God speed, and may the right triumph."[26] Yet apathy among whites did not spare Hays intense and personal attacks. Self-described "T," writing from Demopolis, described him as "objectionable as a man; odious as a politician, and a traitor to the land of his birth."[27] Turning his attention from the Second District, Robert McKee of the *Selma Southern Argus* offered a frank and familiar assessment. Hays had sacrificed his race, family, and section for the sake of political office. The "vilest carpetbagger" or the "worst negro" might be forgiven their Republican transgressions, reasoned McKee. A Southern white native could not.[28]

It was clear before election day (August 3) who would represent the Fourth District in Congress. Hays won a landslide victory. He received 17,343 votes to Read's 4,883 and Dustan's 2,011, capturing ten of the four-teen counties and 72 percent of the vote. John Read triumphed in Bibb, Fayette, Sanford, and Tuscaloosa counties. Entering late, he had confined his campaign to the northern and white counties. In some places Demo-crats did not even know he was running. Read took some votes, but not a significant number from Dustan. The Union general did not carry a single county, running strongest in Marengo and Sumter. He failed completely to forge a white-black coalition. Most Democrats stayed home (over 13,000 more would participate in the next election).

Unlike the white population, the freedmen turned out in large num-bers. What occurred in Greensboro, the county seat of Hale, was repeated elsewhere. Freedmen began filtering into town early on election day, walk-ing, riding, traveling in small and large groups. About seventy-five blacks wearing calico uniforms achieved the height of purpose. Following an indi-vidual holding the American flag, they marched in step to a kettledrum. At Greensboro, and other Black Belt towns, federal troops had recently ar-rived, and they oversaw the contest. Although the Fourth District had been (and continued to be) the scene of political violence, the campaign was uneventful. The freedmen — to a man — placed Republican ballots into the poll boxes. Election day in Greensboro and elsewhere across the Fourth District passed without incident.

Both the margin and the large Republican turnout elated Hays. He wrote Governor Smith just after contest, "I am elected by a large majority." But his elation was tempered by continued political trouble. Hays related an incident involving a white Republican, Sam Brown, and a local Democrat. Brown had been arrested in Eutaw, whites and blacks were excited, and Hays thought a riot was possible. He asked Smith to declare martial law in Greene. In general, he believed, "there is no safety for any Republican."[29]

Hays's request did not bring troops to Greene. It did begin a war of words between the congressman-elect and Joseph Taylor. The outspoken editor of the *Eutaw Whig and Observer* vitriolically denounced Hays for proposing martial law. Replying in the *Demopolis Southern Republican*, Hays mixed tempered reason with caustic diatribe, defending his request for troops due to the dangerous situation that Sam Brown's arrest had caused. The congressman confessed only to hoping to avoid a riot and charged that what he had consistently worked to avoid — violence — Taylor encouraged with his bitter and incendiary editorials. Had not the *Whig and Observer*'s editor warned him that he "would not be permitted to go unpunished?" A thoroughly unintimidated Hays declared, "I fear him nor his henchmen, his threats or his ravings." Hays reminded readers that his father had been one of Alabama's earliest settlers, recalled his own birth at Hays Mount, and stated his intention of remaining in Greene County. He represented Taylor as a "foul-mouthed croaker" and a "crack-brained blatherskite" and recommended to him a self-purgative program that included some enlightening books, cool baths, and communion with his Maker.[30]

Hays was due in Washington in November, and he began putting his affairs in order. Financial problems continued to be burdensome. Earlier, in February 1869, Hays had borrowed $10,000 from William Miller. As he explained in a revealing statement, the money was "to enable me and Mrs. C. O. Hays to make our crop this year." That the formerly wealthy planter was forced to go into greater debt than the year before indicated his precarious economic position. Mention of his wife's name also pointed to Queen's central role. Hays continued to dispose of land. A month after the August election he sold William Miller 1,200 acres for $6,000.[31]

Increasingly Queen would underwrite her husband and the family. In January 1864 she had paid $10,000 to Benjamin P. Hunter for a 1,384-acre tract known as the Means Place. Sebastapol no longer accommodated the Hays family comfortably, and the Means property, near their present home, included a larger house. "Boligee Hill" had been built by Dr. David John Means in 1830. Fourteen rooms and a basement comprised the home

Myrtle Hall, the Hayses' home near Eutaw, Alabama (courtesy of Roberta Hays Lowndes).

Queen renamed "Myrtle Hall" for the colorful crape myrtle plants that dominated the hillside. Fronted by four fluted columns, the residence was simple rather than ornate, commodious but not majestic. Behind the home were a kitchen, smokehouse, brick dairy, and several other structures. Myrtle Hall faced south and from its elevated position commanded an expansive view of the rolling Black Belt stretching west into Mississippi. Queen's attraction to the home was understandable. The family had settled in by the early summer.[32]

That fall, after telling the children and his wife good-bye (Queen was pregnant and would remain at Myrtle Hall), Hays boarded a train for Washington. By 1870 over 100,000 people lived in the capital city, a third of which were black. The Washington that the Hayses spent much of the next decade in had broad appeal. Welcker's rivaled Delmonico's of New York for fashionable dining. Theater patrons enjoyed evenings at either Wall's Opera House or the National Theater (Ford's had recently closed). The main thoroughfare, Pennsylvania Avenue, was lined with fashionable brick residences, hotels of various qualities, churches, and businesses. Among the most elegant Pennsylvania Avenue establishments were the numerous gambling houses, recognizable by their curtained windows and gaslit interiors.[33]

In ensuing years the Hays family would live at the Ebbitt House, the Imperial Hotel, and a residence in Georgetown. Initially Hays resided at the Willard Hotel. Willard's, as the stately hotel was known, was located on the corner of Pennsylvania and Fourteenth Streets, and its handsome brick facade dominated most of the block. Guests often dined there, the bar rarely lacked patrons, and the elegant hotel served as a nightly gathering point for politicians, lobbyists, and other interested parties in a city where "the people inhale politics with the air they breathe and talk and think but little else."[34]

Washington appealed to the refined Hayses. A seemingly endless succession of receptions and parties provided enjoyable, if sometimes tiresome, diversions. While Congress was in session the president and his wife held weekly levees. Fulfilling the obligations of Washington society was imperative. Protocol was strict, and the wives of neophyte congressmen carefully pored over Madeline Vinton Dahlgren's *Etiquette of Social Life in Washington*. Congenial and gracious, Queen thrived in the capital city. The society columnist for the widely read *Washington National Republican* described her as a "leading attraction of Washington society." The couple took full advantage of the theater. On one occasion, mistaking Hays for President Grant, an audience rose and gave the congressman a standing ovation. Their physical similarities — both men were rather short, dark-haired, and bearded — were striking.[35]

A fact of political life for most congressmen was anonymity. In the 240-odd member body few members were well known nationally. Later, as chairman of the Agriculture Committee, Hays gained some stature, and, as the author of the Hays-Hawley letter, unwanted notoriety, but generally he maintained a low profile. The *Washington National Republican* described Hays as "inoffensive" and a "gentleman" who "never assumed to lead." Those who knew Hays well were aware of his quick temper and a harder edge. But on the surface Hays was unobtrusive and obliging. He looked like what he was — a Gilded Age politician with the accent and manners of the South. He always dressed impeccably and, in step with the style, carried a cane. He adapted easily to the relaxed atmosphere that was the U.S. House of Representatives. On Capitol Hill he was soon completely at ease.[36]

House members met in the south wing of the Capitol where the rows of desks rose in successive semicircles from the speaker's chair, creating an amphitheater effect. Visitors to that sanctum were struck by the lack of decorum. An observer found congressmen "obstructing the aisles, talking and laughing in a tone which is audible in any part of the hall, or with their feet elevated on their desks, often times fast asleep." [37] Individually, House members were not paragons of deportment, and, collectively, near bedlam seemed to rule at times. A contemporary wrote:

> until one becomes accustomed to its bewildering noises, its manifold and complicated rules and practices, and its peculiar kind of speech-making, frequently broken by sarcastic retort and impertinent interjections, it is very difficult to understand much of its legislation. A glance at the House will show members absorbed at their desks over piles of books and documents; some are writing letters, others are reading newspapers. Groups here and there are conversing in animated tones, and before the cheerful grate fires in the corners of the hall laughing. . . . On the floor there may be a running fire of debate, with keen, experienced debaters shouting at the top of their voices, for it is necessary to shout to be heard halfway across this huge hall, while others are standing in readiness to join in the discussion as soon as they can catch the Speaker's eye. . . . One is never at a loss for amusement while watching the House during a spirited session. . . . Even to be heard in the hall requires lungs of iron, and to stand against the free and often exceedingly insolent comments and personal remarks, the continual strife for mastery, and the shrewd political manoeuvering [sic] a member who makes speeches and aims to be prominent must have great courage, much endurance, a ready wit, and a very practical way of meeting all difficulties.

Hays became a part of this setting when the second session of the Forty-first Congress opened on December 6, 1869. In the House, controlled by the Republicans (like the Senate), Speaker James G. Blaine sounded the gavel. Joining Hays from Alabama were Republicans Charles W. Buckley, Alfred E. Buck, and Robert S. Heflin. William C. Sherrod and Peter M. Dox composed the Democratic delegation. Hays was assigned to the Naval Affairs Committee and to seat 37-east.[38]

Reconstruction-related issues had dominated the congressional calendar since the war. Attention shifted to pressing economic affairs during the Forty-first Congress. President Grant had devoted more than half of his inaugural address the previous March to the issue of liquidating the public debt. Coping with outstanding financial obligations had been debated by the parties in the fall elections. Republicans pledged to pay the debt in "coin" (gold), and Democrats preferred "greenbacks" (depreciated U.S.

banknotes). Republicans excoriated the opposition as repudiators. Grant recommended a gradual return to specie resumption and a repeal of war-time taxes.

Congress remained in session from December 1869 to July 1870. Most important was a measure aimed at funding the debt that passed both the Senate and the House. No steps toward specie resumption were taken, but the money question gained attention. Debate between "hard" and "soft" money men caused considerable controversy as congressmen voted along sectional lines. A chronic and crippling shortage of currency in the South dictated the position of its representatives. Southern congressmen endorsed a system that combined redistributing and expanding the bank notes in circulation. Redistribution involved correcting the huge sectional imbalance (favoring the Northeast) of circulating bank notes. Alabama's Senator Willard Warner emerged as a champion of currency inflation. Some redistribution and an increase of the bank notes to $54 million was provided by the Currency Act. For soft-money forces, to which Hays belonged, it was a partial victory.[39]

Another economic question, consideration of tariff rates, occasioned Hays's first speech. During its brief existence the Republican party had become identified with protection. During the war Congress had fixed high duties on imports to generate badly needed revenue, and the wall of protection remained high a decade later. In the South and Midwest, where agrarian interests dominated, farmers and planters protested that high duties translated into steeper retail prices. Supporters of a lower tariff rallied in the House to H.R. 1068. Among them was Hays.

Rising from his seat on March 24, 1870, Hays began by placing the trade question in historical perspective. The Alabama congressman cited the tariff of 1816 as a significant demarcation: that measure began a policy of "protection" and shifted the emphasis of preceding "revenue" tariffs. The administration of Andrew Jackson provided the next landmark as rates were lowered. Import duties had risen and fallen since, but regardless, Hays explained, legislators had abandoned the original guiding principle that "revenue should be the object and protection only the incident." Continuing, Hays claimed that he was neither diametrically opposed to protection nor in absolute favor of free trade. Southerners did not object to reasonable duties but were emphatically opposed to "any policy which legalized the act of putting the hand of the manufacturer into the pocket of the producer and consumer to take the lion's share!" Taking exception to standard Republican dogma, he argued that consumers bore the burden of high tariff rates. More specifically, the agricultural South was adversely affected. Manufacturing and agrarian interests could and must coexist, he concluded, but "one should not be allowed to flourish at the expense of the other in such degree that the life of one is the death of the other."[40]

Speeches delivered from the floor did not often change many congressmen's positions. Only rarely did even the most impassioned and well-reasoned argument alter the mind of congressmen who better understood the pressure of the party whip or his constituency. Hays had said nothing new. Essentially, as a contemporary observer pointed out, he had presented "the view of the southern planter." Proponents of lowering and raising the tariff had preceded him. Others in the Forty-first Congress followed the Alabama congressman. Little seemed to matter. Only the slightest tariff reform was carried out later in the session.[41]

The Alabama congressman had touched on various questions in his free-wheeling speech. None who had heard him doubted his determination to lighten the tax burden. The crisis of the Union had passed and so had the need for taxes, Hays maintained. Funding the national debt by paying bondholders in gold was orthodox Republicanism, and Hays stated his opposition to "the disgraceful word of repudiation." But the congressman urged caution; meeting obligations did not justify extreme taxation. There should be no immediate return to resumption of specie payment. Pursuing specie resumption and continued heavy taxation was to invite economic hard times. Hays foresaw panics, the fall of property values, bankruptcy, and misery for all, especially the poor. The so-called "money question" would become more important and Hays's comments anticipated his position.[42]

On economic questions Southern congressmen from both parties often voted together. Other issues drove them apart. Enforcement legislation would often be the subject of emotional congressional debate during Reconstruction. Ratification of the Fifteenth Amendment in March 1870 provided the immediate occasion. Inevitably, the final Reconstruction amendment, prohibiting the denial of suffrage due to race, focused attention on the South. Despite the apparent guarantees in the amendment, black political participation remained highly problematic. Coercion of freedmen during and since the 1868 presidential election provided graphic evidence. Following ratification of the Fifteenth Amendment, Republicans called for the means of ensuring its enforcement. On this occasion and in the future, the lines were clearly drawn. Republicans argued the necessity of extending federal protection to Southern citizens persecuted for their political convictions. Democrats denied that violence occurred, maintained that federal interference was unconstitutional, and warned that the envisioned legislation would create unwarranted centralization of government.

Hays took an understandable interest in the subject. Violence directed at Fourth District Republicans had alternately raged and subsided since Radical Reconstruction began. Persecution had taken the form of economic retaliation, property destruction, and terrorism. Hays had asked that martial law be declared in Greene County the previous August. A case could also have been made for deploying troops in neighboring Sumter County. Ten days after the August congressional election nightriders had attempted to kill two leading local Republicans. Since coming to Washington Hays had received "the most imploring" letters from Republicans throughout the Fourth District describing mistreatment. Worse yet, in early April Hays received a shocking telegram: Alexander Boyd had been murdered.

The Republican solicitor of Greene County was brutally shot to death on the night of March 31. If Boyd was hated as an outspoken Republican, he was feared because of his determination to prosecute several local citizens for murdering two blacks. As Hays would learn, approximately thirty armed men, cloaked in black robes and disguises, had ridden into Eutaw at about eleven o'clock. Most of the klansmen stopped at George Cleveland's hotel. About a dozen dismounted, entered the hotel, and ordered a clerk to lead them up to the second floor. Moments later they charged into Boyd's room. Shocked witnesses downstairs heard scuffling, screams, and then shots. Retreating down the stairs and joining their comrades, the assassins circled the town square shouting final defiance before galloping off. Boyd's corpse was found stretched across the upstairs hall.[43]

Alexander Boyd was William Miller's nephew, and Hays knew him well. Just days after Boyd's murder, in early April, Hays approached Oliver P. Morton, the influential Republican senator from Indiana. He was preparing a major speech calling for federal intervention in districts like the one Hays represented. The outraged congressman related to him the story of Boyd's death, various whippings and beatings, and generally "a bloody epidemic."

Morton took the Senate floor several days later. Speaking on the anniversary of Abraham Lincoln's death, the Indiana senator surveyed political terrorism in several Southern states. Morton cited Hays as his source of information for Alabama. It was not the last time that Morton, a semi-invalid known for his oratorical talent, would quote Hays. Few could have known Hays since he had been in Washington less than four months. Describing the congressman to his Senate colleagues as "a man of unquestioned character," Morton laid before them events in the Fourth District. He admitted that Hays's revelations "made my blood curdle."[44]

The debate continued on Capitol Hill. In the Senate, George Spencer soon corroborated Hays's view of the situation in Alabama. What became the First Enforcement Act emerged from a conference committee in May. The statute, designed to protect black voters and facilitate the more effective prosecution of Klansmen, passed by a strict party vote and became law with President Grant's signature. Under the First Enforcement Act's terms those interfering with elections or discriminating on the basis of race faced trial in federal court. The Alabama delegation split cleanly on partisan lines. The measure's passage represented the most significant legislation of the session.

In the meantime more mundane business occupied Congressman Hays. Naval Affairs Committee duties required attention, and Hays introduced several measures providing for the welfare of the Fourth District and for Alabama. He also sponsored the petitions of individuals proscribed by the Fourteenth Amendment (required until the Amnesty Act became law in 1872) before Congress recessed in mid July.[45]

By then Hays had turned his attention to reelection. Although he had done what he could to prepare for an orderly election from Washington, he was far from confident. Several weeks after the passage of the First Enforcement Act the congressman explained his fears to Governor Smith. "Nothing will stay the bloody hand of the midnight assassin but the presence of troops," Hays advised from Washington on July 24. With the upcoming election in mind, Hays asked Smith to maintain soldiers at Eutaw and station others in Sumter County at Livingston. With troops "we can have a comparatively orderly election." Without them he warned that "the consequences may be disastrous." Hays predicted the loss of lives and of the election. State Republicans had previously faulted Smith for not taking strict enough measures against political outlaws. Hays shared that opinion. "Will you be kind enough," he wrote Smith with measured irritation, "to do the suffering people of these counties this simple act of justice."[46]

Maintaining law and order (and therefore Republican ascendancy) was Hays's highest priority. Not expecting his appeal to have any effect, he addressed a letter the same day to Gen. Samuel W. Crawford, commander of the federal troops in northern Alabama. "As to the present executive doing anything, I have long despaired," Hays complained from Washington. In view of Smith's intransigence, he asked Crawford to make sure that troops remained in Eutaw and that others were dispatched to Livingston. He informed the general that letters arrived daily from citizens in Greene, Tuscaloosa, and Sumter counties describing "murders secretly committed by the organization known as Ku Klux." Hays mentioned specifically the fate of Boyd in Greene and a Sumter County white named James Ethridge. The latter had been seriously wounded by whites who abducted a black cook living with him. Boyd and Ethridge were only two victims. There were many more. Hays wrote Crawford that "our people have suffered for the want of some one who would dare to do his duty as the chief executive of the state." Loyalty to the government had cost Republicans their lives. That same government, Hays protested, had not provided protection, and he blamed the "imbecility of a weak-kneed governor." If the soldiers were sent, Hays predicted a 20,000-vote Republican victory in the upcoming election. He preferred not to ask President Grant or Secretary of War William W. Belknap to authorize the deployment of federal troops. Anticipating the partisan Democratic charges, he explained to Crawford that "it would raise a howl against the President."[47]

Hays heard from Governor Smith in early July 1870. Citing his attempts to establish local militias, Smith pointed to a lack of cooperation among citizens and various inherent difficulties. Full prosecution by the law was also hamstrung by the president's orders limiting the deployment of the soldiers. Unless local officials requested their support, the troops could do nothing. Smith observed that they "might as well be a thousand miles off." He also frankly stated that some officials lacked the will or compulsion to enforce the law. Despite difficulties that he hoped Hays could appreciate, Smith promised strict vigilance.[48] Efforts on those lines would not be nearly enough in what would be the most turbulent election in state history.

I Shall Die Game

Alabama Democrats promised to challenge seriously for control of the state house in 1870. As elsewhere in the South, most state Democrats had accommodated themselves to the freedmen's status. Known as New Departure Democrats, they endorsed the changes mandated by congressional Republicans. Refusing to do so, Democrats decided by 1870, was politically myopic and unrealistic. They generally forsook racial appeals, accepted black suffrage, and actively sought the freedmens' support. As a prominent party member would later recall, Democrats determined "to electioneer pretty strongly with the colored people."[1]

State Democrats met at Montgomery on September 1 and nominated a ticket. Robert Burns Lindsay received the gubernatorial nomination. A former Douglas Democrat, Lindsay had opposed secession but fought for the Confederacy. He had practiced law in Tuscumbia since the war. The party platform faulted Republicans for overtaxing, running up the debt, and assuming power illegally. It was significant that no reference was made to the freedmen. Noting that the Democrats had not outlined a political agenda, the *Montgomery Advertiser* described their platform as "an arraignment of the Radical Party" and added that the voters "are appealed to as a jury to decide whether the facts charged are true or not."[2]

A Republican schism helped the Democratic cause. The interparty fighting involved factions led by Senator George E. Spencer against Republicans loyal to Governor Smith and Senator Willard Warner. Spencer had moved from Iowa after the war and was elected by the legislature to the Senate in 1868. At thirty-two, he was, like many Alabama Republican

George E. Spencer, Republican senator from Alabama (Alabama Department of Archives and History).

leaders, a young man. His political career would be marked by success and controversy. Spencer openly faulted Smith for not taking strong action against night riders. Unlike both Smith and Warner, Spencer also opposed a sweeping amnesty bill that would remove the Fourteenth Amendment's political disabilities, which continued to prevent many Southerners from seeking office. Republican differences were not based solely on ideology. Spencer promoted dissension in order to advance himself. Warner was forced to stand for reelection to the Senate in December. If Democrats could gain control of the legislature they could defeat him. That would leave Spencer in control of federal patronage in Alabama. The Republican breach was well publicized in the months before the state convention at Selma in August.

The role Hays would play in the election was not certain. Early in June, while the congressman was still in Washington, Greene County Republicans met at Hays Mount and named delegates to the state Republican convention. The delegates also passed a resolution thanking Hays for his service in Congress and unofficially nominating him for governor.

That Governor Smith desired a second term was well known. Yet privately and publicly other candidates had been mentioned for the office. How seriously Hays considered seeking the governorship is not known. By design or not, he was not mentioned for a second congressional term prior to the Fourth District convention (to be held at Demopolis on September 6). Nor did Republicans openly endorse him for governor in county caucuses (except in Greene). Republicans in Perry and Hale counties met, appointed delegates to the district convention at Demopolis, and thanked Hays for his congressional service. Yet they did not recommend him for a second term or for the governorship.[3]

More eventful was the scheduled caucus at Livingston on Saturday, August 13. As ever, party duty beckoned, and having returned to Alabama soon after Congress adjourned in July, Hays accepted an invitation to speak. But Queen convinced Hays not to attend when one of their children became ill, and the congressman sent word by his carriage driver Saturday morning. Earlier, on Friday afternoon, several telegrams had reached Livingston warning that armed blacks were en route to the town. One wire from Boligee placed Hays at the head of two hundred freedmen. Livingston whites organized for protection and the town soon resembled an armed camp. A series of events ended the crisis: Republicans and Democrats held conciliatory talks, the blacks dispersed, and the meeting was canceled.[4]

Hays knew nothing of the difficulties until Saturday. His reaction was one of perplexity and concern. Writing Governor Smith that afternoon, he admitted, "I do not know which party is to blame for the feeling in Sumter nor shall I stop to inquire." He did know that "the governor of the state has the right to preserve the peace and to protect all of the citizens." Hays asked Smith to petition President Grant for troops and to station soldiers in Livingston. The congressman pointed to the state's recent economic progress and described himself as a "warm, consistent and uncompromising supporter of your Administration." He had only one reservation: citizens must be protected. "Give us this and your administration will go down . . . as being one of the most prosperous ever written in the annals of the history of *our state*."

The murder of a Sumter County black man five days later poignantly illustrated Hays's point. About twenty mounted men took Richard Burke from his Gainesville (a north Sumter County town) home on the night of August 8 and shot him repeatedly. A former Republican legislator and an elderly Baptist preacher, Burke had been active in the Union League. That the assailants perhaps rode over from Mississippi was as close to identifying them as authorities came.[5]

The murders of Alexander Boyd and Richard Burke were blatantly political. Hays shared Spencer's opinion that Smith had vacillated and left Republicans vulnerable. He stated as much to the governor in their correspondence. Writing Gen. Samuel Crawford, Hays had used stronger language to describe the "weak-kneed" governor. But the congressman could be critical of the executive and still eventually support him. Out of a sense of party loyalty he had never criticized Smith publicly. As lines formed prior to the Selma convention, Hays moved into the Smith camp. He condemned Spencer's self-serving power play and faulted the senator for much of the party's division. Certainly Hays disagreed with Spencer's unmagnanimous amnesty position. Hays was in attendance when the convention met at Selma on August 30. If he had ever seriously considered challenging for the Republican nomination, Hays had put those thoughts aside by that time.

Despite some bitter acrimony, Smith was renominated. The party platform declared support for equal rights, public schools, internal improvements, and amnesty and registered opposition to Democrats' coercive tactics. The ticket included James Rapier. A free black before the war, Rapier's nomination as secretary of state would cost Republicans some core white support.[6]

Hays received the Fourth District congressional nomination the next week when Republicans met at Demopolis on September 6. Col. John A. Farden (Autauga County), Capt. C. L. Drake (Marengo County), and Greene Lewis (Perry County) offered token opposition. Most delegates were loyal to Hays and he was easily renominated. He thanked the convention and promised an all-out effort.

Hays's chances of reelection were less than certain despite the large Fourth District Republican majority. Unlike the previous year, the Democrats would nominate a candidate. And the party was also actively seeking black support. Henry Watson, a Hale County citizen, described in August how the freedmen were being "courted & cajoled by their white [Democratic] brethren to attend political meetings." In Hale County the situation was typical: "A Saturday night rarely passes on without a political meeting of that character."[7]

Anticipated night riding and political intimidation was also working against Hays's cause. Well aware of the building anti-Republican sentiment, editor Pierce Burton predicted that Richard Burke's murder in Sumter County marked "the commencement of a series of Democratic electioneering documents." Less than a week after Hays's nomination, the brutal slaying of another black Republican indicated the grisly truth of Burton's assessment. A band of disguised men took Guilford Coleman from his Eutaw home about three o'clock on the morning of September 12. He had ignored warnings against serving as a delegate at the Republican state convention. Several days later the freedman's mutilated body was found at the bottom of a well.[8]

Hays took the death of Coleman extremely hard. He began a forlorn letter to Senator Warner two days later: "Again it becomes my duty to write of the death by Ku Klux of another colored man." He explained the murder was an act of political retribution, and though he felt safe, "It is hard that others should have to sacrifice their lives because they attend a convention of the party to which they belong." Especially distressing was the death of a man whom Hays had known his entire life. He wrote Warner that "there never was a more innocent man in Greene County than Guilford Coleman."

Beyond the obvious personal tragedy, Hays speculated that the political ramifications might be devastating. "This is the most stunning blow we have yet received after the death of Boyd," he informed Warner. Noting the effect on his black constituency, Hays added, "The party here is terribly demoralized and unless something is done no votes will be cast in the County or Sumter for the Republican ticket."[9] Hays soon traveled to Montgomery and called upon Gen. Robert W. Healy, chairman of the Republican State Executive Committee. He emphasized to Healy the "utter folly" of campaigning in the Fourth District without protection.[10]

At the same time Hays became more concerned for his personal safety than ever before. A frantic note from his mother reached him at Myrtle Hall ten days after his renomination. Anne Miller Womack had continued to live in Eutaw since John Womack's death in 1863. Advised by Probate Judge Attoway Davis of her son's "imminent danger," she wrote, "I cannot sleep one wink at night" and pleaded with him "not to venture out of your own house."[11] An obviously concerned Hays revealed to Warner the next day, "I have received information from various sources notifying me that my life was in danger." He assured the senator that he was "no alarmist and claim to have a reasonable share of courage." Yet Hays did not underestimate the desperation of his political enemies. Enclosing the letter from his mother, he explained to Warner, "I do not know how long it will be before you will hear of my assassination but one thing you may count on with certainty and that is that I shall die *game*."[12]

The Black Belt was only one theater of violence. In June an outspoken Republican had been run out of Tuskegee. Four blacks and one white were lynched by Klansmen at Cross Plains in Calhoun County the next month. The incident gained national attention. Other reports of violence — true, false, and exaggerated — were featured in the *Montgomery Alabama State Journal*. Gen. Samuel Crawford, whose command was increased to about 1,000 by October, dispatched troops to various centers of trouble. As election day neared, Crawford issued a circular directing them to take positions within sight of the polls, and added, "your presence is to prevent violence and intimidation to the voters."[13]

In the meantime, Fourth District Democrats had named Hays's opponent. John Gideon Harris had been selected in party caucus at the Democratic state convention in early September. The relatively unknown nominee had been born into a modest Greene County family in 1834. He had attended Greene Springs School, taught locally for several years, and in 1857 began studying law at Cumberland University in Lebanon, Tennessee. Harris returned to Greene in 1858 and practiced law at Greensboro until the Civil War. He had enlisted as a private, but meritorious service (he was wounded twice) earned promotions to captain and then to major. Harris was a respected lawyer practicing in Livingston when he received the nomination.

Hays and Harris knew each other. Both men were born the same year in the same county and attended the same school (Greene Springs). There the similarities ended. Hays had been raised among the gentry. Harris was of yeoman stock. Nothing better illustrated their respective social positions than the outbreak of war in 1861. Hays received the privileged appointment of aide-de-camp. Harris claimed no connections, and as a private, was pressed into front-line duty. Although their acquaintanceship was long, Harris's opinion of his opponent, like that of other whites who knew Hays, had fallen in recent years. He would privately refer to Hays as "my quondam-friend." Even so, Harris did not denounce Hays publicly in the manner of Ryland Randolph, Joseph Taylor, and other outspoken Democrats. He had never approved of what he termed "excitable" oratory, whether in church, which the nominee attended regularly, or at political meetings.[14]

Simple demographics seemed to dictate certain defeat for Harris. Writing in the *Greensboro Alabama Beacon*, editor John Harvey concluded that "with the heavy radical majority of this District, he can have no expectation of success, unless he can draw several thousand recruits from the ranks of the Republican party.[15] If party editors conceded his defeat, Harris might have wondered about his chances. Yet, the candidate rejected the negative logic. Acting on the premise that "political office should be neither sought nor declined," Harris announced his candidacy in a public letter. He simplified the campaign to a contest between the forces of "intelligence, virtue, and economy" and "ignorance, fraud, and corruption."[16]

Harris quickly assumed the offensive. Speaking at Carrollton on September 29, he attributed financial extravagance, ruinous taxation, and general corruption to the Republican administration. The nominee had sounded the theme of law and order in his letter of acceptance. He repeated that maxim at the Pickens county seat. "Able and eloquent" were the words editors A. Henry and L. E. Gilbert of the *Carrollton West Alabamian* employed to describe Harris's speech. What impressed them was the candidate's "overwhelming and withering argument against radicalism."[17] Traveling north to Sanford County, Harris likened the Smith administration to a spinning ship caught in a whirlpool and out of control. Extending the maritime analogy, Harris advised freedmen to accept passage without demanding to be captain. At the same time he promised the freedmen protection and their constitutional rights. A witness observed that he maligned the Republicans "without gloves" and compared them to "a set of thieves and robbers."

Several days later at Columbiana, the county seat of Shelby, Harris predicted victory. Slandering his opponent was not part of the repertoire of a man who occasionally went to three separate church services on Sunday. As in the past, he did not name his Republican foe. He concluded at Columbiana by eulogizing the recently deceased Robert E. Lee. Hays's opponent proved both a capable and diligent campaigner. In Sanford County, Harris cemented an incongruous coalition of "old Union men, secessionists, old line whigs and democrats, and indeed many good Rads."[18] Elsewhere audiences reacted enthusiastically to his confidence and obvious dedication. The Democratic candidate attracted attention and large crowds, and many citizens responded by registering to vote. A Perry County observer confirmed that "Democracy is on the increase,"[19] and from Pickens County came word that Harris "does not recognize the word fail as being in his vocabulary."[20]

Hays began his reelection campaign auspiciously enough on Septem-

John Gideon Harris, Hays's opponent in the 1870 congressional election (Alabama Department of Archives and History).

ber 26, at Butler in Choctaw County. As he would throughout the contest, the incumbent shared the speaker's platform with several Republicans. Joshua Morse, Sam Browne, and a reconciled William Jones joined him in Butler. Hays connected the constitutional guarantees of citizenship with the Republican party for his largely black audience. He and others were less graciously received in Marion (October 11) and Greensboro (October 20). In Marion a white attacked without injuring a member of Hays's retinue. Outside of Greensboro, "rowdies" threatened Joshua Morse as he spoke. One haranguer drew a knife and jumped on the stage, and only through the interposition of the sheriff did proceedings continue.

Under the circumstances, Hays sharply limited his campaign. He had spoken in every county the year before when he faced Charles Dustan and John Read. But in 1870, at least in Bibb, Fayette, Tuscaloosa, Sumter, Greene, and probably elsewhere, he did not campaign for fear of violence.

It was arranged that other Republicans—not as well known or controversial as Hays—would present the party's case in the Fourth District. In
Demopolis Willard Warner, John Rapier, and Charles Dustan (seeking a
seat in the legislature) spoke on October 19. In Livingston on October 24,
Warner joined former provisional governor Lewis Parsons and Governor Smith. The triumvirate quickly encountered extreme hostility. Local
Democrats, though composing but a small minority of the audience, began
interrupting and insulting Smith moments after he began. Some whites in
the audience carried weapons, and one particularly belligerent individual,
holding and at times brandishing an open knife, assumed a pose very near
Smith. Parsons was received similarly. The Republicans concluded and
retired to a local hotel. But about twenty whites, some armed and most
drinking, followed, making them uneasy. Not without a sense of relief,
Smith, Warner, and Parsons boarded a train that evening for Eutaw.[21]

Thursday, October 25 was an extraordinary day in Eutaw. Both the Republicans and Democrats had planned speaking events. Blacks from the
outlying areas—walking, riding horses or mules, and conveyed in wag-
ons—arrived early for the well-publicized Republican meeting. Among
the many strangers in town were a number of whites who had come over
from Mississippi. By ten o'clock Main Street was crowded with people,
and the courthouse square, where the oratory would soon commence,
filled rapidly. Local proprietors welcomed the crowds and no businesses
thrived like the saloons. Groups of young white men, roughly dressed,
wearing broad-brimmed hats, and often chewing tobacco, congregated in
and about several drinking establishments.

Hays immediately realized the potential for danger when he rode in from
Myrtle Hall that morning. He and other Republicans warily noted the hostility. Some of the whites, in various stages of inebriation, openly carried
pistols, and few hid their distaste for Republicanism. General Crawford
happened to be in Eutaw. Hays warned him of possible trouble and suggested that a joint debate might ease tensions. William Miller, visiting
Eutaw, shared his friend's concern. Hays, Miller, and Sam Cockrell signed
a written invitation to debate. But John Jolly and John Pierce, both outspoken local Democrats, delivered a tersely worded reply that read, "We
do not consider the questions at the present political canvas debatable
either as to men or measures."[22]

Later in the morning the Democratic rally began on the south side
of the courthouse. About noon the Republican meeting commenced on

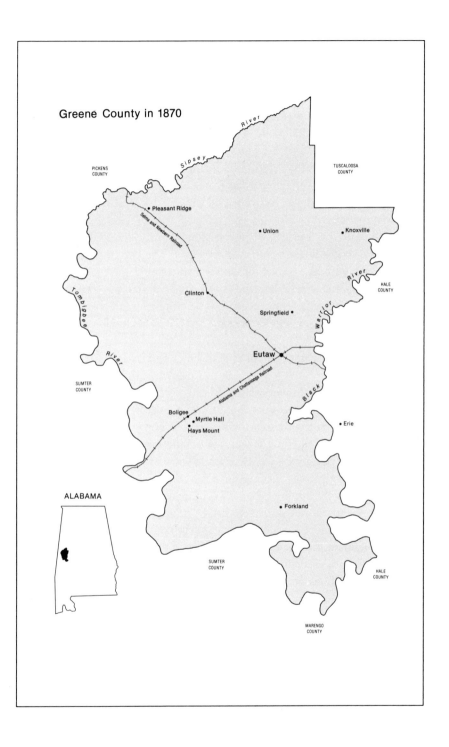

Greene County in 1870

PICKENS
COUNTY

TUSCALOOSA
COUNTY

Sipsey River

Tombigbee River

• Pleasant Ridge

Selma and Newbern Railroad

• Union

• Knoxville

Clinton

HALE
COUNTY

Warrior River

Springfield •

SUMTER
COUNTY

Eutaw •

Alabama and Chattanooga Railroad

Black

ALABAMA

Boligee
• Myrtle Hall
Hays Mount

• Erie

• Forkland

SUMTER
COUNTY

HALE
COUNTY

MARENGO
COUNTY

the opposite end. Governor Smith had fallen sick and remained in his Cleveland Hotel room overlooking the congested scene. As was arranged, Warner and Parsons faced the Republicans from a position just outside the circuit clerk's office. Hays stood nearby with his five-year-old nephew. Despite almost constant heckling from Democrats, Warner spoke for about an hour from atop a small table. The interruptions became worse after the Democratic meeting dismissed and many more whites drifted over. Parsons followed Warner. He attempted to appease the crowd by pointing to his conservative record and praising Robert E. Lee. In no mood to listen, whites responded with derisive remarks, and Parsons concluded his speech under harassment.

At that point, for "burlesque" purposes, as a local Democrat would later state, many whites began to clamor for Hays. The congressman did not plan to make an address, but the duty of adjourning the meeting fell to him. What Warner would describe as "an almost deafening" and "tremendous howl" greeted the congressman as he climbed upon the table. Hays wore a dark suit and, as was his custom, a top hat. He had begun to carry a derringer.

His appearance touched off an uproar. Hays removed his hat and, holding it behind him, waited for the din to subside. At that moment a white man pulled him from the table. Republicans and Democrats never agreed on the rapid sequence of events that followed. Sheriff William White immediately apprehended the man who attacked Hays. As he did so, shots rang out from the courthouse window behind the Republican speakers. The gunfire precipitated a frantic stampede, as blacks trampled over the courthouse fence palings, fleeing for cover and safety. Some whites fired their pistols into the air, but others took more direct aim, and the shooting continued. Calm did not return for fifteen minutes.

Hays escaped injury by taking refuge in the courthouse. Others had not been so fortunate. Estimates of the number injured or killed differed, but as one modern student of the riot has pointed out, casualties inevitably resulted when whites fired at close range into a large crowd of blacks. At least two dozen blacks were wounded. Several may have died. A dramatic ending had been written to the campaign in Greene County.[23]

The incident immediately gained statewide notoriety as the Eutaw Riot. In keeping with past policy of whitewashing political crimes, Democratic editors quickly created a myth to explain the episode. Partisan journalists absolved Democrats and adroitly turned the blame on the Republicans. According to the *Eutaw Whig and Observer*, Hays had fallen from the table and then ordered his black supporters to fire. In fact, Joseph Taylor charged, Hays had probably fired the first shot. Black Republicans were the aggressors, white Democrats the victims, and "the responsibility of the whole affair rests upon the radical leaders and especially upon Charles Hays."

Despite like-minded contentions to the contrary, Democrats were plainly responsible for the violence at Eutaw. Some Republicans claimed that the opposition planned the disturbance. That is possible. More likely, there was no premeditation. Many of the whites were drunk, some were armed, and the incident involving Hays triggered the gunfire. It is easier to evaluate what did not occur. Neither Hays nor any other Republicans did any shooting. It was no small incident for a former governor and a sitting governor, congressman, and U.S. senator to be mobbed. The Eutaw Riot, the most spectacular extension of violence directed at Fourth District Republicans, marked the end of the 1870 campaign for Hays.[24]

In the meantime Harris had continued to present his case effectively. The Democrat's campaign achieved the definition and continuity that Hays's lacked. Harris spoke convincingly and often and campaigned, as he stated, "from one end of the district to the other." On some occasions significant numbers of freedmen came to hear him. If his promises to blacks could not be confused with Hays's egalitarian message, Harris was a firm New Departure apostle. He pledged respect for the freedmen's newly gained rights and made clear his opposition to political violence. He recalled, "I took an open and bold stand against all Ku Kluxism, and all disguised men, and denounced it, and denounced all secret political organizations."[25] Hale County freedmen listened in early November to the Democrat document his "strong opposition to everything that savors of lawlessness."[26]

Harris might have hoped to attract some blacks, but he received more encouragement from the large numbers of whites who heard and cheered him. The candidate met Robert McKee as he passed through Selma. He impressed the learned editor of the *Southern Argus*. McKee wrote that Harris was "as confident as if the majority against him was only hundreds instead of thousands."[27]

Voters in the Fourth District and across Alabama went to the polls on November 8. Hays barely held off Harris's challenge. He received 18,373 votes and carried Autauga, Hale, Marengo, and Perry counties. Harris polled 16,400 votes and triumphed in eight counties. He ran well as expected in counties with as many or more whites than blacks. The Democrats claimed Bibb, Choctaw, Fayette, Pickens, Shelby, and Tuscaloosa counties. What was considerably more surprising — truly startling — were the Democratic victories in heavily black Sumter and Greene counties. Harris received thirty-five more votes than Hays in Greene and more than a six-hundred-vote plurality in Sumter.

The Republican falloff in the Black Belt cost William Smith the election. Expected Republican majorities were minimized or, as in Greene and Sumter, eliminated altogether. Robert Lindsay received 2,000 more votes than William Smith in an election where over 157,000 citizens participated. The Democrats also picked up a congressional seat and gained control of the state House of Representatives.[28]

Gideon Harris had undoubtedly inspired previously apathetic whites and received some black support. He was personally instrumental in revitalizing the Democratic party in the Fourth District. Other explanations for the political reversal in Greene and Sumter counties, offered by Hays and others, were also valid. Intimidation and fraud had played a role. Certainly the murders of Richard Burke and Guilford Coleman, and the riot at Eutaw, had terrorized blacks in Greene and Sumter counties. Although troops oversaw election duty in the Fourth District, they only discouraged the most open violence. And in Eutaw, they accomplished not even that. Nothing could prevent whites on routine workdays from making threats with impunity. As an army officer in Sumter County concluded, "The vote count in this county will prove the fact that a systematic plan of intimidation had been made and most effectively carried out."[29] It is also likely that the Republicans were counted out in numerous precincts in Greene and Sumter. Greene County's Probate Judge Attoway Davis and Circuit Clerk Arthur Smith attached with cause an appeal to the copy of the official returns. They declared that the election was "not a true voice of the people, and we further believe that there was not only fraud but intimidation resorted to for the purpose of preventing the colored men from voting the Republican ticket."[30]

The curtain had not yet fallen on the contest. Citing the irregularities in the Black Belt and elsewhere, Governor Smith refused to leave the capital when Robert Lindsay arrived later in November to assume office. The standoff ended — Smith had barricaded himself in his office — several weeks later when the Republicans reluctantly yielded. Also in December, the legislature elected a Democrat, George T. Goldthwaite, to replace Willard Warner in the Senate. The Republican defeat was nearly complete.

Hays maintained as did other Republicans that the party had been robbed. But he had no choice but to go forward. Attending to various plantation affairs, mainly overseeing the picking and baling of the cotton crop, delayed his return to Washington. He faced more severe financial problems than ever. Low cotton prices and poor crops forced him further into debt each year. As the election had neared its end, on the last day of October 1870, William Miller had loaned Hays the large sum of $18,000. Miller still held the collector of customs position at Mobile. As security, Hays put up twenty-four mules, six wagons, and the cotton and corn crops to be made at the Sebastapol, Hays Mount, and Means places. The mortgage replaced previous debts Hays owed Miller. Borrowing so much money was one indication of Hays's difficulties. The defaulting judgments in Greene that were returned against him from ten separate parties were another. Miller faithfully assumed the past debts that Hays had incurred and could not meet in 1870.[31]

The congressman, Queen, and their children, Mary Hairston, Anne Miller, and Ormond, returned to Washington early in the new year. Arriving well after Congress convened, Hays missed over a third of the lame-duck session. Had he been present at the outset he would have heard the clerk read to an assembled House and Senate President Grant's remarks. Among other matters, they concerned Spanish atrocities in Cuba, civil service reform, and the establishment of the Third Republic in France. Grant began, however, by surveying the situation in the South. Alabama and the Fourth District were only one center of unrest. No Southern state had been spared the night-riding antics of passionately anti-Republican forces during the recent midterm elections. The president regretted that "violence and intimidation" had prevented a fair contest in some areas and that "the verdict of the people has thereby been reversed." He mentioned federal safeguards. Benjamin F. Butler, Radical senator from Massachusetts, responded by drafting comprehensive enforcement legislation. Yet little was accomplished during the brief session.[32]

The Forty-first Congress adjourned on March 3, 1871, and the Forty-second began the next day. Three Republicans and three Democrats represented Alabama in the House. Incumbent congressman Charles Buckley returned for a second term with Hays. Benjamin S. Turner, a former slave, joined them on the Republican side of the House. Peter Dox, William A. Handley, and Joseph Sloss represented the Alabama Democrats. Despite some losses in the House, the Republican party remained in comfortable control of Congress and dictated the agenda.

Enforcement legislation was the highest Republican priority during the brief forty-eight-day session. Recent disturbances in the Carolinas, Mississippi, Alabama, and elsewhere caused Grant in late March to request the passage of strong federal deterrents. An extended discourse followed. Over eighty congressmen spoke on the issue, including Alabama Democrats Handley and Sloss. The Republican-sponsored bill clarified and expanded the protection guaranteed by previous enforcement measures. It defined what constituted a conspiracy, provided federal court review in related cases, and allowed the executive to suspend the writ of habeas corpus in areas deemed ungovernable. Republican spokesmen justified sweeping federal interdiction by pointing to Southern conditions. Scalawag congressman Oliver Snyder of Arkansas stated that members of the "White Brotherhood, Secret Empire, Ku Klux Klan . . . bound by terrible oaths" had declared war on Southern Republicans. Democrats claimed the bill was politically inspired, unnecessary, and unconstitutional. Taking the floor, Alabama congressman Handley read a letter written by John Pennington, a state Republican, arguing that what Alabama most needed was "to be let alone." Representative Joseph Sloss described the measure as a dangerous step toward despotism. In the House, on April 6, and soon thereafter in the Senate, Republican majorities overcame the opposition. Grant signed the Ku Klux Klan Act into law later that month.[33]

With the exception of Hays, who did not vote, the Alabama delegation split for and against the measure on partisan lines. Hays's abstention was calculated. Two days after the legislation passed, Democratic congressman Sloss wrote recently elected Governor Lindsay, "I take pleasure in doing justice to Mr. Hays, by saying, that during the discussion of what is known as the "Ku Klux Bill," he has proved himself a friend of peace and conciliation." Citing Hays's influence with the Grant administration, Sloss urged the governor to keep lawless elements in check and to provide the Republican congressman leverage. Hays, Sloss emphasized, was "violently opposed to sending United States troops to Alabama."[34] Why an outspoken opponent of political violence from a district racked by terrorism did not support the measure seemed illogical. Among others, Hays surprised Ryland Randolph by abstaining. The perplexed editor of the *Tuscaloosa Independent Monitor* asked, "What's up?" and superciliously wondered "if Charles is going to turn somersaults from loyal leaguism to Ku Kluxism?"[35]

Hays's tentativeness was more bewildering in light of recent trouble in the Fourth District. The previous month, in March 1871, William Blackford had paid Hays an unscheduled visit in Washington. As the Hale County probate judge informed Hays, a group of disguised men had visited his Greensboro home on the night of January 19. He believed they meant to kill him, and he simply could not live in Greensboro any longer. Blackford had resigned his probate judgeship. His friend's experiences alarmed Hays. If violent elements were bold enough to harm a white probate judge, they certainly would not hesitate to deal harshly with a black sharecropper. In April, Hays received a letter from a doomsaying Greene County Republican. Anonymously signing himself "Your Friend," the author informed Hays that "the devil seems to be loose in Greene County." The informant reported that recently one black had been threatened and two others abducted by a posse. As Hays read on, he learned of an attempt to poison one freedman's entire family. On another occasion, "the K.K.K. in full regalia and about 30 strong" rode out of the Hays Mount vicinity and administered twenty lashes to a black man. The letter's author knew Hays well enough to guess his angry response. He advised the congressman to "take things cooly" and not "fly into any sudden fit of temper."[36]

Despite such direct evidence of atrocities that seemed to cry out for federal intervention, Hays hesitated that spring. He had never been blind to white public opinion. The "Ku Klux Bill" represented the harshest piece of Reconstruction enforcement legislation proposed up to that time. Passage of the measure did not ensure that Alabamians would feel overnight the throttling brunt of federal intervention, but Hays correctly assumed that great resentment would result. Another consideration influenced the politically shrewd congressman: another election was less than two years away. For now, he commented, "I think the patient wants rest."[37]

The House also considered amnesty legislation. By 1870 the issue of political amnesty, long a point of contention, was gaining a certain inevitability. A large Southern majority, irrespective of party, favored removing the restrictions on officeholding imposed by the Fourteenth Amendment. As matters stood, proscribed individuals were forced to petition Congress to have their rights restored. The continued reality of political exclusion forced Southern Republicans to take a defensive position. And, as Hays and others realized, there was no defense against continued sanctions five years after Lee surrendered to Grant. An amnesty bill, H.R. 370, gained bipartisan support and passed on April 10. Hays's Republican state colleague, Charles Buckley, was among those who spoke in its favor, and every Alabama congressman supported the measure. Despite the House support, the Senate did not consider the bill before adjournment on April 20.[38]

Hays remained in Alabama from late spring to December of 1871. Various problems distracted him. Litigation difficulties stemming from the Eutaw Riot were one source of irritation. In late October 1870, soon after the trouble, a U.S. marshall had arrested several young men and charged them with complicity in the riot. Within days they appeared before a U.S. commissioner and a grand jury in Demopolis. Hays was among those summoned to give testimony, but he convinced Circuit Judge Luther R. Smith that other eyewitnesses would serve just as well. Even so Hays remained a central figure in the continuing controversy. The case was referred to the U.S. Circuit Court (Southern District) in Mobile in December 1870, and fourteen indictments based on violations of section six of the Enforcement Act were handed down. Hays had been subpoenaed in Washington to appear as a witness in the trial scheduled for the April 1871 term in Mobile. He had no intention of doing so. The congressman favored dropping all charges. The riot was over, and, as he explained, convictions after the fact "would stir up a bad feeling." That was one consideration. Hays also worried privately that to testify risked the safety of his family and property. Sam Cockrell, his Republican lawyer friend in Eutaw, had provided evidence against some of the defendants. For his efforts, Cockrell was severely beaten upon his return to Mobile. Although threatened with legal action, Hays refused to take part in these proceedings, which went forward in January 1872.[39]

Hays also involved himself between sessions in a bitter patronage battle. In Alabama as elsewhere, Republicans vigorously pursued office. That pursuit frequently divided native Republicans and their Northern counterparts who had more recently taken up Alabama residency. Attempts in the spring and summer to remove William Miller from the customs collector post in Mobile had begun a bitter struggle among state Republicans. Recently denied a second term, U.S. senator Willard Warner promoted himself as Miller's successor. Faced with a choice between an intimate friend and a political colleague, Hays strongly backed Miller. The congressman praised Miller highly in a letter to Secretary of the Treasury George Boutwell in May. Citing Miller's service to the party and his connections, Hays concluded that the collector's "removal will result in the most disastrous consequences to the Republican party in Alabama."[40] As the possibility of Miller's exit became more likely, Hays appealed to Thomas M. Peters, a Lawrence County Republican and a state supreme court justice. Miller was being forced out because he was a "native Republican" as opposed to a "carpetbagger." Awarding Southern patronage positions to Northerners was a source of extreme disagreement between party members throughout the former Confederate states. Hays warned that Warner's appointment threatened the party. The congressman pointed to the critical necessity of rewarding Republican converts among native white Alabamians. Would Peters write President Grant and Secretary Boutwell? Hays worried that if those "who have passed through the fiery ordeal of Republicanism . . . must be turned out for the purpose of allowing [preference for] the patriotic carpetbagger" then "the days of the party is [*sic*] at an end." Hays claimed that Grant supported Miller, but that Warner had the backing of Boutwell, and was visiting him "every day and making misrepresentations."[41]

Peters began a letter to Grant several days later: "I beg to call to your attention to the letter of Hon. Charles Hays herewith inclosed." Peters protested replacing Miller. The prominent Republican wrote further, "I concur with Hays" and added that "the Republican Party in this state must go to pieces under the policy of which he complains."[42]

Hays wrote Boutwell again on the last day of June. He made clear that he considered replacing Miller a grave mistake. Concerned about weakening the state Republican organization, he explained to Boutwell that Miller had lived in Alabama for over fifty years and was well connected. Envisioning the worst scenario, a Democratic victory in 1872, he reasoned, "I cannot afford to give up my property and leave the state." Hays expressed "the kindest personal feelings for ex-Senator Warner," but concluded that the Republican "has had his day."[43]

Nevertheless, the appointment of Warner was announced in July. Hays voiced his disapproval directly to the president in a telegram later that month. Soon thereafter, in early August, he indicated his displeasure to a Mobile acquaintance. "What encouragement have we to keep up the organization of the party, when we see the party receiving its death wounds from the authorities at Washington?" Hays asked rhetorically. He hoped that the president, whom he described as "a just man," would revoke the dangerous appointment. Otherwise, "it is the death knell of the Republican Party in Alabama."[44] Ever worried about the state party's precarious position, Hays communicated the same thoughts to Anthony W. Dillard. The chancellor of the Western District wrote him back in late August, "It is but the dream of a sick man's brain to even hope to build up a Republican party in Alabama without putting native men at its head." Like Hays, he understood that Republican longevity depended on attracting white Alabamians to the party. "No people relish being ruled over by strangers," he wrote the congressman. Pressure on Grant, much from Spencer, caused the president to withdraw Warner's nomination early in 1872.[45]

How Hays felt about the past and the future he made clear when he testified before a congressional committee that summer. Created the previous March by Congress, the Joint Select Committee to Inquire into the Condition of Affairs in the Insurrectionary States was commissioned to establish the true nature of affairs in the South. Hays testified in Washington on June 2. As he explained to former vice-presidential candidate Francis Blair, he held out hope for peaceful coexistence between Alabama Democrats and Republicans. Unfortunately, in the past that had not been the case. The most skeptical Democrat on the committee must have been moved by the litany of violence Hays recounted. The congressman described how Alexander Boyd had been brutally murdered in a Eutaw hotel by masked men. He also mentioned the execution-style death of Guilford Coleman. Queried further about such agitation, Hays provided an extended version of the Eutaw Riot. He related how he and other Republicans had attempted to head off trouble and described the insults suffered by Warner and Parsons as they spoke. He recalled attempting to dismiss the meeting, the following fusillade, and how he and others scrambled frantically for their lives.

In general, Hays continued, "There is a very great hostility to every man in that section of the country connected with the Republican party." He noted that young former Confederates, many of whom had lost their land, were responsible for the violence. Even if the more affluent and propertied element had not usually participated in the crimes, they still had silently acquiesced. That class had hoped the vigilantes would destroy the Republican party. Hays recalled being concerned about his own safety during the previous campaign. He informed Vermont congressman Luke Poland that friends advised him to "go out of the county for awhile" because "I was in an unsafe situation there."

Although the congressman still doubted that a Republican speech could be delivered in Eutaw, he stressed that conditions had improved. His hopes for toleration, which rose and fell, were presently high. Hays spoke of letters he had received from leading Alabama Democrats who promised reason and peace. The Ku Klux Klan Act, he felt, had frightened some into obeying the law. Over sixty defendants had recently been indicted in Alabama federal court. A general amnesty bill, Hays speculated, would also have beneficial results. "I believe the county will quiet down," he advised. Hays held out serious hope that the Republican party would be permitted to function as a viable organization by the election of 1872. Even so, he sounded a note of warning, advising against publishing the testimony he and others had provided the committee. Doing so might upset the delicate balance. He maintained that "there are men who are perfect desperadoes, who have nothing to do except to go about, and who think it is a popular thing to hound a man because he is a Republican."[46]

Hays was the second Alabamian called to testify before the committee. William Miller had been the first. About 150 followed. Many were Democrats and among them were John Jolly and John Pierce. Agreeing with Hays that peace prevailed, both Eutaw lawyers took the opportunity to fault their congressman. Jolly stated that whites in Greene considered Hays "a man who has floated to the surface by the mere force of circumstances" and dismissed him as duplicitous and justifiably out of favor. Asked whether all Republicans encountered such scorn, the barrister hedged, "We do not like them."[47] Pierce flatly commented that Hays was objectionable "personally, individually, politically, and every other way." Neither was he "a man to be trusted by friend or foe." If community leaders felt that way, objective observers might well have questioned Hays's optimism.[48]

6

The Sacred and Inalienable
Rights of Liberty

Late in 1871 Hays, Queen, and their children made what by then had become a familiar trip to Washington. The family had increased in size since it was last in the nation's capital. Queen had given birth to a boy on August 10, 1871, at Myrtle Hall. Charles Hays, Jr., was the couple's fourth and last child. About this time the Hayses moved from the Willard Hotel to larger quarters offered by the equally elegant Ebbitt House. Hays and Queen continued to lead an active social life. There was every opportunity to do so. Wives of congressmen were expected to make "calls" and leave their cards, and to be "at home" on designated days. Elaborate receptions and parties were frequent, and the Gilded Age's ostentatious display of wealth was nowhere more apparent than in the nation's capital. Writing in the mid 1870s, an observer claimed that in other cities "the mansions of the opulent and hospitable are thrown open because the host and hostess desire to see their guests. In Washington this order of things is reversed." Alexander Shepherd may have set the most garish pace among the nouveau riche. By 1871 the former gas fitter's assistant had become head of the Board of Public Works. "Boss Shepherd," as he became known, hosted some of the most elaborate soirees at his L Street and Connecticut Avenue mansion. His and Hays's relationship was destined to be less agreeable.[1]

Congress convened in early December 1871. In the House James G. Blaine sounded the gavel and the roll was called. Within the next few days the president's remarks were read and new committee assignments made. Hays was becoming accustomed to the ritual. He remained on the

Committee on Naval Affairs and was also assigned to the Agriculture Committee. The appointment to Agriculture of the only self-described "cotton-planter" in the congressional directory was appropriate.

Committee work necessarily involved some of Hays's energies. At other times, as when he introduced a petition from Sumter County citizens requesting a refund of the federal cotton tax, he acted independently. Hays also personally fought to increase federal appropriations for Alabama. Consideration of a River and Harbor Bill (H.R. 2208) provided the occasion. Willard Warner had struggled to gain money for improving Mobile's harbor. Hays took up the burden in April 1872. Noting that Mobile was one of the South's busiest ports, Hays asked that $50,000 for improvements be doubled. Congressman Omar D. Conger of Michigan immediately objected. Taking exception, Hays replied that the secretary of the Treasury recommended a $100,000 allocation. Even so, he convinced few, and the effort failed.[2]

Tariff reduction was the most important issue of the session. Southern and midwestern interests were responsible for the Tariff of 1872, the first meaningful downward revision of duties since before the war. Although Hays missed various votes (increasingly not an unusual occurrence), he joined low tariff forces in May on the key showdown. The cause of tariff reduction had precipitated Hays's first speech two years earlier. Lowering the duties pleased him, but Hays did not speak in behalf of doing so. More crucial in his mind was enforcement legislation. On this subject—partisan and controversial—Hays did take the floor.

No session of a Reconstruction Congress seemed possible without some discussion of this controversial topic. In his opening remarks, President Grant had stated that "the condition of the Southern states is unhappily not such as all true patriotic citizens would like to see." Political violence in South Carolina had recently caused the president to suspend the writ of habeas corpus in nine counties. An effective federal crackdown followed. For some congressmen, albeit fewer than previously, enforcement legislation remained a priority. Attention was briefly focused on the South when the Committee Upon the Condition of the Late Insurrectionary States reported in February 1872. Blending conciliation and coercion, the Republican majority recommended granting amnesty to former Confederates and extending section four of the Ku Klux Klan Act. That provision, authorizing the president to suspend the writ of habeas corpus, expired in June.

The reference to amnesty reflected the building momentum for that cause. Except for the tariff, amnesty received as much attention as any issue. Efforts to remove political disabilities had carried the House previously but had stalled in the Senate. But now men with backgrounds as disparate as Senator Daniel Pratt of Indiana and South Carolina congressman Joseph Rainey both spoke for the measure. Rainey, a former slave, spoke magnanimously in favor of lifting disabilities. From a Northern-Democratic perspective, Pratt advised that the continued penalties made for political discontent and excluded able men from government service. In May, the Amnesty Bill cleared the House and Senate and was signed by Grant. Thousands of Southerners regained full political rights. Hays felt the statute repealing the Fourteenth Amendment's officeholding restrictions long overdue.[3]

Extending section four of the Ku Klux Klan Act also vitally concerned Hays and other Southern Republicans. But interest in the "Southern question" by 1872 was clearly declining. Democrats, who had long sought a hands-off policy from the government, now found an increasing number of Republicans in agreement. Fewer and fewer congressmen thought like Hays and other Southern Republicans who realized the hazards of removing federal protection. Hays understood the mindset of violently anti-Republican Alabamians. He realized that "Ku Kluxism" was not an aberration of the past. A year earlier, when Congress was considering what became the Ku Klux Klan Act, Hays had declined to vote. But his objections to the legislation had since vanished, and he had testified to the measure's practical benefits before the "Ku Klux" committee.

On May 4, Hays rose to appeal for an extension of section four. He spoke at length, making several points. The most basic was that Southern Republicans, and especially black Republicans, remained at the mercy of political vigilantes. Had not the damning investigative committee findings dispelled any doubts, he asked? Despite the graphic testimony of Republicans, Hays maintained that the "half has not been told." He pointed to a history of persecution suffered by Republicans. Citizens continued to be "dragged from their firesides and shot and hung because they dared to express Republican sentiments." Hays mentioned the trouble in South Carolina. Passage of the Ku Klux Klan Act had deterred some, but he warned, "The moment this act expires the reign of blood and terror will once more commence." Hays also advised Congress of the threat to the future of the Republican party in the South. In the approaching election a fair and free vote was not possible without sanctions. Using Alabama for illustration, Hays attributed the Democratic victory two years earlier to a campaign of terror and election chicanery. The verdict could be reversed if federal deterrents and sanctions were in place. Otherwise, he did not doubt Republican defeat because "Ku Klux pistols and midnight scourgings will do the work." More philosophically, Hays recalled his conversion to the Republican party. He explained that he accepted what Democrats rejected: black citizenship. Both the freedmen and the cause of humanity had been served by emancipation. Yet Democrats rebelled at this. Instead, "They denounced, vilified, and abused those of us who believed it was right and just." The observation brought the scalawag congressman back to the subject at hand — extending the provisions of the Ku Klux Klan Act. What were theoretical constitutional guarantees to vote worth if many blacks feared to exercise them? The situation in Alabama and the South demanded extension. Without protection, allowing the freedmen the franchise was "a farce and a fraud." He could have added that, without protection, he might not return to Congress.

Hays's arguments sounded more contrived than convincing to many who listened. His impassioned appeal had no effect. Neither did that of Senator John Scott of Pennsylvania who provided a broader indictment of political outlaws. Speaking from his experiences in Tennessee, Republican congressman Horace Maynard provided a history of Democratic recalcitrance and predicted, "You will see at once a revival of the same old atrocities." Yet the sense of egalitarianism that had previously galvanized Republicans was noticeably lacking. Later that month, just before the session broke up, an attempt to suspend the rules in the House and extend the Ku Klux Klan sanctions failed.[4]

Congress recessed in June 1872. Returning to Alabama by way of New York City, the Hays family spent two nights at the exclusive Fifth Avenue Hotel. Meals, various services, and two bottles of champagne and sherry cost Hays $75.93. He would not be able to afford such luxury much longer. Several days later, following the train trip south, the family rode up to Myrtle Hall after a seven-month absence.

Word of Hays's comments advocating extending the Ku Klux Klan Act had preceded him. Joseph Taylor, now editing the *Tuscaloosa Times*, pronounced the speech "vindictive" but facetiously doubted Hays's authorship since he was "mentally incapable of writing."[5] The *Marion Commonwealth*'s newly installed editor, E. A. Heidt, attributed Hays's remarks to political motivations. The congressman was simply bidding for reelection. Enforcement legislation represented by 1872 an anachronism, Heidt claimed. The *Commonwealth*'s editor termed the speech "inexcusable" and called Hays a "vile, dirty wretch," addressing him directly: "You must soon resign the seat in Congress you have so long disgraced."[6]

Attention had turned to the election of 1872 by the time Congress recessed. Ulysses Grant was renominated at Philadelphia in June. Vice-president Schulyer Colfax, discredited by the Credit Mobilier railroad-stock scandal, was replaced on the ticket by Massachusetts senator Henry Wilson. Dissension also threatened the Republicans. Some members objected to the administration's preoccupation with Reconstruction and the failure to promote various domestic reforms. The so-called Liberal Republicans met at Cincinnati in May and nominated Horace Greeley for president. The Democrats opted not to nominate a candidate. Despite objections to Greeley—the *New York Tribune*'s editor had denounced the Democrats for years—the party endorsed the Liberal Republican nominee. In Alabama and throughout the South, party members generally fell in line and supported Greeley with varying degrees of enthusiasm. Although Greeley had campaigned stridently against slavery, he had more recently helped free Jefferson Davis from prison.

In Alabama both parties met in the summer of 1872 to select state tickets. Assembling in July, the Democrats rejected incumbent governor Robert Lindsay in favor of Thomas Herd Herndon. The Mobile lawyer and former Confederate headed a ticket composed entirely of former secessionists.

State Republicans convened in mid August at the capitol. Acting to deflect criticism that outsiders controlled the state party, Republicans nominated a straight native-Unionist slate of candidates. Senator George Spencer, who had come to an understanding with former enemies, lined up with a united party. Hays and Spencer had reached something of a personal rapprochement. Spencer took his seat beside Hays on the House Speaker's stand with several other Republican congressmen when the convention convened on August 14. David P. Lewis, a Huntsville lawyer, received the gubernatorial nomination.[7]

In Hays's congressional bailiwick, Democrats had speculated on the upcoming congressional contest. Several candidates received mention before the Fourth District Democratic convention met in Tuscaloosa in August. Many leaned toward Gideon Harris because of his strong showing two years earlier. Harris himself was interested, and in April 1872 had written

Robert McKee, editor of the *Selma Southern Argus*, "I say to you that there is but one office I have any desire for . . . and it is to defeat . . . Hays."[8] Editor Heidt began running Harris's name on the *Marion Commonwealth*'s editorial masthead in May and predicted his candidacy would "redeem our District and defeat the ignoramus Hays."[9] Referring to Harris's run at Hays in 1870, editor Benjamin F. Herr of the *Livingston Journal* reasoned that "it would be a great hardship for him [Harris] to do the work and someone else reap the benefit."[10] Harris ruined their plans in late May by formally declining to run. He explained in a public letter to Cooke that the Amnesty Act now allowed almost anyone to seek office. Circumstances had changed since 1870 when few were eligible and he had answered the party's call. No longer duty bound, Harris also expected keen competition and a large field. "I am," he wrote, "unwilling and adverse [*sic*], to having my name thrown upon the political arena in a wrangle or scramble for office."[11] Qualifying his statement later that month in a letter to Robert McKee, he expressed a willingness to serve, "But to enter a hurdle race — I am unwilling."[12]

In the meantime, William Russell Smith, a well-known antebellum politician, picked up support, and Tuscaloosa County's delegates pledged their loyalties to him. E. W. Smith of Sumter County also actively sought the nomination. Despite his protest, other Democrats persisted in promoting Harris through the convention. Democrats met at Tuscaloosa on August 7. On the first ballot Harris received fifty votes, William Smith forty-eight, and E. W. Smith forty. After Harris's name was withdrawn and E. W. Smith capitulated as a third ballot began, William Smith was nominated unanimously.

Smith was fifty-seven years old and a man of considerable political experience. He had been raised in Huntsville and Tuscaloosa and spent several years at the University of Alabama without graduating. In 1834 he began studying under George W. Crabb, a prominent Tuscaloosa barrister, and he soon was admitted to the bar and began practicing law at Greensboro. A lengthy political career began with his election to the Alabama house in 1841. Originally a Whig, Smith converted to the Democratic party in the early 1840s, and later he joined the Know-Nothing party. He sat in the Thirty-second, Thirty-third, and Thirty-fourth Congresses during the 1850s. Smith's doubts about secession did not keep him from serving two terms in the Confederate Congress. He had run unsuccessfully for governor in 1865 and had more recently filled a two-year term as

William Russell Smith,
Hays's opponent in the
1872 congressional elec-
tion (Alabama Depart-
ment of Archives and
History).

president of the University of Alabama. Few could doubt William Brewer, a contemporary and an able historian, who wrote that "no one in our annals has had a career more checkered than that of Judge Smith."[13]

The Democratic standard bearer quickly gained the endorsement of the district newspapers and also the *Selma Times*, *Mobile Register*, *Huntsville Advocate*, and *Montgomery Advertiser*. With more hope than evidence, editors claimed that he would provide a formidable test for Hays. Smith's stature, popularity, and oratorical gifts were frequently mentioned attributes, and the editor of the *Eutaw Whig and Observer* predicted that his candidacy would "be the means of bringing out many votes in the northern counties, who heretofore have taken no interest in politics."[14]

That Hays planned to seek a third term was understood. Returning to the life of a planter did not appeal to him in 1872. Politics was the livelihood of many Southern Republicans, and public office provided a secure existence. Hays's alternatives were limited. Cotton prospects were bleak, and he knew nothing else but planting. For practical as well as ideological reasons Hays was a vital part of the Republican party's future in Alabama and the South. He based continued Republican success on various contingencies. More native whites needed to be attracted to the party. That could not be done, he complained, by giving outsiders patronage positions. Neither would anything be achieved when the national party refused to pass enforcement legislation. Maintaining the high level of political participation among freedmen was essential. But at this stage, despite privately expressed fears, Hays was not pessimistic. He was even thinking of seeking a Senate seat.

Fourth District Republicans held their district convention in Uniontown in Perry County on August 28. A few delegates had united to block the incumbent's nomination, but their effort collapsed. Hays had previously displayed a facility for positioning himself. Using the office bonds he signed for leverage, he had first captured the congressional nomination in 1869. He had since consolidated his place by a solid performance in Congress and by awarding patronage appointments and other favors a congressional seat provided. Politics was in its most basic form about power, and Hays understood the art. He was nominated by acclamation that evening.

The campaign started tentatively for William Smith. Unlike Gideon Harris, Smith had political experience and enjoyed name recognition. He soon learned that being well known was not always an asset. Noting his prior affiliation with the Know-Nothing party, several European-born Demopolis residents asked him to clarify his ideas concerning immigration. Smith immediately repudiated the Know-Nothing philosophy in a printed response.

In Demopolis on September 17, the Democratic nominee reiterated in person his aversion to anti-immigrant prejudices, and, putting the charges behind him, he moved on two days later to Marion where he attacked Hays. Noting that William Jones was campaigning with his opponent, Smith quoted the Marengo County Republican's public and critical letter of Hays (written four years earlier).[15]

In September Hays began a round of speaking engagements. In Livingston on September 21, he formed part of a Republican battery with Sam Cockrell and William Jones. Cockrell, a Eutaw lawyer and one of but a few white Greene County Republicans, enumerated Hays's qualities. As he did throughout the campaign, Hays avoided controversy. The man who had recently framed matters in apocalyptic terms on the House floor did not resemble the candidate who spoke in Livingston. Even Benjamin Herr, the partisan *Livingston Journal* editor, admitted that Hays delivered "a very fair speech; and said nothing that we heard that could offend anyone." [16] Just what he did say, as usual, went unreported. The next week, at the Hale County seat of Greensboro, John Jolly accepted a late invitation and debated Hays, Jones, and Andrew Bingham, candidate for state treasurer. Editor Harvey of the *Alabama Beacon* acknowledged that the Radical speakers "displayed a spirit of commendable courtesy." [17] Hays and other Republicans addressed a largely white audience at Calera (Shelby County) on September 27. Extreme political partisanship was avoided, and self-styled "VERITAS" decided Hays's remarks were "designed more to conciliate than to provoke the people." [18]

Hays, Jones, and Bingham spoke at Eutaw on October 5. The editor of the *Whig and Observer* attempted to correlate poor attendance with black disillusionment and labeled the gathering a "complete failure." [19] The reporting was scarcely objective, and if the rally was unsuccessful at all, it was not indicative of Republican strength. An observer with a different perspective predicted "everything is working well in Greene. We count on a good majority for the Republicans." [20]

A large crowd of freedmen listened to Republican oratory in Tuscaloosa on October 9. Handbills had advertised several speakers, but only Hays appeared. Relations between the congressman and an old nemesis, James Taylor of the *Tuscaloosa Times*, had not improved. The editor faulted both Hays's style and substance: "He bawled at the top of his voice, intoned like a colored exhorter in the midst of a high religious excitement, and reddened in the face like a boiled lobster." As for content, Hays's speech "lacked only words and ideas of being a speech" and was pitched to the intellectual level of "the most ignorant corn-field negro." [21]

Slandering Hays provided more satisfaction than political benefit. William Smith faced the same problem that confounded former Democratic candidates: overcoming the black Republican numbers. The editor of the *Marion Commonwealth*, E. C. Heidt, conceded a 4,000 Republican majority but felt that the margin was not insurmountable. He reduced the election to strictly pragmatic terms; a 143-vote shift (from the 1870 results) in each of the fourteen counties would provide deliverance. In Tuscaloosa, editor

Taylor of the *Times* outlined Smith's mathematical chances to defeat "a man universally odious to the white people." [22]

For his part, Smith denounced Hays and spoke to as many voters as possible. Like Gideon Harris two years earlier, he made special appeals to freedmen and sought their trust. Even so, Smith's assurances usually failed to impress blacks. Equally unproductive was his strained praise for Horace Greeley.

Hays matched Smith's diligence. Little of the animosity that had marred the previous contest was evident in 1872. That Hays even spoke in Eutaw and Livingston indicated a marked improvement in the political climate. According to the *Montgomery Advertiser*, the congressman "everywhere asserts openly in his speeches that the District is perfectly peaceful" and that "no one has obstructed or interfered with him." [23]

If Hays acknowledged comparative peace, he welcomed the arrival of federal troops. Earlier that fall he had asked Senator Spencer to use his influence and arrange for troops to be sent to the Fourth District. The Alabama senator passed on Hays's request to William E. Chandler, secretary of the National Republican Committee. Spencer advised Chandler that Hays "ought to have help." Authorities complied with the request. Hays read from the Enforcement Act in Livingston on October 29 and explained that soldiers would be nearby. That observation surprised no one since a contingent from the 7th U.S. Cavalry had arrived in Livingston several days earlier. Soldiers also took up positions at other Fourth District localities as election day approached. [24]

Hays probably never doubted his reelection. He received 20,171 votes to Smith's 15,817. As usual Hays gained huge majorities in the predominantly black counties. In Perry County, where he ran strongest, the incumbent received 4,139 votes to Smith's 1,399, or 75 percent of the vote. Republicans reclaimed Greene and Sumter counties by large pluralities. Decided Republican victories in both, under peaceful circumstances, seemed to substantiate Republican charges of corruption and intimidation in 1870. As expected, William Smith dominated elsewhere. In the predominantly white counties, like Fayette, where a citizen had predicted, "Hays will not get a single white vote," Smith ran strongly. He decisively defeated Hays in Fayette, Bibb, Pickens, Shelby, and Tuscaloosa counties and more narrowly in Choctaw and Marengo.

Hays could also take great satisfaction in the statewide Republican victory. David Lewis defeated Thomas Herndon by 10,000 votes as the Republicans recaptured the governorship. Adding to the sweeping Republican victory were gains in the legislature and the outcome of the congressional contests. Alabama's representation had been increased to eight seats, and Republicans claimed five of them.

Grant carried all but six states and easily defeated Horace Greeley. Although the Liberal Republicans had once hoped to run well in the South, few significant Republicans backed Greeley. The most important to do so in Alabama was an embittered Willard Warner.[25] As one observer wrote a prominent Mobile Republican, "It seems that the liberal movement has amounted to nothing."[26]

Victory placed Alabama Republicans in control of the House and insured the election of a party member to the U.S. Senate. George Spencer, the incumbent, was the likely choice. Others considered challenging him. Benjamin Turner, a black congressman from Selma representing the First District, was mentioned. So was Hays. Despite his reelection to Congress, Hays at least considered seeking the seat. Saffold Berney, who had replaced Joseph Taylor as the editor of the *Eutaw Whig and Observer*, declared that Hays was "infinitely" preferable to Spencer. "If we are compelled . . . to choose from the Republican ranks," the editor wrote shortly after the election, "we prefer him."[27] Whether Hays meant to challenge Spencer is uncertain. Judging from a letter President Grant wrote to Hays on November 16, he may have. Grant praised Spencer in the postelection congratulatory note. Informing the congressman that "I take no part in contests for office between party members of the party to which I belong," Grant made it clear that he favored retaining Spencer's services in the Senate, and delicately concluded, "I feel it due to Senator Spencer, and to myself, to say this much." Hays abandoned his ambitions, and Spencer gained reelection in December 1872.[28]

The Hays family returned to Washington early in 1873. Queen had been anxious to leave their hotel accommodations for a home, and she now got her wish. The family moved into a residence on the corner of Dunbarton and Washington streets in Georgetown. Writing a friend on Easter, Queen praised their home but mentioned that talk of bonnets and dyed eggs was driving her "to St. Elizabeth's as a retreat." St. Elizabeth's was Washington's institution for the insane.[29]

Little was accomplished during the final and brief session of the Forty-second Congress. Hays had arrived late. Even after his appearance in January 1873, his attendance at roll calls, never exemplary, was sporadic. He spoke from the floor only once for any length. A comprehensive River and Harbor Bill provided the occasion. Emerging from the House Committee on Commerce, such bills were seized on by congressmen who attempted to attach their pet projects as pork barrel measures. Discussion on February 21 was under way on the River and Harbor Bill (H.R. 3922) when Hays proposed an amendment. He unsuccessfully attempted to fund a survey of the Black Warrior River. Three days later the congressman again rose as consideration of the wide-ranging bill continued. Hays did not give up hopes of increasing the money designated for harbor improvements at Mobile. Holding the floor for several minutes, he asked Congress to double the designated $50,000 sum. He offered solid arguments. He pointed out that better port facilities benefited the mercantile interests of New York, Philadelphia, Boston, and other shipping centers. Improving Mobile's port was "momentously important to the commerce of the entire country." The representative was prepared with facts and figures. The U.S. Corps of Engineers had estimated $200,000 for the project, and Hays reasoned, "I only ask one-half the amount." He cited a report from the secretary of war as further corroboration. As with many local questions, a majority of congressmen took no interest in floor proceedings. Of those bothering to vote, a slight plurality rejected Hays's proposal. Moments later, Ohio congressman James A. Garfield added insult to injury by attempting to deduct $20,000 from the allocation of $50,000. Resorting to a parliamentary maneuver, Hays appealed to Speaker James G. Blaine that debate was not in order. The speaker sustained him. Despite the initial setback, Hays's efforts did not pass unrewarded. The final version of H.R. 3922 allocated $100,000 for the harbor improvements.[30]

The Forty-second Congress concluded in March 1873. Myrtle Hall would serve as Hays's base for the next nine months. In August 1872 he had been appointed to the State Republican Executive Committee. And, as a party official and a leading Alabama Republican politician, he could not remain aloof from a divisive patronage battle that spring. The characters, but not the plot, were new. Replacing in office a native Alabamian with an outside Republican once again created trouble. The struggle grew out of an attempt to appoint Lou H. Mayer as collector of internal revenue in the Mobile district. A New Yorker in his late twenties, Mayer had the support of Senator Spencer. Other state Republicans (mostly natives) favored extending the tenure of the present collector, John T. Foster, an established resident.

Hays, predictably, supported Foster. He wrote the commissioner of internal revenue in Montgomery that Foster was a "true and active Republican" who had "been very valuable to the party in the recent election."[31] Hays's approval of Foster was matched by his disapproval of Mayer. The congressman had consistently argued that native Douglas-Bell men must form the basis of the state Republican party if it was to survive. Bypassing Alabamians and offering the rewards of office to outsiders doomed the party. He concurred totally with Chancellor Anthony Dillard, who wrote him that "it would be fully as absurd to put Alabamians at the head of the party in Ohio, or Illinois, as to put strangers at its head here in Alabama."[32] Aside from Mayer's New York background, Hays faulted him for his role in the Republican defeat of 1870. The former Union soldier had edited a newspaper that was critical of William Smith, the Republican candidate for governor. It was small wonder that Hays declared his opposition to the "Spencer-backed young Mr. Mayer" in a letter to Secretary of the Treasury William A. Richardson.[33] Despite the congressman's efforts, Mayer received the appointment. To Hays he remained "a disgrace to the Republican party in Alabama."[34]

Compared to intervals in the past and difficult times ahead, political feelings in 1873 were not as intense in the Black Belt. Notice of some improvement was indicated by the public thanks the *Eutaw Whig and Observer* tendered Hays for copies of the *Congressional Globe*. Before leaving his editorial post later that year, Saffold Berney made the surprising admission that Hays was "identified with the interests and welfare of Alabama."[35] Hays welcomed the respite and unaccustomed words of praise. About the same time he made clear in a letter to B. Perry of New Jersey that party passions were cooling. "Thank heaven we have no trouble to contend with of a political nature," he informed him. Writing from Myrtle Hall in June, Hays invited Perry to visit the area and offered to act as his guide, adding, "I have traveled all over the United States" and claiming that "there is no country or state that can compare with ours in point of fertility of soil, climate, good water, healthfulness, etc." All the area lacked was Yankee frugality and money, and he urged Perry to consider moving to Greene County.[36]

Hays's reference to money was revealing. His financial position had continued to deteriorate. Prosperity in the late 1860s and early 1870s was sporadic, and the congressman had fallen further into debt. Unable to make promissory note payments to William Miller, Hays lost almost all of his property to his creditor-friend. The once affluent planter was reduced in 1872 to renting the Sebastapol, Hays Ferry, and Cainfield places from Miller. Renting what had once been part of his inheritance was painful to accept. Hays was now a glorified sharecropper. He agreed to provide Miller with one-fourth of the crop in return. In addition, Miller loaned Hays $3,500 and received a lien on the entire crop.[37]

Adding to Hays's financial worries, worse than ever by now, were the hard times gripping the nation. A banking panic and the collapse of the railroad boom in the fall of 1873 had triggered a crippling economic downturn. Declining prices for crops had begun before the so-called Panic of 1873. The nationwide depression only exacerbated Hays's situation. Under the worst economic circumstances in years the Forty-third Congress convened just before 1873 ended.

The prevailing economic distress meant that monetary debate would dominate congressional proceedings. Although President Grant had provided no sure direction in his opening address, inflationists and their opponents in Congress carried the debate forward. Most southern and midwestern Senate and House members held out currency expansion as a panacea. Hard-money proponents warned against straying from financial orthodoxy. Most significantly, the soft-money camp forced through the so-called Inflation Bill in April 1874. The measure provided for increased greenback circulation and established a $46 million bank note fund to be divided among states with adequate currency. A southern-midwestern axis delivered the votes, but Grant vetoed the Inflation Bill. Hays numbered among those supporting that measure and other attempts to increase the money supply. A more modest achievement awaited the soft-money interests. A statute framed largely in the House (H.R. 1572) released greenback reserves, set a maximum greenback circulation, and allowed a redistribution of $55 million in bank note currency.[38]

Congress also considered civil rights legislation. Grant had endorsed in his opening address passage of a civil rights statute. Such bills had been proposed but not acted upon in recent years, and the divisive question caused extensive debate during the first month of 1874. Among the legislation's most vigorous champions was Senator Charles Sumner of Massachusetts. Citing constitutional objections, Democrats referred to the recent *Slaughterhouse* Supreme Court decision, which transferred many civil rights from federal to state protection. Opponents also objected to the legislation on practical grounds. Congressman Robert B. Vance, a North Carolina Democrat, argued typically that statutory coercion would cause "antagonism of the races."[39]

The civil rights debate revealed much about Charles Hays. Advocacy of the Fourteenth Amendment and black enfranchisement had initially earned him the enmity of white Alabamians. But endorsing legislation thrusting the races into daily and intimate contact was considered more heretical (even if, de facto, that situation already existed). A civil rights statute, opponents insisted, invited everything from miscegenation to race war. That Hays openly advocated the legislation was a measure of his Radicalism. That he spoke in behalf of a bill authored by Massachusetts senator Benjamin Butler—reviled by Southerners as "Beast Butler"—confirmed it. Butler's bill provided penalties for persons or corporations that denied individuals on account of race equal access to inns, railroad cars, schools, and other public accommodations.

As he had done previously (especially when explaining his attraction to Republicanism) Hays couched a Radical position in conservative terms. He addressed the emotional subject with admitted "diffidence" and "caution" on the last day of January 1874. The congressman emphasized the innocuous nature of Butler's proposal. The bill merely gave legal sanction to what was and had been an accepted part of the pattern of Southern life, he argued. Integration was already practiced. He invited the skeptical to "get upon the cars tomorrow morning and start South, take your seat in the finest palace car, and you will find southern women traveling and sitting side by side with colored women as nurses and servants." Why should anyone object to a black buying a ticket and traveling independently? The close association of whites and blacks was a historical fact, and the civil rights measure did not portend social revolution. Critics who claimed the bill "blotted out the lines between knowledge and ignorance" were guilty of misrepresentation. What Butler proposed should not be confused with social equality. The measure did not "force anything" and "no possible harm can come to the white man by the passage of the law."

Hays concluded his brief remarks by falling back on his personal catechism. Extending civil rights to blacks was morally correct and served the cause of justice. Recalling that the freedmen had built the South, remained loyal to their masters during the war, and had since acted with credit, he judged them deserving as well. Hays expected criticism, but ridicule "shall not deter me from . . . a duty which God, reason, and conscience tell me is right."[40]

His comments and those of others preceded an extensive civil rights debate later that spring. In May the Senate approved a comprehensive measure drafted by Senator Frank Frelinghuysen of New Jersey (and inspired by the recently deceased Charles Sumner). The bill faced tougher going in the more conservative House. Among those urging passage was Hays's black colleague, James Rapier of Alabama. Efforts to bring the measure (often called the Sumner Bill) to the floor for debate failed. Hays consistently supported the efforts of Benjamin Butler to do so. Ultimately the House delayed consideration of the measure until after the midterm elections.[41]

Hays was more active during the first session of the Forty-third Congress than at any past or future period. He introduced twenty-five bills, three sets of resolutions, and thirteen petitions. Days after the session had opened in December 1873 he asked the House to compensate Alabamians for the cotton that Treasury agents had illegally confiscated after the war. Hays also introduced a bill that would have provided reimbursement for the burning of the University of Alabama by federal troops during the war. On January 13 he took the floor again. He had come to an appreciation of the navy during several years of committee service, and efforts to subtract funds from a naval appropriations bill caused him to protest. Noting that European rivals were busily adding to their strength, Hays maintained that the United States could not "stand idly by, hugging the elusive phantom that arbitration . . . and compromises can always avert war and strife." He argued that naval strength was vitally important and warned against the dangers of false economy, charging that more rather than less money was needed. Hays made a passing reference to the situation in Santo Domingo. The congressman obviously supported the administration's controversial attempts to annex that island. To him, it was clear "that little gem of an island . . . sooner or later must be ours."[42]

Less than a week later Hays rose in behalf of education. On the same day, January 19, he introduced two bills that would increase the number of public schools in the South. The first required the federal government to grant Alabama all the undisposed public lands in the state for the benefit of the Free Public School Fund. More grandiosely, the other measure called for federal underwriting of public schools throughout the former Confederacy. Neither emerged from the Committee on Education and Labor.

Hays had earlier become a member of the Agriculture Committee, and as the session opened he was named chairman. That appointment reflected his seniority and, as Hays would soon demonstrate, his fierce interest in the country's agricultural welfare. As Agriculture chairman he protested on April 24 an attempt to reduce the pay of a Department of Agriculture employee. The issue at hand—involving only $600—was itself not of great consequence. It took on more meaning when viewed as part of a pattern. A man of his agricultural background took offense at colleagues who funded various projects but raised "a howl for retrenchment" when agricultural concerns were involved. It was to congressmen who "know more of Blackstone" than the "agricultural needs of our nation" that Hays addressed himself on April 24. He remained more concerned with the "poor farmer of the West" than "the rich banker of the East." The congressman recalled the Morrill Act of 1862 (establishing the agricultural colleges). Did not attempts to reduce reasonable allocations violate that statute's spirit? Hays closed, "Let us know who is the farmer's friend and who is his enemy." [43]

In the meantime, Hays received discouraging economic reports from home. Destitution had not been so widespread since the immediate postwar years. Tight money and low crop prices had caused extensive suffering in the Fourth District. Bad weather compounded problems as heavy rains ruined crops. In a letter to Probate Judge R. L. Maupin of Marengo County, Hays mentioned his distressed constituents. The congressman cited their pleas for help in "the great number of letters daily received by me." He advised the judge and his fellow Marengo County citizens to petition Congress formally for relief. [44]

Conditions worsened dramatically in the spring. Unprecedented rainfall in April and May caused the Tombigbee and Black Warrior rivers to flood, sweeping away soil, livestock, and even houses and leaving many without the most basic necessities. As the situation reached a crisis, the editor of the *Eutaw Whig and Observer* advised victims to put their faith in the Lord. Hays took a different approach. He personally lobbied for federal aid. Hays and fellow Republican congressman Charles Sheats appeared before the Senate Appropriations Committee. On May 18 Hays introduced a desperately worded petition from Fourth District citizens and another resolution asking for emergency relief in the area affected by Alabama's flooding rivers. The petition, read by the House clerk, reasoned that although "man cannot live by bread alone . . . it is just as true that physically he cannot live without bread." A sympathetic House approved, several days later the Senate concurred, and President Grant signed the measure in early June.

The joint resolution allowed the president discretion to issue army rations and clothing to victims in areas where swollen rivers had overflowed banks and inundated the countryside in vast sheets of water.[45]

Hays considered the relief measure a major victory, but he learned soon of opposition to it back home. He returned to Alabama after Congress recessed in late June. Political opponents maintained that the congressman planned to make political capital from what they considered a boondoggle. In Marengo County Probate Judge Maupin publicized the letter Hays had recently sent him (urging county citizens to petition Congress for aid). The *Eutaw Whig and Observer* published the communication and commented that "the General Government, as Mr. Hays knows — or should know — had not a particle of constitutional right to do what he would have it do in this matter."[46] Other Democratic editors took various tacks, all critical. "If the Govt. commences to issue rations," the *Demopolis Marengo News Journal* claimed, "there will be at least a thousand plows stopped." Hays took exception and pointed out that many Democrats had written him to requisition relief.[47] The issue would not die. Some points seem certain. Although Hays claimed to have "acted from no other than pure motives," he was not blind to political benefits. But that was not his overriding concern. Relieving suffering was.[48]

Other matters were beyond debate. When some Republicans doubted the wisdom of a color-blind society and the ideological underpinnings of Reconstruction, Hays reaffirmed his commitment to fundamental justice. Justifying the extension of the Ku Klux Klan Act, he had paraphrased the Declaration of Independence, reminding colleagues that "all men are born free and equal."[49] The congressman advocated civil rights legislation and spoke of "the sacred and inalienable rights of liberty."[50] Hays had recently eulogized Thomas J. Speer in Congress. He praised the Republican House member from Georgia for his personal qualities and paid his respects to the deceased congressman's family. Less conventionally, Hays noted the unpopular but brave political stand Speer had assumed. Hays compared him to a solitary rock in the ocean withstanding storms and waves. Hays's words for Speer applied equally to himself: each man had "embraced the humanizing cause of equal rights and exact justice for all men." Hays had become a Radical by 1874. As has been pointed out, the meaning of that term had changed. Early in Reconstruction, Radicals favored political equality for blacks and the proscription of some white Southerners. By the early 1870s black participation in politics was a reality and political penalties against

whites had been removed. The term "Radical" had taken on a new con-
notation. It referred to Republicans who favored something approaching
real equality for the freedmen and also a continued federal presence in
the South. Authorship of the Hays-Hawley letter would confirm Hays's
Radical credentials.[51]

7

The Hays-Hawley Letter

The 1874 midterm elections would be decisive to the future of Republicanism in the South. Republican influence, having peaked soon after congressional Reconstruction began, was in visible decline. Democrats had returned to power in Tennessee, Georgia, and Virginia. The party claimed a majority of the legislature in Hays's Alabama. Only in Arkansas, Louisiana, Mississippi, and South Carolina was Republican control still absolute. Sentiment among northern and midwestern Republicans for the inherent Reconstruction promise of interracial democracy was waning. It would be wrong to describe the flagging spirit in terms of desertion or capitulation. The Republican party had not lost its soul— concern for the freedmen. But a weariness had set in. The number of Reconstruction skeptics was increasing, and the Radicals were on the defensive.

Southern Democrats were organized and optimistic about consolidating their power in the elections. In their zeal, as before, some members did not stop at electioneering, but covertly pressed a violent campaign against Republicans. Various factors contributed to the unrest and their blatant defiance. The pending civil rights legislation and the specter of racial mixing increased the normally turbulent political passions of Reconstruction. Contributing too was the growing perception that the administration favored a hands-off policy in the South. Under the circumstances a small but active minority of Southern whites formed political societies (the most common being the White League) and revived the night-riding tactics of the Ku Klux Klan. Other political outlaws lacked any affiliation but shared a sense of purpose—preventing blacks from voting and repudiating Radicalism. However carried out, formalized or not, a campaign of terror was on by summer 1874. A black candidate for the Tennessee legislature was murdered. Pitched battles took place between blacks and whites in North Carolina and Kentucky. In September, in Louisiana, Democrats staged a violent coup d'etat and temporarily removed from power Republican governor William P. Kellogg. Embattled Republicans were soon petitioning Washington for troops. A partisan Republican press had at times exaggerated Democratic political crimes and ignored trouble instigated by Republicans. But with reason the *Washington National Republican*, the unofficial party organ, publicized the "new rebellion."[1]

Violence certainly escalated in Alabama. Reports of political unrest had begun to reach Hays during the preceding spring in Washington. Mixed with reports of flooding waters from his constituents were appeals for protection. Particularly diligent in his correspondence was James K. Greene, a Greene County freedman, who wrote Hays in Washington "continually and repeatedly." Anticipating the contest, he strongly argued against campaigning unless troops were present.[2] Hays learned more clearly of the political mood when he returned to Alabama that summer. Writing to him at Myrtle Hall, William Taylor, a Sumter County freedman, described the treatment meted out to Nelson Doyle, another black. Doyle had crawled to Taylor's door early one morning after being "tremendously whipped." About the same time, during July, Hays visited James Abrahams in Livingston. The Republican probate judge confirmed the worsening conditions.

Hays had decided to seek a fourth term. He was a young man—only forty in 1874—and he still allowed himself to speculate about a Senate seat. Also, from a political standpoint, as he realized, his retirement would be tantamount to surrendering the Fourth District to the Democrats. There were other considerations. Living in Washington did not prevent him from overseeing what lands he had left between sessions. Queen enjoyed the amenities of the city. Among them was a fine Catholic school that Mary Hairston and Anne Miller attended. There was no compelling reason to return to Alabama and every reason to stay in Washington. Under the circumstances Hays made known his intention to seek a fourth term.

Hays had moved with purpose toward political office and its rewards. Once he secured a seat in Congress, he beat back Democratic opposition with that same determination. He was less accustomed to challenges from Republicans. Yet Alexander Curtis, a Perry County freedman, now openly sought the nomination. His efforts failed, however, and Curtis endorsed Hays when the incumbent congressman was renominated on July 29 at Uniontown in Perry County. In an otherwise unremarkable acceptance speech, Hays included a warning, stating that order must be maintained in the Fourth District and troops might be necessary.[3]

His words proved tragically prophetic. On August 1 a Fourth District Republican, Walter P. Billings, was shot as he rode home after addressing a Republican audience at a Sumter County rally. Billings had moved from Missouri to Alabama the previous year and opened a law office in Livingston. According to the *Meridian Mercury* (in nearby Mississippi), he was a "mischief-making carpetbagger." His murder gained statewide attention and a familiar debate followed. Republican charges of Democratic complicity were met by denials.[4]

Hays became involved when the *Mercury* accused him of agreeing to meet with Republican governor Lewis to plan retaliation. Hays had known Billings, but not well. The congressman had received a letter of introduction from him the previous March in Washington. Later that spring, Billings had written Hays several follow-up letters regarding the civil rights question. Rebutting the *Mercury* in a public letter, Hays mentioned meeting Billings at Uniontown for "the first and last time." He denied any plot with Governor Lewis. Some Democrats claimed that on the day of his death Billings had boasted of having $10,000 in campaign money on his person. It followed, according to rationale, that his assailants had wanted to rob him. Hays countered that Billings had not been robbed and it "would be mockery to doubt . . . that he was murdered because he was an [*sic*] Republican."[5]

Hays was in Montgomery on August 20 when Alabama Republicans held their state convention. The killing of Billings—though the most spectacular murder—was by no means an isolated example of Republican mistreatment. Discussion of political terrorism dominated the proceedings. A hastily formed Committee on Outrages weighed evidence, concluded that a critical situation existed, and recommended that Governor Lewis appoint a commission to conduct an investigation. More immediate action was taken in secret caucus: Hays, Congressman Alexander White, and Senator Spencer were designated to travel to Washington and request military protection from the president. At the convention, Hays had placed the name of incumbent governor David Lewis in nomination to succeed himself. Lewis was nominated by acclamation.

Democrats met the next month in Montgomery. George Smith Houston, a Limestone County Unionist, received the gubernatorial nomination. More important was the party platform. In Alabama, as elsewhere in 1874, the so-called "white-liners" dictated party strategy. The accommodationist-minded Southern New Departurists had been repudiated. Past Democratic efforts to attract blacks now yielded to the interest of energizing Alabama whites through racial appeals. Men like John Forsyth, editor of the *Mobile Register*, accentuated the differences rather than the similarities between the Republican and Democratic parties. Alabama Democrats unabashedly raised their platform on "the preservation of white civilization."[6]

In the meantime, Hays and the other designated Republicans met with President Grant. The chief executive was at his Long Branch, New Jersey, retreat when the Republicans reached the city. Attorney General George H. Williams first listened to their pleas, which he described as "very threatening and full of trouble." He briefed the executive at Long Branch on September 2. Several days later, the Alabama delegation, joined by several Republicans from South Carolina and Louisiana, visited Grant there. Little of what was said is known. Much can be surmised. Appealing to the administration was a tried and tested strategy of Southern Republicans. Yet Grant's response had often been more capricious than consistent. He had recently refused to help struggling Republican regimes in Arkansas, Mississippi, and Texas. In spite of what happened in the past, he did not hesitate now. He empowered the attorney general and secretary of war to ready soldiers for election day.[7]

What Hays said to Grant at Long Branch, though not documented, may be assumed. That he was incensed is certain. Several days earlier the Alabama congressman had been wired news of the murder of another Fourth District Republican, Thomas Ivey, a mail agent on the Chattanooga Mobile Railroad who had campaigned for Hays in the past. On the afternoon of August 29, a band of whites stopped the train on which he was riding in Sumter County, and shot and killed the freedman. Less than a month had passed since Billings's death. Hays undoubtedly used strong language at Long Branch. He spoke in the same terms several days later to Joseph B. Hawley.

Hawley was one of the country's better known congressmen. The Connecticut politician had recently presided over the Republican National Convention of 1872. Hawley also edited the well established *Hartford Daily Courant*. As fellow Republicans in the Forty-third Congress, Hays and

Joseph B. Hawley, who collaborated with Hays on the Hays-Hawley letter, which exposed to a national audience the extreme acts of violence committed against Republicans in Alabama (Hartford Collection, Hartford Public Library).

Hawley knew each other, but apparently not well. On the evening of September 6, somewhere in the city, Hawley overheard Hays privately discussing the violence directed at Alabama Republicans. The editor-congressman listened to Hays's rendition with empathy and indignation. Maintaining that such conditions begged to be exposed and rectified, he asked the Alabamian to reduce his comments to writing and permit their publication. Hays consented without hesitation. Hawley followed up the next day, September 7, with a formal written request. He referred to the previous evening's "informal narration of late occurrences." Would the congressman provide "the substance of what you have told me?"[8] Such was the beginning of a collaboration that caused a nationwide controversy.

Hays began at once. The words came easily. He underlined some for emphasis and struck out others, and the length of the letter increased. Drawing upon newspapers, telegraphic dispatches, correspondence, and his general knowledge, the congressman completed his work within days. Hawley read and approved the narrative and, after forwarding the lengthy letter to the *Courant*, went hunting.

The shocking exposé was spread across the front page of the *Hartford Courant* on September 15. A devastating picture of Fourth District conditions began with a survey of Sumter County. Hays summarized the shootings of Walter Billings and Thomas Ivey. In Hays's estimation, Billings had been killed because he was a "Yankee" and a "Republican." Hays referred readers to Billings's widow for further details of the "revolting murder." He also recounted how a local citizen who had attributed the Republican's death to politics was severely beaten by several whites and ordered to "keep his mouth shut about that d——d Yankee, Billings." Ivey was likewise executed because he was a "meddlesome" Republican and a "nigger." Without imparting any blame (but the implication was clear), Hays also mentioned the recent murders of five Sumter County freedmen in one night. He attributed the carnage in that county generally to "a murderous band of Democrats."

Affairs were not dramatically better in Hale County. Hays recounted that John Stokes, former editor of the *Montgomery Alabama State Journal*, had delivered a speech at the county seat of Greensboro on July 20. That night two pistol-carrying whites visited Stokes in his hotel room and warned the Republican against speaking in Greensboro again. On another occasion masked men had sought out Jonathan Bliss, a delegate to the Republican state convention. The freedman fled moments before they arrived. As of yet, Bliss had not returned to Hale.

Incidents elsewhere in the Fourth District indicated a similar pattern of brutal political repression. Joseph Speed, the former state superintendent of public instruction, was one of the few white Republicans in Perry County. Hays claimed that a crowd mobbed Speed in Marion. Republicans in Choctaw and Marengo, also in the Fourth District, lived constantly in danger. A rumor that freedmen were preparing to wage race war had recently precipitated tragedy in Choctaw. Whites organized, conducted a search, and, failing to find the nonexistent private army, killed ten blacks and wounded thirteen others returning from church. In Marengo County, William Lipscomb, a white man, was found shot to death in the road. Hays let his Northern readers draw their own conclusions concerning the death of the "earnest Republican."

Unrest prevailed in Choctaw, Hale, Marengo, Perry, and Sumter counties, but Republican mistreatment was worst in Pickens County. "This is a county in West Alabama," Hays began, "where the white men publicly boast that no white man ever cast a Republican vote and lived through the year." Hays described Pickens as an inbred bastion of white supremacy. Landowners still worked blacks as slaves on "secluded plantations" in a region "untouched by the civilizing influences of railroads and rivers." Rarely did notice of outrages escape Pickens, but Hays offered two exceptions. A group of whites had lynched four blacks in mid August. At about the same time a raft bearing the decomposing bodies of two freedmen and one white man was discovered floating down the nearby Tombigbee River. Around the necks of the two black men were placards reading, "to Mobile, with the compliments of Pickens County."

Republicans outside the Fourth District also suffered. Three southeastern counties—Coffee, Macon, and Russell—and Madison in the north provided the settings for more political terrorism. In less detail, Hays outlined trouble there. The letter, carrying over from the *Courant*'s front page (and including accounts that Hays lifted verbatim from newspapers), was about 5,000 words in length.

Descriptions of Democratic-inspired terrorism were standard fare in large northern and midwestern Republican newspapers. A highly partisan and national newspaper press, divided into Democratic and Republican camps, had long disputed the political violence in the South. Republicans used the accounts to justify enforcement legislation and troops during elections. Democrats argued that the reports were manufactured for self-serving political reasons and pejoratively referred to the "outrage mill." The debate was beyond resolution. Even so, the imprimatur of a congressman lent a legitimacy that other so-called "outrage" accounts from the South lacked.[9]

Neither Hays nor Hawley could have predicted the uproarious reaction that ensued. The correspondence quickly became known as the "Hays-Hawley letter" and created a furor among America's highly partisan newspapers. The collaborative effort eventually drew comment from major dailies in every section of the nation. If not "copied through the country,"[10] as the *Indianapolis Sentinel* insisted, or "read from a hundred stumps, like the Declaration of Independence,"[11] as a *Cincinnati Commercial* journalist remarked, the letter was spread far from Connecticut. Commenting that "the entire nation stood aghast," the *New York Tribune* reasoned that "one of the vexed questions of the day" concerns "whether Alabama is really under a rule of terror."[12]

The Democratic press questioned Hays's motives, veracity, and charac-

ter. Critical of another St. Louis daily that publicized Hays's narrative, the
Post-Dispatch wondered why a paper should bother to publish the correspondence of a Southern Republican "at war with his people, his race, and
his color." His motives were transparent. If troops were sent to Alabama,
the *Post-Dispatch* pointed out, Hays's election chances improved. The *Post-
Dispatch* declared that "the Southern scallawag [*sic*] wants to go back to
Congress through the ministration of federal troops to hunt imaginary
Ku-Klux."[13] Other papers, not bothering to discern Hays's motivation,
simply condemned him. The *Nashville Union and Telegram* referred to Hays
as "Alabama's unapproachable fabricator of political sensations."[14] The
Democratic defense extended to the West Coast, where the *San Francisco
Examiner* condemned the "startling letter" as political hyperbole and called
Hays the "veriest lying knave that ever went unhanged." Evaluations in the
Richmond Dispatch, the *New York Times*, the *Charleston News and Courier*,
and the *Atlanta Constitution* read similarly.[15]

The judgment of the *New York Sun* was also negative. The noted Charles
A. Dana presided over the Democratic paper as editor. The name of
Charles Hays meant nothing to Dana, and the *Sun* concluded that the
congressman cut a slight figure in the House. If a "sudden providence"
vacated his seat, the paper maintained, only his landlady and the sergeant-
at-arms would miss him. Referring to Hays's position on the Agriculture
Committee, the *Sun* concluded that the suddenly highly visible Republican might know about "the long and short staple of his cotton bolls," but
"there his faculty, if he has any, begins and ends."[16]

Only a few Southern Republican newspapers existed, but several Northern party editors rushed to Hays's defense. The *Cincinnati Gazette* published the letter in its entirety. Noting the Alabama situation, the *Gazette*
recommended Hays's comments to the "reader who desires accurate information respecting the condition of affairs in the South."[17] The *Washington New National Era* featured the letter on its first page and decried the
"frightful outrages and midnight murders" of "the rebels of Alabama."[18]
Accepting the congressman's allegations at face value, the *Boston Globe*
made the point that a Democratic press could not refute the testimony of
a Southerner who had owned slaves and fought for the Confederacy. More
support was provided by the *Washington National Republican*. Acknowledging that the congressman had been "written into unexpected notoriety,"
the paper described Hays as inoffensive, modest, and incapable of promoting himself or a cause at the expense of the truth.[19]

The editor of the *New York Tribune* took special concern in the controversy. Whitelaw Reid had recently assumed control of the influential daily. Reid considered himself a Republican, but he objected to the Grant administration, and he opposed the federal government's continued interference in the South. Having made a much publicized Southern tour in 1865–66, Reid continued to be interested in the former Confederacy. In early October, the paper announced that it had a reporter in Alabama investigating Hays's allegations.

Zebulon L. White, the *Tribune*'s chief Washington correspondent, had headed south in late September. Instructed to visit and report from centers of Republican-Democratic strife, he was attracted to Alabama by Hays's revelations. White reached Montgomery about the first of October. The journalist carried a copy of the Hays-Hawley letter with him. White passed almost a week there interviewing prominent Democrats and a few Republicans. Among the Republicans he talked to was Gen. Robert Healy, U.S. marshal of the Southern District of Alabama. Healey confirmed the terror Hays had publicized to the nation. William Screws, editor of the *Montgomery Advertiser*, was of another opinion. Having long since dropped what little regard he had for Hays, he was especially anxious to correct the congressman's account. He denounced the Fourth District congressman and completely rejected his statements. His and other arguments impressed White. A systematic refutation of Hays's position, under the bold caption, "The Slandered State," soon thereafter appeared on the front page of the *Tribune*. The journalist also revealed his plans to visit the scene of the "most excitement" — Sumter County.[20]

A westbound Selma and Meridian train took White through the Black Belt's rolling prairies to his destination. He reached Livingston on October 6. Arriving at midnight after a rough and cold wagon ride of eight miles from the nearest depot, the newspaperman found the village "as still as the grave." A closer inspection the next morning revealed a town of about two or three hundred people. A wood-frame courthouse, two hotels, a tavern, and a series of offices and shops composed the unremarkable and apparently quiet village.[21]

The *Tribune* correspondent remained in Livingston for three days. He talked with numerous whites, a few blacks, Capt. William Mills (in command of a detachment of troops present to supervise the upcoming election), and even two detectives, Joseph Hester and Josiah Beach, who had been dispatched to Sumter County by the Post Office Department and the Treasury Department to investigate internal revenue matters and the murder of mail agent Ivey. Having represented themselves as tobacco peddlers, Hester and Beach had learned in confidence from local whites of crimes against Republicans. Both men provided the *Tribune* reporter with evidence of White League activity. Hester described "a terrible state of affairs." Yet White discounted most of what the detectives told him. Admitting that Billings and Ivey might have been killed because they were outspoken Republicans, the journalist insisted that most Sumter County whites condemned the murders. Nothing resembling the desperate situation Hays had described existed. Overall, the newspaperman's *Tribune* articles exonerated almost everyone except Hays, whom he charged with blatant misrepresentation of the facts. White, having made his case, dropped plans to visit the other counties mentioned by Hays. Nor did he make any attempt to see the congressman.[22]

As the story received protracted national attention, Hawley himself was inevitably criticized. The self-described "radical abolitionist from my earliest days" refused to repudiate Hays. Hawley wrote Charles Dana at the *Sun* a week after the letter appeared. He defended Hays as an "honest man" and asked why the *Sun* had criticized the congressman without printing his letter. Hawley hoped that a fellow editor could appreciate that he "wanted the readers of the *Courant* to hear one report from somebody on whom they could put their fingers."[23] Hawley soon received a note from Stephen A. Hubbard, the *Courant*'s managing editor. Hubbard informed Hawley that many Alabama newspapers were "pitching in . . . quite severely" on the letter.[24]

Alabama's overwhelming Democratic state press had attacked Hays without mercy. Refuting the allegations became a ritual among party editors. As unofficial spokesman for the state Democratic party, William Screws of the *Montgomery Advertiser* began the process in a lengthy rebuttal published soon after the letter's publication. In the Fourth District, other editors denied Hays's allegations and excoriated the congressman. Greensboro's *Alabama Beacon* editor John Harvey denounced Hays for slandering the people of Hale County. In Pickens County, allegedly the scene of mayhem, Hays's charges were categorically denied, and the editors of the *Carrollton West Alabamian* mocked Hays by running his lurid description of Pickens on its masthead for weeks. Epithets were employed, evidence to the contrary amassed, affidavits sworn to, and one presumed victim even resurrected from the grave. Upon the appearance of William

Lipscomb, whom Hays had erroneously charged had been shot to death in Marengo County, the *Demopolis Marengo News Journal* marveled at his return from "the land of the ghosts." Because of the paucity of state Republican newspapers, the debate was one-sided."[25]

If much of what Hays charged cannot be proved or disproved, evidence provides a basis for some conclusions. Generally, more than what Democrats admitted, and less of what Hays charged, represented the truth. Hays had falsely implied that the death of five Sumter County blacks were due to politics. An ambush of Choctaw County blacks, written about in the letter, had been put to rest before Hays had taken up his pen. Hays had promised readers "to narrate no rumors, to color no atrocity . . . but simply to give you well authenticated facts." Yet he had given credence to various rumors and sensationalized alleged incidents in melodramatic prose.[26]

The congressman can also be defended. In a few instances he relied on published information that he did not know was false. Reports of William Lipscomb's death, which Hays repeated, were printed and widely believed. Other portions of the Hays-Hawley letter represented the literal truth. Despite *Tribune* reporter White's findings, martial law could have been declared with justification in Sumter County. Both Walter Billings and Thomas Ivey were killed because of their close Republican associations. Elsewhere, in Hale County, two whites had accosted John Stokes after he spoke at Greensboro. It was also true that a lynch mob of Pickens County citizens was guilty of hanging four freedmen.

An observer, removed but not unconcerned, made an accurate summation. Stephen Hubbard of the *Hartford Courant* wrote Hawley several weeks after the letter's release. "If Hays has overstated anything, I am sorry; there has evidently been enough persecution there to establish a good case without alluding to acts of violence not well authenticated."[27]

Hays was anything but repentant. Defending himself to a Greene County Democrat, he claimed that he had taken the information from opposition party newspapers. Even granting some false allegations, he maintained the letter could stand on its merit. His license with some events represented little when compared to the fear and suffering Alabama Republicans had experienced since Reconstruction began. Rationalizing was easy. It was almost irrelevant that certain names, places, and circumstances might not always bear close scrutiny. There was no recrimination.

Hays had more to worry about than the fallout from the Hawley correspondence. His reelection was at stake. In Alabama and throughout the

South, the civil rights issue was causing extreme consternation. A *Cincinnati Commercial* journalist reported while traveling through Alabama in the summer that "the talk, talk, talk about civil rights and 'nigger equality' would drive a man crazy if he was not used to it." [28] The question presented Democrats an issue and Republicans a dilemma. In the past Southern Republicans had attempted to broaden the party base by redirecting debate from the race question to economic issues. Endorsing the Civil Rights Bill risked alienating carefully cultivated white support. In Montgomery, at the state convention, Republicans had drafted a platform that failed to mention the measure and warily distinguished between "social equality," not desired, and "equal advantages," which were. Even so, the *Commercial* journalist predicted the desertion of north Alabama Republicans from the party and Democratic victory in November. He might also have foreseen Republican defections as well in south Alabama.

In the Black Belt, unlike the Tennessee Valley or the piney woods of southern Alabama, Reconstruction politics had always been absolutely predicated on race. Since 1867 blacks had voted Republican. With few exceptions, whites had cast Democratic ballots. Without changing the political agenda in the Fourth District, the "white-line" emphasis on race sharpened the focus. Some previously apathetic Fourth District whites might vote, but generally Hays stood to lose little support that he did not automatically forfeit as a Republican.[29]

In Montgomery, when the Democrats held their state convention in September, Fourth District Democrats had caucused and nominated James Jones as the congressional challenger. The forty-two-year-old Marengo County citizen had attended Princeton University and studied law at the University of Virginia. After serving the Confederacy, Jones returned to Demopolis and was practicing law with Francis Strother Lyon when he agreed to challenge Hays.

Whereas fellow Democrats Gideon Harris and William Smith had failed to unseat Hays, Jones had some hope of succeeding. Hays had provided him some leverage by both speaking and voting in favor of the Civil Rights Bill. Jones rarely failed to make the direct connection between Hays and the controversial measure. Although Jones did not denounce blacks in the savage manner of a later school of demagogues, he made it clear that the present social distance between the races should not narrow. The Democrat presented the cause of caucasian superiority at Linden in Marengo County on August 11. To maintain otherwise, he stated, was to dispute

John J. Jones, Hays's opponent in the 1874 congressional election (Alabama Department of Archives and History).

the historical record. "We will never submit to social equality," Jones concluded.[30] He advanced the same theme at Jemison in Chilton County on August 29. A warm reception was assured in a county where Democrats had earlier passed a resolution condemning "any man, or set of men, who attempt to force upon us the 'Civil Rights bill,' Social Equality, and amalgamation of races."[31]

Associating Hays with "black equality" formed only part of the stratagem. Jones regularly referred to irregularities surrounding the distribution of federal supplies to flood victims and charged Hays with political profiteering. Sometimes undeserving parties had claimed the pork. Foes now derisively referred to Hays as "Side-Meat Charley." A Hale County Democrat wrote an acquaintance in September that the rations were "being distributed in Greensboro and other favorable voting places." He accused Hays of bribery. "What stuff are the American people made," he continued, "that they can quietly allow this proceedings . . . under the flimsy veil of humanity."[32] The Hays-Hawley letter provided Jones more anti-Republican material. He incorporated into his standard remarks a bitter critique and read, depending on where he spoke, appropriate sections of the celebrated letter. Jones left an Autauga County rally early in October with "the mendacious 'Side-Meat' Charley impaled upon infamy's high pinnacle."[33]

In the meantime, Hays directed operations from Myrtle Hall. As before, the Hays Mount–Boligee area ten miles south of Eutaw was a center of Republican activity. Numerous Fourth District Republicans traveled the dusty, hot road leading to Myrtle Hall. No friend of the congressman described Hays Mount that summer as "a perfect Mecca" for those who "cast their lots with Hays and his mongrel crew, swallowing civil rights, social equality, and all the disgusting dogmas of Radicalism."[34]

Hays did not begin campaigning until October. As was his practice, he traveled with other Republicans. Samuel Reid, former editor of the *Montgomery Advertiser* and a belated Republican convert; Anthony Dillard, chancellor of the Western District; and Alexander Curtis, a Perry County freedman, often composed the entourage. Recent violence and Hays's notoriety demanded unprecedented security: a U.S. marshal usually accompanied the Republican. U.S. soldiers, who took up posts in various Black Belt towns, provided further protection.

Hays, Reid, and several others filled a date in Marion on October 13. Hays spoke first, defending his much-publicized letter, and if "Old Perry" was correct, the other speeches were anticlimactic. "When I say [Hays] more than surprised his audience by the ability and power with which he gave an account of his stewardship and of the issue between the Republican and Democratic parties," the Perry County resident assured, "I give him but a faint expression to the general feeling of admiration and enthusiasm with which his remarks were received by thousands of his old constituency." If the observer lacked objectivity, he correctly pointed to Hays's continued bedrock support among blacks.[35] The Republican caravan crossed into Greensboro and Hale County the next day where another large crowd of freedmen congregated. Hays answered Democratic objections to troops in a speech described as a "vigorous vindication." The scenario was the same in Tuscaloosa on October 16. Freedmen assembled, a crude speaker's platform was erected, and four to five hours of Republican oratory followed. The next day, in Eutaw, the congressman again justified the presence of soldiers and defended the Hays-Hawley letter. Republicans congregated a week before election day in Livingston. As always, Hays spoke of equality and opportunity. He also mentioned federal troops and of maintaining the peace and informed his audience that in view of recent crimes, President Grant had promised to establish a permanent garrison in Sumter County.[36]

A merciless Democratic press challenged and ridiculed Hays as he carried his campaign forward. In Marion, Hays received what must have been a mixed reception. "This pistol-carrier and whiskey-drinker," began E. C. Heidt of the *Marion Commonwealth*, "boasts of having written the 'Hawley letter,' and declared that he stood ready to write another of the same character."[37] With Ryland Randolph, by then editor of the *Tuscaloosa Blade*, Hays's differences were long-standing. After Hays spoke in Tuscaloosa, Randolph ridiculed the "champion liar and remorseless slanderer" who would be more at home in the devil's kingdom or a penitentiary than in Congress.[38]

Although Hays drew close scrutiny, attention remained focused on civil rights. Custom, if not law, had traditionally separated the races, and James Jones warned through election day of Republican efforts to alter that natural arrangement. E. C. Heidt put the question in practical terms for readers of the *Marion Commonwealth*. Voting the Republican ticket was tantamount to endorsing mixing with former slaves in theaters, hotels, hacks, streetcars, steamboats, the University of Alabama, and the recently founded Agricultural and Mechanical College at Auburn. When Hays spent the night at a black's home, the *Birmingham Independent* reported he was "ready not only to preach but to practice social equality."[39] That such appeals raised racial consciousness in the Black Belt is certain. Even so, unrestrained opposition also stoked Republican sentiment in the predominantly black counties. The political implications in a district where there were three times as many blacks as whites were obvious. In fact, editors like Benjamin Herr of the *Livingston Journal* had warned against the pitfalls of totally writing off the black vote. Corresponding with Robert McKee, editor of the *Selma Southern Argus*, Herr maintained that "a race alignment will involve serious consequences to the 'black counties.'"[40]

Hays easily won reelection on November 3. An appreciably increased turnout of white voters did not offset the unprecedented number of blacks who voted Republican in the Fourth District. Hays received 23,813 votes to Jones's 18,438. The methodology was familiar to Democrats: the incumbent carried every black county except Choctaw and Pickens (where freedmen constituted a bare majority). In one black county (Perry) Hays claimed only sixty-nine fewer votes than Jones combined in Bibb, Choctaw, and Fayette counties.

But the Black Belt was one of the few areas where Alabama Republicans ran well. The Democratic party dominated elsewhere, gaining control of the legislature, six of eight congressional seats, and the governorship. George Smith Houston received 107,118 votes to Lewis's 93,934. The civil rights issue had provoked more white participation than any other Reconstruction question. Intimidation and possible fraud also contributed to the verdict. On election day, in Eufaula and Mobile, fatalities resulted when whites fired on black voters. Economic coercion also had an effect. What remained, for a combination of reasons, was the fact of Democratic redemption in Alabama. That was not lost on Hays.

There was more bad news from a Republican standpoint. Democratic candidates triumphed almost everywhere nationally and turned a 110-seat House deficit into a 60-seat majority. The depression and Grant administration scandals partly accounted for the worst defeat in Republican party history. The connection between Republicanism and continued federal interference in the South also contributed. Republican misrule in South Carolina, sensationally revealed recently by reporter James S. Pike in the *New York Tribune*, pointed to Reconstruction excesses. An increasingly skeptical public had grown tired of the situation. In Ohio and Indiana, as well as in other midwestern and northern states, the much discussed Civil Rights Bill helped Democratic candidates. The question's effect on Southern Republican prospects was devastating. Only in Louisiana, Mississippi, Florida, and South Carolina did Republicans cling to power. What Hays had always feared, that the Republican party in the South would not survive its infancy, was closer to reality than ever before. Returning to Congress provided him little solace. He realized the prospect of a Republican renaissance was bleak.[41]

We Shall Not Falter in the Struggle

Hays, Queen, and their four children returned to Washington late in 1874. The couple continued to enjoy their home in Georgetown. Among other attractions, Queen wrote a friend, Georgetown was "not so hot as down in the city," and "the children can stay out and play all day."[1]

Hays was uncharacteristically present when the final session of the Forty-third Congress opened on December 7. Two weeks later, just before the Christmas recess, he asked for an inquiry into the recent Alabama election. State Democrats and Republicans, he explained to his colleagues, disputed the alleged violence and disorder. Without alluding to the Hays-Hawley letter, he mentioned that Northern newspapers had denied the reported political violence. No House member was uncertain about what Hays was referring to. The House consented, and a committee composed of three Republicans and two Democrats began hearings almost immediately at Washington on Christmas Eve, 1874.

Republican party members in Congress during the session acted on the basis of political reality. Democrats would control the Forty-fourth Congress. The party set a partisan agenda that included enforcement, civil rights, and currency legislation. Gaining a consensus among Republicans on the money question would become increasingly difficult. Specie resumption, proposed by the hard-money wing of the party, necessitated a contraction of the currency. That alternative was unpopular in money-short areas like the South. A Republican-sponsored measure requiring partial resumption and actually allowing an expansion of bank notes was acceptable to most party members. The Specie Resumption Act passed over the objections of the Democrats. Hays and every Alabama Republican (except James Rapier) followed the party line.[2]

More partisan legislation followed. Early on Republicans agreed to a diluted version of the Civil Rights Bill drafted during the last session by Senator Frelinghysen. The measure assured all races equal access to public accommodations and travel facilities but, unlike the original bill, did not extend the principle to education. Hays appreciated both the vision and limits of the proposed statute. Several months earlier, in behalf of another civil rights measure, he had spoken of the "sacred and inalienable rights of liberty and freedom." House Republicans triumphed in a February show-down, Senate clearance was gained, and President Grant signed the Civil Rights Act of 1875.[3]

The Specie Resumption and Civil Rights Acts were the most signifi-cant statutes passed during the session. Attempts to provide protection for Southern Republicans would fail. Caucusing at night, House and Senate Republicans began constructing what became the Force Bill. The most re-cent attempt to insure fair elections described and set penalties for election fraud, provided that offenders would be tried in federal court, and, most controversially, empowered the president to suspend the writ of habeas corpus. Taking issue with fellow party members whom he labeled "ex-tremists," Ohio congressman James Garfield argued for a "government of law and not the bayonet" at one late-night caucus. Hays believed bayonets were necessary to achieve law.

On February 18, as speculation concerning the Force Bill mounted, the Select Committee on Alabama Affairs reported out. Over 350 witnesses had provided testimony in the last two months. The three-member Re-publican majority concluded there had been widespread intimidation in Alabama. The Republicans also stated that the testimony generally cor-roborated the Hays-Hawley letter allegations. Although no model of ob-jectivity, their conclusions bore closer resemblance to the truth than the Democratic version. The two Democrats who signed the minority report categorically denied violence and charged federal troops with interfering in the election.

More important, the debate concerning the Force Bill continued. Presi-dent Grant joined Republican forces supporting the measure. It was not coincidental that Hays met with Grant three times at the White House between February 2 and 23. The author of the Hays-Hawley letter had become a leading spokesman for the cause of enforcement. Despite some lukewarm Republican support and a Democratic filibuster, Indiana congressman John Coburn succeeded in bringing the Force Bill to the floor during the session's final week. Debate dominated the proceedings of February 26–28 and carried over well into the night.[4]

Hays was one of thirteen Republicans who presented the administration position. The congressman began on the evening of February 26 by citing the recently released findings of the Select Committee on Alabama Affairs. Two Democrats on the committee had signed the minority report claiming that much of Hays's publicized allegations were apocryphal. Hays took strong issue. Admitting every word of "my HAWLEY letter" did not represent the literal truth, he contended that the charges were generally applicable. He pointed to the conclusions of the three member majority that substantiated his views. Numerous other crimes, which the congressman made general reference to, would never be publicized. Hays also pleaded innocent to any wrongdoing in what he termed the "bacon affair." Some of the government pork provided for flood victims had been claimed by undeserving parties, and fellow congressman John Caldwell of Alabama had even called for an investigation. Hays recalled that he was campaigning and did not control the pork's distribution. The episode, magnified by enemies for political purposes, represented "a matter of small consideration to me."

But all of this he considered mostly extraneous. There was the matter of the pending Force Bill. The situation in Alabama pointed to the necessity of approving the legislation. Hays maintained that the evidence gathered by the committee only hinted at the Republican holocaust in Alabama. He advised against accepting the "whitewashed" minority interpretation and claimed that Democratic professions of peace and tranquility were specious. "That peace is the peace that the wolf gives to the lamb," he continued. What was true in Alabama was written large elsewhere in the South. House members listened with empathy, or strained tolerance, as Hays predicted that "if the Republican party allows this session of Congress to end without throwing some protective aegis over the soldiers of Republicans in Southern states, our doom is sealed." He further argued that suspending the writ of habeas corpus and depending upon soldiers would not intimidate white voters. Democrats had contended otherwise. "What we want," he emphasized, "is a fair chance to express ourselves at the ballot box." Any sense of justice demanded the freedmen's protection.

The debate continued. Alyett Buckner, a Missouri Democrat who had sat on the Committee on Alabama Affairs, pointed to inflated "outrage" reports that appeared in the Hays-Hawley letter. Georgia congressman Phillip Cook also numbered among the Force Bill's opponents. Over thirty Georgians had been indicted under various federal enforcement acts, but a limited number had been convicted. Cook's explanation was simple: very few were guilty. Even some Republicans advised that less federal coercion and more home rule was needed in the South. Yet Congressman John Coburn drew a fearful picture of mistreatment of Southern Republicans, concentrating on the situation in Arkansas and Alabama. Enough Republicans supported the Force Bill two days later to achieve passage, but the Senate did not consider the measure. The short but eventful final session of the Forty-third Congress closed a week later in early March 1875.[5]

By then Hays was greatly concerned with the intentions of Alexander Shepherd. The former District of Columbia governor was threatening legal action against him. More than a year earlier, in January 1874, Hays had borrowed $2,000 from a Washington broker. Senator George Spencer had convinced Shepherd, then governor, to assume responsibility for the note. Little of the debt had been paid when the note matured in January 1875. Shepherd was forced to assume the difference.

Two months later, after attempts to pass the Force Bill failed, Congress concluded and Hays left Washington. Shepherd, some $1,600 poorer, believing that Hays was "absconding," referred privately to him as a "damned scoundrel" and threatened the congressman with a writ of attachment. Shepherd mentioned seizing Queen's trunks and the furniture in their Georgetown home. (Shepherd's virtuous position must have struck Hays as somewhat hypocritical. As the former driving force on the District Board of Public Works, "Boss Shepherd" had earned a reputation for total financial irresponsibility.) Spencer once again intervened. Aware of Hays's financial condition, he persuaded the former governor against a lawsuit. Spencer convinced Shepherd that William Lilly, a friend of Hays's and a lawyer, might be able to collect the money. Whatever his business failings, Hays inspired devotion among his friends. Lilly no less than Spencer wanted to help the congressman. He offered Shepherd several paintings in return for the note. Later, under examination, Lilly frankly stated, "I have got more paintings than any private gentleman in America today." He was willing to part with a few for Hays's sake.[6]

Hays spent almost all of 1875 in Greene County. The time when he would return permanently to Alabama was drawing near. Although the Republicans in Alabama had received 47 percent of the vote in 1874, the party had now begun to unravel. In February 1875 the Democratic-controlled legislature redrew the congressional districts. The Fourth District, formerly a Republican stronghold, was gerrymandered. Greene County became part of the predominately white and Democratic Sixth District. There was more. In almost all the Southern states, following Redemption, Democrats rewrote the Republican-authored state constitutions. The constitutional convention referendum that August in Alabama was a gloomy portent of the Republican party's future. The referendum resulted in the election of a convention totally different from the one Hays had served in eight years earlier. Eighty of the approximately one hundred delegates were Democrats. The convention drafted a document providing for economic retrenchment and a legislative apportionment scheme favoring Democrats. Working further against Republican success was an election provision of the new constitution. The requirements forced voters to cast ballots in their home precincts. Blacks had preferred to vote in the county seats where there was protection. In November, aided by a confused and divided Republican opposition, ratification was easily achieved. Implementing the Constitution of 1875 marked the permanent changing of the political guard in Alabama.

Hays could find little to be optimistic about in 1875. The fortunes of the state Republican party had never been lower. Financial problems confronted him personally. Others were plowing the prime Black Belt furrows he had inherited. Part of the money Hays had borrowed in Washington he used to buy livestock and tools. Even so, as the loss of land at a Greene County sheriff's sale indicates, his situation did not measurably improve.[7] Late in 1875 Hays returned to Washington and moved into new quarters at the Imperial Hotel. He and Queen had sold the home in Georgetown, and she and the children presumably remained at Myrtle Hall. The Imperial, shabby in comparison to the opulent Willard or Ebbit, was all Hays could afford. The poor accommodations pointed graphically to the congressman's long, steady, and now nearly complete financial fall. Hays did, however, begin making payments to Alexander Shepherd.

There were fewer "scalawags" in the Forty-fourth Congress than at any time since Reconstruction began. Hays was one of only seventeen Southern Republican congressmen. He was in his seat on December 6, 1875, when the Democratic House Speaker convened the session. He was not present very often after that. Hays introduced one bill, presented a single petition, and voted infrequently during the nine-month session ahead.

Hays had been absent periodically for stretches before. Yet his record during the first session went well beyond truancy. The explanation is uncertain. Money was a constant source of worry, and he was undoubtedly disillusioned politically. Another explanation is possible. Some evidence indicates that he was already suffering from the effects of Bright's disease. A kidney affliction with lingering and debilitating effects, the illness was usually fatal. For whatever reason or combination of reasons, office had clearly become a burden.

Compounding his concerns was a situation threatening his censure or even expulsion from Congress. The extended ordeal began when Burwell Boykin Lewis took the floor three months after the Forty-fourth Congress opened. The freshman Democratic congressman from Alabama, rising on March 9, 1876, asked the House to investigate the recent appointment of Guy Roosevelt Beardslee to the U.S. Military Academy at West Point. Lewis pointed to allegations that Hays had falsely represented Beardslee as a resident of the Fourth District (a congressman could only nominate a resident from his district). Hays may, Lewis continued, have collected $3,000 from the young man's mother. Several days later, on March 14, a twelve-member House Judiciary subcommittee began hearings. The committee took testimony periodically for the next two months.[8]

The narrative that unfolded dated from February 1875, when Helen C. Beardslee, a New York widow, and William Lilly, Hays's attorney friend, began business transactions. In return for $3,000 Lilly had promised to secure for her son an appointment to West Point. Guy Beardslee lived with her in New York. Lilly had asked Hays to nominate Beardslee just as the Forty-third Congress concluded in March 1875. Assured he was a resident of Choctaw County (in the Fourth District) and a deserving young man, Hays consented. Beardslee reported to the military academy several months later. Hays presumably thought no more of the appointment until several months into the Forty-fourth Congress. Lewis had somehow discovered Lilly's subterfuge.

Well aware that the situation offered the chance to discredit Hays and the Republican party, he moved quickly. To Lewis, who had observed during the recent 1874 contest that the only issue was the "supremacy of white men of Alabama," the opportunity to bring Hays down was inviting.[9] Hays, Beardslee, his mother, and other involved parties were subpoenaed soon after the subcommittee formed. Lilly's testimony confirmed his guilt and, at least in the estimation of some, Hays's innocence. As for his role, Lilly admitted to "an innocent deception on my part practiced on Mr. Hays." Other witnesses also maintained that Hays was an unwitting party to Lilly's profiteering. John Stokes, Hays's friend and former clerk of the Agriculture Committee, had been present when Lilly had first mentioned the subject. He assured the committee that Hays had believed Beardslee was a Fourth District resident.

Different evidence suggested otherwise to some committee members. There was a chance encounter between the congressman and Guy Beardslee to consider. Hays had met Beardslee at Lilly's home unexpectedly, but he had quickly wished him well and departed. Chairman Scott Lord, a New York Democrat, inferred that Hays knew the young man did not live in Choctaw County, and by avoiding conversation, was protecting himself. Hays's financial problems were also raised. Alexander Shepherd took the stand and recited their difficulties. The point—that Hays needed money and likely received it from Lilly for nominating Beardslee—was unstated but obvious.[10]

Hays presented his version of events on April 29. He assured the committee that he did not know of any financial transactions between Lily and Mrs. Beardslee. Lilly had "thoroughly convinced" him that Guy Beardslee lived in Choctaw County. Hays emphatically stated his disappointment in Lilly. The congressman maintained that he was a victimized instrument of the attorney's designs.

Hays was one of the final witnesses. He released a written statement declaring that if any evidence indicated his guilt, "I am unworthy a seat in the Congress." He also requested an immediate report in another letter to the House Judiciary Committee. That did not happen. The findings would not be laid before Congress until August. Hays was forced to wait, as he wrote, for "the vindication of my good name."[11]

Despite his sporadic attendance, the Fourth District's congressman missed less than he might have. The Democrats' enthusiastic pursuit of various investigations limited the consideration of legislation. Irregularities in the Naval Department were alleged, and Secretary of the Navy George M. Robeson's activities were closely examined. The much-publicized Whiskey Ring scandal required more attention. Bribery charges were leveled at Senator Spencer. In the House the impeachment proceedings against former secretary of war William Belknap demanded consideration. With reason, the *New York Times* commented that the "number and extent" of investigations was "unprecedented."

Some legislative headway was made. As congressional priorities shifted, the money question supplanted all others. Democrats had opposed the Specie Resumption Act. They now attempted to repeal the measure or at least delay resumption (scheduled for 1879) indefinitely. The first volley in the struggle between gold and silver forces was also fired. Leaving the bimetallic standard, or demonetizing silver, had attracted little attention when the Coinage Act of 1873 had passed. Changing conditions since then—primarily the falling value of silver—caused silver and soft-money interests to call for a return to bimetallism. Reading the pages of currency debate in the *Congressional Record* would test the endurance of even the most devoted student of finance. Tracking and fixing Hays's position is difficult due to his excessive absences. When the congressman did vote, he resisted Republican financial orthodoxy. In March 1876, Hays sided with Democrats who supported the repeal of the Specie Resumption Act, and later, following the lead of one of the most outspoken silverites, William D. Kelly, he supported restoring the standard silver dollar to legal tender status. Both were futile causes.[12]

By spring attention had turned on Capitol Hill to the approaching presidential election. The Democrats, meeting in June at St. Louis, nominated Samuel J. Tilden of New York. The Republican choice was not clear-cut. Among the most widely mentioned candidates were James G. Blaine, Benjamin H. Bristow, Oliver P. Morton, and Rutherford B. Hayes. The Republican convention was scheduled for June in Cincinnati.

In Alabama, Republicans did not settle on a candidate before the convention. The failure pointed to division within the party. The feud between former governor William Smith and George Spencer, dormant since the early 1870s, had broken out with a new intensity. The specifics—disagreement over membership in the state Republican Executive Committee—pointed to a broader power struggle.

Although Hays no longer sat on the Executive Committee, he inevitably became involved. Samuel F. Rice, a friend and fellow Republican, led the attack on Spencer. In a public letter to Hays in April 1876, he argued, "Spencerism and Republicanism are very different things. The prosperity of the former signally fails to bring prosperity to the latter." Hays was unconvinced. Spencer had reconciled himself with many state Republicans including Hays, since earlier problems. The senator's recent efforts to extricate Hays from his financial problems provided some indication of their relationship. If Hays owed him a debt of gratitude, he was also philosophically sympathetic with Spencer. That wing of the party was more genuinely committed to the freedmen's rights. Practical application of Republican racial ideology had always divided state Republicans. It was significant that James Rapier, the best known black state Republican, supported Spencer. Hays, who once compared the congressman and Frederick Douglass, had long admired Rapier. Both men refused to compromise full citizenship.

Unreconciled state Republicans, meeting separately in May at Montgomery, nominated two state tickets. Both factions also selected rival slates of delegates to the national convention at Cincinnati. The Spencer faction endorsed Oliver Morton, the candidate of the Southern Radicals. (As recently as January, Morton had demanded that Congress enact enforcement legislation.) Hays, in Washington, was selected in absentia as one of the four at-large delegates. Benjamin Bristow or James Blaine was the choice of the Smith-Rice camp.

The Republican Convention opened at Exposition Hall on June 14. Leaving Washington, Hays and Spencer, expecting controversy, traveled by train to Cincinnati. Refused accommodations by the proprietor of the Walnut Street House because some of their party were black, Spencer's group made their headquarters at the Spencer Hotel. The rival Smith-Rice delegation enjoyed plush arrangements at the Gibson House. Determining what Alabama delegation to recognize provided an early floor fight. Although the Smith-Rice faction was seated, the narrow margin (375 to 354) was an indication of Blaine's tenuous status as favorite. Eventually, Rutherford B. Hayes, governor of Ohio, received the nomination. Among those nominated for vice-president was Joseph Hawley.[13]

Hays continued to miss more roll-call votes than he made during his two remaining months in Congress. A great burden, however, was lifted when the Beardslee subcommittee findings were laid before Congress on August 2. Committee Democrats criticized Hays in their conclusions but recommended against further action. A Republican minority (joined by one Democrat) completely exonerated the congressman. Although the outcome provided Hays some satisfaction, the episode had, by August, continued for six months. The question of Hays's integrity had again been raised. Unsympathetic and sympathetic summaries, depending on political points of view, had appeared in the national press. The *New York Tribune* had printed Hays's name across its front page, prematurely pronouncing him guilty.[14] The congressional recess days later in mid August 1876 further relieved Hays.

Ordinarily, in the summer of every other year, Hays would be organizing for his reelection. But doing so was not on his agenda in the summer of 1876. Earlier that spring the congressman had written former governor William Smith of his plans to retire. Hays's health may have been crucial in that decision. Political reality could also have influenced him. Chances of returning to Congress from the newly constituted and gerrymandered Sixth District were slight. His poor record during the last congress suggests another consideration: simple political weariness. A decade of strife had worn him down. It was time, as Hays wrote Smith, to return to private life.

Hays did not participate in the 1876 contest. Alabama Republicans superficially smoothed over differences, but they failed to offer strong opposition. George Smith Houston defeated the Republican gubernatorial nominee by 40,000 votes in August. Samuel Tilden easily carried Alabama in November, and the Democrats claimed seven of the eight congressional seats. In the Sixth District, where Hays sat out the election, the Republicans did not even offer congressional opposition.

The victor in the presidential election would remain uncertain for several months. Although Tilden claimed more electoral votes than Hayes, the returns from Florida, South Carolina, and Louisiana were disputed. An Electoral Commission established soon after Congress convened in November would make a final determination.

In early November Hays returned to Washington as a congressman for the last time. He did not take the floor and continued his absentee pattern during the three-month lame-duck session. Attention was focused on the Electoral Commission. On March 2, 1876, Rutherford Hayes was certified the victor.

In one of his last official acts, on the final day of the Forty-fourth Congress, Hays wrote the president. The letter, dated March 3, coincided with the day of Hayes's private inauguration at the White House. He recommended the appointment of James L. Alcorn to the cabinet. The Mississippi Republican's Senate term was expiring. Hays had consistently recommended extending office to native Southern whites. By now he realized something else. Patronage was about all the Republican party could claim in the South. Eight years of service in the House of Representatives concluded for Charles Hays on March 3, 1877, when the Forty-fourth Congress adjourned.[15]

The final two years of Hays's life are clouded in obscurity. That they were filled with adversity is certain. Hard times continued for all Southern farmers, and Hays was no exception. Although he owned some of the rich Black Belt land that George Hays had sought out fifty years earlier, tight money and low cotton prices frustrated his efforts. At the same time his health deteriorated. Anne Miller Womack, almost seventy years old, had moved from Eutaw to Columbia, Tennessee, to live with her daughter George Anne. Her son's health obviously worried her. In June 1877 she wrote him, "I want either to draw you nearer me, or I want to come to you . . . but I must see you."[16]

Hays found it impossible to divorce himself entirely from the political world. In 1877 local elections in Greene County underscored his status according to the *Eutaw Whig and Observer* as "the Republican leader of this country."[17] The next year, as a point of symbolic honor, Hays was elected president of the Republican state convention. The convention met in Montgomery on July 24, 1878. By then the party could claim little more than an ideology and did not even field a gubernatorial candidate.

As president, Hays spoke to the assembled black and white audience. His political convictions had not changed. Neither had those of his opponents. "They oppose today, as they opposed heretofore," Hays claimed, "the exercise of the colored man of the rights of citizenship and of suffrage." Hays ridiculed the "white man's party," pointing to the indignation caused by two blacks who attended the recent Democratic state convention. He scorned the opposition for fraudulent vote counts in past elections and for failing to enforce federal election laws since they had come to power. For this reason, he claimed, the Republicans chose not to designate a candidate or participate in the "mere mockery of an election." Many in his audience realized that the reality, Republican political impotence, had more to do with the decision than alleged fraud, and they were equally skeptical of Hays's claim that the party was as strong as ever. Hays called Republicans to arms. He pledged the party to fight on despite "terrible odds." The Democrats possessed money and controlled the press. Republicans lacked financial resources and journalistic spokesmen. Even so, he declared the party could claim "truth and right" and predicted ultimate victory. Hays closed by promising, "we shall not falter in the struggle to this end." Those were his last public words.[18]

In Montgomery, Hays had predicted eventual vindication for the Republicans, but he also acknowledged that some who were present "may only behold the fruition of our labors from the borders of eternity."[19]

The former congressman had himself in mind. Hays knew he was dying. Bright's disease was gradually wearing him down. The slowly debilitating illness caused great pain at times. There was no cure for the disease and he had recently taken out a $10,000 life insurance policy. Six months after speaking in Montgomery, Hays wrote his mother, "I have been at death's door." That was in March 1879. He had three months to live.

As Hays's world collapsed around him, he faced absolute insolvency. "If I could succeed in raising money on my real estate I would gladly do so," he continued. But "no one in this country has any money to loan." Economic necessities compelled him to send the boys, Ormond and Charles, to a public school "where I have to pay nothing." Queen tutored Mary Hairston and Anne Miller "in the spare moments she can give them from household affairs." The once affluent planter wanted his mother to move back to Alabama and live at Myrtle Hall, but admitted, "The truth is I have not the money for Queen to come for you at this time." Hays held out hope that he would see her before long and felt "some good spirit will soon cause a meeting that will provide a happiness in our family."

In the last months at Myrtle Hall there was time for reflection. Several months before he died, Hays wrote his mother of "all my misfortunes." The political principles he had battled for no longer commanded the priority they once had. Republicanism in Alabama had been totally repudiated. His land and wealth were gone. But most unacceptable was the inevitability of his imminent death. Hays was literally waiting to die. At some earlier point he and his sisters, George Anne and Mary, had erected a large memorial to George Hays at his grave site. The twenty-foot granite marker stood near Hays Mount. Hays requested to be buried there. Noting the death of an aunt, he wrote Anne Womack in words of measured fatalism: "soon we shall follow her and be happy." The realization of his mortality was devastating. He and Queen had been married fifteen years. In one sense it did not seem so long since he had proposed to her in Tuscaloosa the year before the Civil War ended. But measured in terms of events—triumphs and setbacks—an epoch seemed to have passed. In fact, it had. Mary Hairston, their oldest child, was fourteen. Anne Miller was twelve, and Ormond was eleven. The youngest, Charles Hays, Jr., was only seven.[20]

Hays had mentioned to Anne Womack that he planned a trip with Queen to Mobile when he was strong enough. He never made that journey, failing quickly in June 1879. On Tuesday night, June 24, he died at

Myrtle Hall. He was forty-five. The Democratic press, having maligned him in life, was respectful in death. As the *Eutaw Whig and Observer* briefly noted, Hays had succumbed to a "lingering and painful disease." He was buried within a mile of Myrtle Hall in the family cemetery. Reverend A. K. Hall of Livingston officiated at the service. There on a wooded hillside in Alabama's Black Belt, he was laid next to his father.[21]

Epilogue

A significant number of former Southern Whigs and Unionists gravitated into the Republican party after the Civil War. Demographics and economics caused many to change affiliations. As has been traditionally assumed, most native white Republicans were small hill country farmers. Many had Unionist antecedents. Charles Hays's approach was different. A Black Belt planter, he had owned slaves, voted Democratic, and served the Confederacy. But these credentials did not prevent him from embracing Republicanism.

Hays never authored a manifesto explaining what, by any standards, was an astounding political reversal. Even so, his reasons seemed clear. Hays rejected Conservatives who were unwilling to bend to a "new order" that christened freedmen full citizens. Granting blacks' ignorance, he did not doubt the race's potential for achievement and development. Hays did not in the truest sense consider the freedman the white man's equal. Such a position was barely entertained in the late nineteenth century. But Hays's was a compassionate approach to an oppressed race he believed capable of improving its status if provided the opportunity. Guaranteeing that opportunity defined his career. As Hays attested before Congress, the freedmen would eventually overcome the obstacles of two and a half centuries of slavery. Emancipation represented, the former owner of over a hundred slaves insisted, "the moral . . . advancement" of the nation. Continued resistance was immoral. If the Republicans anticipated the future, Hays linked the Democratic party with a "dead past." For him the party represented an anachronism. Its limiting vision relegated over four million blacks to permanent secondary citizenship. Myopic and detrimental to the country's development in Hays's view, the Democratic position was also unconstitutional following the passage of the Fourteenth and Fifteenth Amendments. Yet Democrats condemned both amendments in name and often honored neither the spirit nor the letter of either. This unreconstructed outlook, obvious by 1867–68 as the lines of congressional Reconstruction took form, Hays considered unconscionable. He faulted Democrats for not respecting federal authority and a seeming obliviousness to the consequences of the war. Impatient with Conservative-Democratic intransigence, he broke with his former party.[1]

Yet Hays's background predisposed him against drastic Northern-imposed solutions, and he acted on the axiom that Republicanism must be made respectable in Alabama. His positions early on as a constitutional convention delegate and as a state senator were moderate. It was significant that Hays first spoke in Congress for tariff reform. There was a cause that both Alabama Democrats and Republicans could endorse. Hays held out hope for the toleration of Southern Republicans. Late in his career the arch-Republican recalled feeling that Southerners "would forget the animosities and antipathies engendered by the war" and accept the resulting new order and consequences. That did not happen.[2] Instead, lines hardened and an unforgiving mindset developed in every Southern state.

Although Hays looked for common ground with Alabama whites, his search grew fainter as Reconstruction became more bitter, and he finally abandoned the quest altogether. Various events, especially crimes committed against Republicans, inexorably pushed the congressman in a more confrontational direction. Speaking in behalf of enforcement legislation in 1875, he reasoned, "I was forced into the position I occupy upon this floor."[3] Advocacy of the Force Bill, extending the Ku Klux Klan Act, and what became the Civil Rights Act of 1875 reflected a partisanship and alienation from his native region. Hays had cautiously entered the Reconstruction waters. But as the current became turbulent, he was swept into the rapids, from where there was no political return. The author of the Hays-Hawley letter bore little resemblance to the equivocating state senator who had considered returning to the Democratic party. His personal political evolution, however illogical, was complete. Hays's Radical credentials were indisputable.

As an outspoken Republican, Hays drew constant condemnation from a dominant Democratic press in Alabama. The extremely personal criticism was not unique. Fellow Southern Republicans faced similar hostility. That Hays and other Southern-born Republicans often defied party orthodoxy and voted their region's economic interest did not matter. These considerations were drowned in the maelstrom of Reconstruction hate. Although important, and sometimes stridently debated in Congress, consideration of the money question or the tariff did not color Reconstruction for what it was: one of the most fratricidal political eras in the nation's history. Varying interpretations of the former slaves' place in society did. "In the Southern states," a Georgia Republican wrote former attorney general Amos Akerman in 1875, "few men, if any, have taken their side in the present politics from any opinions concerning currency, taxation, expenditures, civil service, foreign policy or Indian policy." Akerman continued, "men are Republican or Democratic according as they are or are not attached to the last three amendments of the Constitution."[4]

In time, Hays became the foremost Southern apostle of enforcement legislation in the House of Representatives. The vein of political violence in America runs long and deep. But not before or since has intimidation and terror been so endemic to a political epoch. Although this study has concentrated on the trials of a single congressman's efforts to protect Republicans, the dilemma for party colleagues was equally critical. Scalawag representative Clinton Cobb of North Carolina provided a list of some fifty-six Republicans who had been beaten or whipped in Alamance County in 1871. For the edification of the Forty-second Congress he enumerated over a dozen other counties (the setting for the Kirk-Holden war) where outrages were also frequent. Emancipation and application of the Reconstruction amendments unleashed forces unprecedented in their political, economic, and social repercussions. These concerns produced a pyrotechnic mixture that burst into searing and episodic violence. Men like Cobb and Hays often knew the victims and frequently also had a reasonable idea of the perpetrators. They also realized only the consistent federal pursuit of the various terrorists would make a difference.

Nowhere in the South was political intimidation more consistently prevalent than in the Fourth Congressional District of Alabama. Making for the political combustion was a black majority galvanized by a forceful and defiant figure in the person of Charles Hays. In Sumter, Greene, Hale, Perry, and other Black Belt counties where Republicans had seized control, violence became common. Championing white supremacy justified for some orchestrated Klan–White League assaults. Basic human instincts compelled Hays to demand punishment of the "raiding white-leaguer" and the "southern desperado."[5] So did political reality. Without a large black turnout on election day his return to Congress was always jeopardized. Hays spoke long and passionately for federal intervention. Other Southern Republicans did also. Agreeing with Hays in 1871 that the Ku Klux Klan Act merited extension, Republican congressman Horace Maynard of Tennessee warned that otherwise "it will not be twenty-four hours before it will be known in every Ku Klux den in the South."[6] But nobody in the approximately 250 member house was as relentless and outspoken on the subject as Hays. Alleged and real crimes against Alabama Republicans would bring the otherwise unknown congressman suddenly to the nation's attention when he authored the Hays-Hawley letter on the eve of the 1874 midterm elections. And it was also fitting that the next year, as the Grant administration marshalled support for the Force Bill, Hays was a central liaison.

The Force Bill did not become law, and generally the federal government had limited success in protecting Republicans during Reconstruction. Terror prevented a fair count at some point in every Southern state. In predominantly black populated areas like Hays's district, where freedmen were at the economic, physical, and psychological mercy of their former masters, the carnage took on staggering dimensions. Events in the Fourth District suggest that action short of declaring martial law and suspending the writ of habeas corpus (done with some success elsewhere) was futile. Troops and national statutes did not prevent the Eutaw Riot. A litany of Republican victims shot down between 1868 and 1874 in Hays's district includes M. T. Crossland, Alexander Boyd, Richard Burke, Guilford Coleman, Walter Billings, Thomas Ivey, and others. Hundreds of individuals (usually black) were beaten, burned out, and threatened. And that was just in the Fourth District. Under the circumstances Hays often felt less like a congressman than the embattled commander of a frontier fort. In this context the Hays-Hawley letter may best be understood. Whatever the inaccuracies, the charges accrued from a personal and real sense of frustration and tragedy. Hays wrote truthfully that "the killing has all been on one side."[7]

Well before Hays wrote the editor of the *Hartford Courant*, he had become the object of a virulent hatred reserved for the scalawag ingrate. The degree of ostracism that he experienced is impossible to determine. Evidence suggests that it was considerable. Editors blasphemed Hays in print for a decade. And he was treated publicly with attitudes ranging from quiet contempt to open hostility. A Republican in neighboring Marengo County spoke to the intensity of emotion. He related, "I feel and have felt in my own county and among my own people just as a soldier of an invading army would feel in traveling in a foreign country."[8] Hays appreciated the full pathos of the statement. Although he took satisfaction in defying political foes he considered reactionary and disloyal, Hays was also plainly affected by his extreme unpopularity. Particularly injurious were allegations of his disloyalty to the South and Alabama. The congressman felt it necessary to reiterate his love and interest in his region and state. Speaking for a final time before the House, Hays denied wanting to "malign my own people."[9] He added, "The last tie that I have got upon earth is to Alabama." Hays was sincere. But whites never were reconciled to his words and actions. The Greene County Republican was an emblematic reminder of everything Democrats considered reprehensible about Radical Reconstruction. As James G. Blaine stated in his memoirs, all Southern Republicans were "doomed to a hopeless struggle against the influence, the tradition, the hatred of a large majority of the white men of the South."[10] Respectability was impossible.

Accepting at face value the Democratic criticism of Hays would be misguided, but dismissing the epithets as political rhetoric also seems inadvisable. Hays could never serve as a perfect foil for the school of Dunning historians who caricatured Southern Republicans as self-serving and corrupt. Recurring indiscretions in his public and private life point to a troubling pattern. It is conceivable that the congressman accepted money for nominating Guy Beardslee to West Point. His transactions with Alexander Shepherd also hint at a certain impropriety. Certainly the congressman realized that the allegations he made to Joseph Hawley were not totally factual. Neither was Hays guileless. Duncan Dew, a respected Greene County citizen, grew up with Hays and the two remained friendly despite political differences. Dew refused to denounce Hays, but did describe him as a "wire-worker."[11] The term denoted calculation and self-promotion in the political vernacular of the nineteenth century. It was not entirely inappropriate.

If flawed, Hays was not the charlatan his political enemies described. Much of the invective directed at him was a consequence of his success. Testifying before the Select Committee on Alabama Affairs in 1875, U.S. district attorney John Southworth reasoned, "They do not like him [Hays] because he is a leader." [12] Hays was that. A figure of messiah proportions for the freedmen, Hays bestowed blacks with a sense of hope, self-respect, and confidence. A more precise estimation of Hays's appeal to the former slaves escapes documentation. Most freedmen could not read or write and have left no record. But they could vote, and they did so, repeatedly, for Hays. Some risked their life doing so. That a strong visceral relationship existed is certain. The victorious campaigns that Hays waged in 1869, 1870, 1872, and 1874 represented far more than exercises in self-aggrandizement and political survival. Although Democrats refused to endorse anything re-sembling racial parity, and many Alabama Republicans were equally unen-thusiastic, Hays vigorously made the case for black advancement. Speaking for the last time before the House, Hays digressed and recalled the disre-pute into which he had fallen. But he argued that a sense of "duty" (he used the word six times in less than a paragraph) overshadowed all con-siderations.[13] That duty, as Hays described it, was to the freedmen. In his bailiwick the high-sounding Republican words about the "privileges and immunities" of citizens and "equal protection of the law" would take on their greatest meaning, or ring most hollow. Hays attempted to give them resonance. As he moved across the Fourth District, the Republican articu-lated the hopes of the former slaves. In that outback setting, at Livingston, Tuscaloosa, Eutaw, Marion, and elsewhere, the vision of Reconstruction architects achieved close application. Charles Hays played no small role.

By the late 1870s the Republican party had ceased to contend seriously for control of Southern state government. Total Democratic hegemony in the region existed until the 1890s when the agrarian-based Populists evolved. Blacks supported the Populists. So did many upcountry white farmers with Unionist backgrounds. The Republican party had always drawn its white support from the north Alabama hills. Bourbon Democrats turned back the Populist challenge and soon disenfranchised the blacks. Yet Republicanism remained viable in the hill counties. Large numbers of north Alabama Populists became Republicans and were attracted to the Progressive wing of the national party. In 1912 these elements supported Theodore Roosevelt and the Bull Moose party. Republicanism remained a strong presence in north Alabama until the advent of Franklin Roosevelt and the New Deal. In keeping with their reform heritage, many of these Republicans then embraced the Democratic ideology.

Long before, blacks had ceased to figure politically. Bourbon Democrats excluded the blacks from the political process across the South. The constitution of 1901 in Alabama, as did similar documents in each Southern state, effectively stripped the suffrage from blacks. The Supreme Court sanctioned social exclusion and Jim Crow accommodations. The more equitable order that Hays and other Republicans had struggled for seemed as far away as ever by the turn of the century.

That fact does not reduce the significance of Hays's efforts. Hays's incongruous switch from a slaveholding Democrat to an egalitarian-minded Republican endowed his career with an importance that transcends the Alabama Black Belt. His experiences have implications for the Reconstruction experiment that went bad. His voting record, speeches, and, above all, the notoriety he accepted as a scalawag were eloquent testimony to this commitment. In Eutaw, at the Greene County courthouse, records reveal that Hays died intestate. He had nothing to bequeath. That was not totally accurate, however, because Charles Hays died without realizing the power of his legacy.

Notes

Preface

1. John Cox and LaWanda Cox, *Politics, Principle, and Prejudice, 1865–1866: Dilemma of Reconstruction America* (London: Free Press of Glenscoe, 1963).

2. Eric Foner, *Reconstruction: America's Unfinished Revolution, 1863–1866* (New York: Harper & Row, 1988), 278.

3. Walter Lynwood Fleming, *Civil War and Reconstruction in Alabama* (New York: Columbia University Press, 1905), 750.

4. John Witherspoon DuBose, *Alabama's Tragic Decade: Ten Years of Alabama, 1865–1874*, edited by James K. Greer (Birmingham: Webb Book Co., 1940), 246.

5. For a selective look at state Reconstruction studies see Sarah Woolfolk Wiggins, *The Scalawag in Alabama Politics, 1865–1881* (Tuscaloosa: University of Alabama Press, 1977); William C. Harris, *The Day of the Carpetbagger: Republican Reconstruction in Mississippi* (Baton Rouge: Louisiana State University Press, 1979); Elizabeth S. Nathans, *Losing the Peace: Georgia Republicans and Southern Reconstruction, 1865–1871* (Baton Rouge: Louisiana State University Press, 1968); Jerrell H. Shofner, *Nor Is It Over Yet: Florida in the Era of Reconstruction, 1863–1877* (Gainesville: University of Florida Press, 1977); Joe Gray Taylor, *Louisiana Reconstructed, 1863–1877* (Baton Rouge: Louisiana State University Press, 1974); Gordon B. McKinney, *Southern Mountain Republicans, 1865–1900* (Chapel Hill: University of North Carolina Press, 1978); Carl H. Moneyhon, *Republicanism in Reconstruction Texas* (Austin: University of Texas Press, 1980).

6. Allen Trelease, "Who Were the Scalawags?," *Journal of Southern History* 29 (November 1963), 448; rejoinder provided by David Donald, "Communications," *Journal of Southern History* 30 (May 1964); William C. Harris, "A Reconsideration of the Mississippi Scalawag," *Journal of Mississippi History* 32 (February 1970); for

Alabama see Sarah Woolfolk Wiggins, "Five Men Called Scalawags," *Alabama Review* 17 (January 1974) and *The Scalawag in Alabama Politics, 1865–1881*. See also Lawrence Powell, "The Politics of Livelihood: Carpetbaggers in the Deep South," in *Region, Race, and Reconstruction Essays in Honor of C. Vann Woodward*, edited by J. Morgan Koussar and James M. McPherson (New York: Oxford University Press, 1982).

7. Lillian A. Pereyra, *James Lusk Alcorn: Persistent Whig* (Baton Rouge: Louisiana State University Press, 1966); Donald Bridgman Sanger, *James Longstreet: Soldier, Politician, Officeholder, and Writer* (Baton Rouge: Louisiana State University Press, 1952); William Garrett Piston, *Lee's Tarnished Lieutenant: James Longstreet and His Place in Southern History* (Athens: University of Georgia Press, 1987).

Chapter 1: An Aristocratic Background

1. Will of Charles Hays (Office of the Chancery Clerk, Chester, South Carolina), Book H, 59; *U.S. Bureau of the Census, Seventh Census, 1850 (Population)* 421, 429–31; Mary Hairston Hays to Thomas M. Owen, November 7, 1913, in Hays Surname File, Alabama Department of Archives and History, Montgomery; V. Gayle Snedecor, *A Directory of Greene County for 1855–56* (Mobile, Ala.: Strickland & Co., 1856), 61–68; Mary Morgan Glass, ed., *A Goodly Heritage: Memories of Greene County* (Eutaw, Ala.: Greene County Historical Society, 1977), 10, 13.

2. Civil Register County Officials, I (1819–1832), 94, Alabama State Department of Archives and History (hereinafter cited as ADAH); *Journal of the House of Representatives, 1829* (Tuscaloosa: McQuire, Henry & Walker, 1839), 3; Deed Book of Greene County (Office of the Probate Judge, Eutaw, Ala.), A: 2, 4, 8, 276–77; B: 250; Index to Alabama Track Book (Greene County), A: 6–8, 16, 19, 61; C: 196–98, 463, 475; E: 627; G: 168–71; H: 211, 214–15, 259–60, 274; ADAH; Glass, ed., *A Goodly Heritage*, 84, 94, 98, 175; interview with Mrs. Roberta Hays Lowndes, May 24, 1986, Decatur, Georgia.

3. Will of George Hays, Will Record Book B (1826–1840), (Office of the Probate Judge, Eutaw, Alabama), 204–06; "Gould, Executor of Hayes [*sic*] v. Womack and Wife," *Alabama Reports* (1841) II (Tuscaloosa: Hale & Pheland, 1842), 93; Pauline Jones Gandrud, comp., *Marriage Records of Greene County, Alabama 1823–1860* (N.p.: Milestone Press, 1969), 65; Hays Family Bible, in possession of Mrs. Roberta Hays Lowndes (this and other material cited hereinafter as in possession of Lowndes).

4. John W. Womack to Lewis Womack, August 27, 1869, in Marcus Joseph Wright Papers, Southern Historical Collection, University of North Carolina, Chapel Hill, North Carolina (cited hereinafter as SHC); John Buckner Little, *The*

History of Butler County Alabama, From 1815 to 1885 (Cincinnati: Elm St. Printing Co., 1885), 200.

5. William Garrett, *Reminiscences of Public Men in Alabama for Thirty Years* (Atlanta: Plantation Publishing Co., 1872), 57–59.

6. John Womack to Lewis Womack, September 29, 1844, Marcus Joseph Wright Papers, SHC.

7. *Catalogue of the Students of the Greene Springs for the Sixth Scholastic Year, Ending May 25, 1853* (Tuscaloosa: J. D. J. Slade, 1853), n.pag.; Marcus Joseph Wright, comp.; "Memoranda for Biographical Sketch of Charles Hays," in Hays Surname File, ADAH (hereinafter cited as "Sketch of Charles Hays"). Wright, Hays's brother-in-law, compiled the brief biographical summation of Hays in 1913. Clay Lancaster, *Eutaw, the Builders and Architecture of an Ante-Bellum Southern Town* (Eutaw, Ala.: Greene County Historical Society, 1979), 18, 142–43, 180.

8. *Greensboro Alabama Beacon*, August 10, 1850.

9. *Congressional Globe* (42nd Congress, 2nd session), IV: 3077; Garrett, *Reminiscences of Public Men*, 57–59. For mention of Womack's political activities see the *Greensboro Alabama Beacon*, June 30, 1843, April 14, May 5, July 29, 1849, April 13, 1850.

10. "Minutes of the Faculty, 1850–1873," on file at University of Georgia Archives, University of Georgia Library, Athens; *Catalogue of the Trustees, Officers, Alumni, and Matriculates of the University of Georgia at Athens, Georgia, from 1795–1906* (Athens: E. E. Stones Press, 1901), 68; *A Catalogue of the Officers and Students of Franklin College, Athens, 1851–52* (Athens: Christy & Lelsea, 1851), 11, 14; *A Catalogue of the Officers and Students of Franklin College, Athens, 1851–53* (Athens: Christy & Lelsea, 1852), 9, 15; Phi Kappa Treasurer's Book, 1848–1855, on file at Georgia Room, University of Georgia Library, Athens, 229; *University of Virginia Matriculation Book*, 2 (N.p., n.d.), n. pag.; *Catalogue of the University of Virginia Session of 1852–53* (Richmond: H. K. Ellyson, 1853), 19, 30; Garrett, *Reminiscences of Public Men*, 58.

11. "Gould v. Hays et al.," *Alabama Reports* XIX (1851) (Montgomery: J. H. & T. F. Martin, 1852), 438–63; Glass, *A Goodly Heritage*, 88.

12. William Proctor Gould, *Diary of William Proctor Gould of Boligee, Greene County, Alabama*, 4 vols., 3:18 (hereinafter cited as *Diary*).

13. *Diary*, 4:45; "Gould v. Hays et al.," *Alabama Reports* 25 (1854) (Montgomery: Cowan & Martin, 1855), 426–33.

14. John Womack to Pauline Womack, n.d., Marcus Joseph Wright Papers, SHC; Charles Hays to Cornelia Hays, n.d., in possession of Lowndes.

15. Deed Book of Greene County (Office of the Probate Judge, Eutaw, Ala.), U: 50, 124; *Alabama Manuscript Agricultural Census*, 1850, II (DeKalb-Morgan), 13–14; *Alabama Manuscript Slave Census*, 1850, I (Autauga-Madison), 93–94.

16. John Womack to the editors of the *Philadelphia Saturday Evening Post*,

August 16, 1855, in *Eutaw Observer*, n.d., John Womack Scrapbook, Manuscript Division, ADAH.

17. John Womack to Col. C. W. Lee, July 27, 1859, in *Eutaw Independent Observer*, n.d., Womack Scrapbook, ADAH.

18. Charles Hays to Andrew Johnson, August 1, 1865, U.S. Adjutant General Records, Record Group 94, National Archives, Washington, D.C. (hereinafter cited as Amnesty Papers, NA).

19. Open letter from John Womack addressed to Syndenham Moore, December 4, 1860, in Womack Scrapbook, ADAH; "Proceedings of the National Democratic State Convention of Alabama, held in the City of Montgomery on June 4, 1860" (Baltimore: John W. Woods, 1860), 11, 13, Womack Scrapbook, ADAH. For the history of secession in Alabama see William L. Barney, *The Secessionist Impulse: Alabama and Mississippi in 1860* (Princeton: University of Princeton Press, 1974).

20. Gould, *Diary*, 4:114; *U.S. Bureau of the Census, Eighth Census, 1860 (Agriculture)*, 23.

21. John Womack to Syndenham Moore, December 4, 1860, Womack Scrapbook, ADAH; Walter Lynwood Fleming, *Civil War and Reconstruction in Alabama*, 27–28, 37.

22. U.S. Congress, House Report No. 262, "Affairs in Alabama" (43rd Congress, 2nd session), Duncan Dew, 522 (hereinafter cited as "Affairs in Alabama"); "Exemptions Granted by the Governor of Alabama from Military Service in the Confederate States Army," compiled by Clyde Wilson, Military Records Division, ADAH; Wright, Sketch of Charles Hays." For information on Marcus Joseph Wright see Mark Mayo Boatner, *The Civil War Dictionary* (New York: David McKay Co., 1959), 950; *Eutaw Whig and Observer*, October 29, 1863.

23. Ledia Gale to Cornelia Hays, December 25, 1863, in possession of Lowndes; interview with Lowndes, May 24, 1986; Thomas McAdory Owen, *History of Alabama and Dictionary of Alabama Biography* (Chicago: S. J. Clarke Publishing Co., 1921), IV: 1303.

24. Charles Hays to Cornelia Hays, May 1864, in possession of Lowndes.

25. Charles Hays to Cornelia Hays, November 2, 1864, in possession of Lowndes.

26. Charles Hays to Cornelia Hays, May 1864, in possession of Lowndes.

27. *Demopolis Southern Republican*, September 29, 1869.

28. *Congressional Record* (43rd Congress, 2nd session), III: 1852.

Chapter 2: The Fall of the Son

1. Eric Foner, *Reconstruction: America's Unfinished Revolution, 1863–1877*, 178–84, 225–27; Kenneth M. Stampp, *The Era of Reconstruction, 1865–1877* (New York:

Knopf, 1966), 62–64; Michael Les Benedict, *A Compromise of Principle: Congressional Republicans and Reconstruction, 1863–1869* (New York: Norton, 1974), 106–8; LaWanda Cox and John Cox, *Politics, Principle, and Prejudice, 1865–1866: Dilemma of Reconstruction America*, 198–99, 201.

2. *Congressional Globe* (42nd Congress, 2nd session), IV: 3077; Peter Kolchin, *First Freedom: The Response of Alabama's Blacks to Emancipation and Reconstruction* (Westport, Conn.: Greenwood Press, 1972), 4–5; William Warren Rogers, *The One-Gallused Rebellion: Agrarianism in Alabama, 1865–1896* (Baton Rouge: Louisiana State University Press, 1970), 4, 10; George R. Bentley, *A History of the Freedmen's Bureau* (Philadelphia: University of Pennsylvania Press, 1955), 49, 104–5, 186–87. For a discussion of the Freedmen's Bureau in Alabama see Elizabeth Bethel, "Freedmen's Bureau in Alabama," *Journal of Southern History* 14 (February 1948). For accounts of Alabama after the war see Whitelaw Reid, *After the War: A Southern Tour* (London: Moore, Wilstach & Baldwin, 1866) and J. T. Trowbridge, *The South: A Tour of its Battlefields and Ruined Cities* (Hartford: L. Stebbins, 1866).

3. Charles Hays to Andrew Johnson, August 1, 1864, Amnesty Papers, NA; *Montgomery Advertiser*, October 7, 1865; Jonathan Truman Dorris, *Pardon and Amnesty Under Lincoln and Johnson* (Chapel Hill: University of North Carolina Press, 1955), 111–12; Michael Perman, *Reunion without Compromise: The South and Reconstruction, 1865–68* (New York: Cambridge University Press, 1973), 122–23. For material on dilemma of planters, see James L. Roark, *Masters Without Slaves: Southern Planters in the Civil War and Reconstruction* (New York: Norton, 1977) and Roger Ransom and Richard Sutch, *One Kind of Freedom: the Economic Consequences of Emancipation* (New York: Cambridge University Press, 1977).

4. *Congressional Globe* (42nd Congress, 2nd session), IV: 3077.

5. C. C. Thomas to Lewis Parsons, July 4, 1865, Amnesty Papers, NA.

6. *Eutaw Whig and Observer*, quoted in *Greensboro Alabama Beacon*, September 1, 1866; *Montgomery Advertiser*, October 14, 1866; U.S. House Executive Document 16, "Final report of the names of persons engaged in rebellion who have been pardoned" (39th Congress, 2nd session), 17; Jonathan M. Weiner, *Social Origins of the New South Alabama, 1860–1885* (Baton Rouge: Louisiana State University Press, 1978), 53–56; Kolchin, *First Freedom*, 33–34.

7. George Clemenceau, *American Reconstruction, 1865–1870* (New York: Dial Press, 1928), 230; Benedict, *A Compromise of Principle*, 137, 156, 169; Foner, *Reconstruction*, 256–61, 268–69; Perman, *Reunion without Compromise*, 235–36, 256–57; Cox and Cox, *Politics, Principle, and Prejudice*, 208–12.

8. Perman, *Reunion without Compromise*, 271–73, 290, 305, 315; Cox and Cox, *Politics, Principle, and Prejudice*, 202, 207–10; Foner, *Reconstruction*, 276–77; Sarah Woolfolk Wiggins, *The Scalawag in Alabama Politics, 1865–1881* (Tuscaloosa: University of Alabama Press, 1977), 21–25; Malcolm Cook McMillan, *Constitutional Development in Alabama, 1798–1901: A Study in Politics, the Negro, and Sectionalism*

(Chapel Hill: University of North Carolina Press, 1955), 111–12; Michael W. Fitz-gerald, *The Union League Movement in the Deep South: Politics and Agricultural Change during Reconstruction* (Baton Rouge: Louisiana State University Press, 1989), 46, 113, 116; Loren Schweninger, "Alabama Blacks and the Congressional Reconstruc-tion Acts of 1867," *Alabama Review* 31 (July 1978), 189–90, 195–96.

9. U.S. Senate Reports, No. 704, "The Subcommittee of the Committee for Privileges and Elections Reports [on] Elections of 1874, 1875, and 1876" (44th Congress, 2nd session), 40.

10. William Miller to Lewis Parsons, August 8, 1865, in Governor Lewis Par-sons Papers, Governors' Papers, ADAH; *Montgomery Daily State Sentinel,* August 30, 1867; *Demopolis Southern Republican,* April 14, 1869; *Testimony Taken by the Joint Select Committee to Inquire Into the Conditions of Affairs in the Late Insurrectionary States, Alabama,* I: William Miller, 11 (hereinafter referred to as *Alabama Testi-mony*); Kolchin, *First Freedom,* 51–76; Fitzgerald, *The Union League Movement in the Deep South,* 37, 116.

11. A. S. Mock to C. Cadle, n.d., in Papers of the Bureau of Refugees, Freedmen, and Abandoned Lands, Record Group 105, NA (hereinafter cited as Freedmen's Bureau Papers).

12. *Congressional Globe* (42nd Congress, 2nd session), IV: 3077–78; *Congressional Globe* (43rd Congress, 2nd session), III: 1852. For a declaration of Republicanism from a prominent Democrat, see letter of Joshua Morse to *Montgomery Advertiser,* May 7, 1867.

13. Charles Hays to Charles W. Pierce, September 18, 1867, in "Reports of Operations from the Sub-Districts," Freedmen's Bureau Papers, NA.

14. Charles W. Pierce to O. D. Kinsmen, June 11, 1867, Freedmen's Bureau Papers; *Tuscaloosa Independent Monitor,* October 16, 1867; *Greensboro Alabama Bea-con,* December 28, 1867. Robert S. Rhodes, "The Registration of Voters and the Election of Delegates to the Reconstruction Convention in Alabama," *Alabama Review* 8 (April 1955), 126–29, 133–35.

15. Henry Deedes, *Sketches of the South and West* (Edinburgh & London: William Blackford & Sons, 1869), 142–43. See, for Montgomery, J. Wayne Flynt, *Mont-gomery: An Illustrated History* (Woodland Hills, Calif.: Windsor Publications, 1980).

16. *Montgomery Advertiser,* October 12, 1867; McMillan, *Constitutional Devel-opment,* 115–22; see also Richard L. Hume, "The 'Black and Tan' Constitutional Conventions of 1867–1869 in Ten former Confederate States: A Study of Their Membership" (Ph.D. dissertation, University of Washington, 1969), James D. Thomas, "Alabama Constitutional convention of 1867" (M.A. thesis, Auburn Uni-versity, 1947).

17. *Montgomery Daily State Sentinel,* November 16, 1867; McMillan, *Constitu-tional Development,* 119–20, 122, 124, 127–28; Hume, "Constitutional Conven-tions," 17–20; Benedict, *A Compromise of Principle,* 214, 232, 242–43.

18. *Montgomery Daily Mail*, November 11, 1867; *Official Journal of the Constitutional Convention of the State of Alabama, 1867* (Montgomery: Barrett & Brown, 1868), 22.

19. *Journal of the Constitutional Convention*, 30–37; Hume, "Constitutional Conventions," 17–19.

20. *New York Herald*, November 29, 1867; *Journal of the Constitutional Convention*, 21–22, 97–99.

21. McMillan, *Constitutional Development*, 131–32, 140, 143–46, 148–49; Hume, "Constitutional Conventions," 23–24, 31; Wiggins, *Scalawag in Alabama Politics*, 24–30, 35.

22. *Greensboro Alabama Beacon*, quoted in *Eutaw Whig and Observer*, November 26, 1874; John Witherspoon DuBose, *Alabama's Tragic Decade: Ten Years of Alabama, 1865–1874*, edited by James K. Greer (Birmingham: Webb Book Co., 1940), 246–47.

23. "Affairs in Alabama," Duncan Dew, 543.

24. U.S. Congress, Executive Document No. 238, "Report of General George Meade" (39th Congress, 2nd session), 2; McMillan, *Constitutional Development*, 169–72.

25. "Affairs in Alabama," Samuel F. Rice, 507; Wiggins, *The Scalawag in Alabama Politics*, 35–38. For material on the resentment of Republicans see Wiggins, "Ostracism of White Republicans in Alabama During Reconstruction," *Alabama Review* 27 (January 1974), 56–62.

26. *Tuscaloosa Independent Monitor*, October 12, 1869. For material on animosity toward Republicans in Greene County see the account of a contemporary of Hays's, E. C. Meredith, "Reconstruction in Alabama," unpublished manuscript in possession of the estate of Roy Swayze, Eutaw, Alabama.

27. "Affairs in Alabama," Charles Hays, 15.

28. *Tuscaloosa Independent Monitor*, November 27, 1867.

29. *Congressional Record* (43rd Congress, 2nd session), III: 1097.

Chapter 3: Apostasy Confirmed

1. Deed Book of Greene County (Office of the Probate Judge, Eutaw, Alabama), W: 535–36, 667–68. For an examination of the postwar situation, see James L. Roark, *Masters Without Slaves: Southern Planters in the Civil War and Reconstruction* (New York: Norton, 1977).

2. John A. Yordy to Charles A. Miller, February 11, 1868; John Yordy to Gen. Julius Hayden, February 24, 1868, in Gov. William Hugh Smith Papers, Manuscript Division, ADAH; Charles Pierce to Bvt. Maj. George Shorkley, March 31, April 30, June 30, 1866, Freedmen Bureau Papers, NA; William War-

ren Rogers, Jr., "The Eutaw Prisoners: Federal Confrontation with Violence in Reconstruction Alabama," *Alabama Review* 43 (April 1990), 101–11.

3. Voluminous information of a primary and secondary nature regarding Reconstruction violence exists. This study has drawn heavily from two congressional investigations that resulted in printed testimony. Against the backdrop of Klan activity, the Forty-second Congress created a twenty-one-member joint committee to assess the situation in the South. Between June 1871 and January 1872 the committee took testimony relating to affairs in North Carolina, South Carolina, Georgia, Mississippi, Florida, and Alabama. Over 150 witnesses were examined in Alabama, and three volumes of testimony (more than any other state) were compiled. See *Testimony Taken by the Joint Select Committee to Inquire into the Conditions of Affairs in the Late Insurrectionary States, Alabama.* Several years later, the Forty-third Congress authorized an investigation of the circumstances surrounding the 1874 elections in Alabama. Over 350 witnesses testified. Their observations are found in U.S. Congress, House Report No. 262, "Affairs in Alabama" (43rd Congress, 2nd session). For a masterful study of political intimidation from the end of the war to the early 1870s see Allen W. Trelease, *White Terror: The Ku Klux Klan Conspiracy and Southern Reconstruction* (New York: Harper & Row, 1971). Overlapping somewhat with Trelease, and documenting violence further into the 1870s, is William Gillette, *Retreat from Reconstruction, 1869–1879* (Baton Rouge: Louisiana State University Press, 1979). Eric Foner also deals ably with the subject in *Reconstruction: America's Unfinished Revolution, 1863–1877.* See also George C. Rable, *But There Was No Peace: The Role of Violence in the Politics of Reconstruction* (Athens: University of Georgia Press, 1984). Reconstruction violence in Alabama is best covered by William Bell Dudley, "The Reconstruction Ku Klux Klan: A Survey of the Writings on the Klan with a Profile and Analysis of the Alabama Klan Episode, 1866–1874" (Ph.D. dissertation, Louisiana State University Press, 1973). See also James LeRoy Taylor, "A History of the Ku Klux Klan in Alabama, 1865–1874" (M.A. thesis, Auburn University, 1957).

4. George Meade to Andrew Johnson, April 5, 1868, in Andrew Johnson Presidential Papers, Library of Congress, Division of Manuscripts.

5. *Alabama Testimony*, I: Charles Hays, 16; Trelease, *White Terror*, 82–88; Dudley, "The Reconstruction Ku Klux Klan," 206–8, 222.

6. William S. McFeely, *Grant: A Biography* (New York: Norton, 1981), 277; William B. Hesseltine, *Ulysses S. Grant: Politician* (New York: Dodd, Mead, 1935), 120–21, 124.

7. *Journal of the Senate of the State of Alabama, 1868* (Montgomery: James G. Stokes, 1868), 13–18; Wiggins, *The Scalawag in Alabama Politics*, 38–39; Michael Perman, *Road to Redemption: Southern Politics, 1869–1879* (Chapel Hill: University of North Carolina Press, 1984), 32–34, 42–48.

8. *Montgomery Daily Mail*, July 28, 1868; *Journal of the Senate, 1868*, 36. Richard

H. Abbott argued that the political disabilities issue severely hurt Republican political chances in *The Republican Party and the South, 1855–1877: The First Southern Strategy* (Chapel Hill: University of North Carolina Press, 1983), 165–71.

9. Benjamin H. Screws, "The 'Loil' Legislature of Alabama: Its Ridiculous Doings, and Nonsensical Sayings" (Montgomery: R. W. Offutt & Co., 1868), 36–37; *Journal of the Senate, 1868,* 96–97; *Montgomery Daily Mail,* August 3–6, 1868.

10. *Demopolis Southern Republican,* September 29, 1869; *Journal of the Senate, 1868,* 104, 125; *Mobile Daily Register,* August 13–14, 1868; *Montgomery Mail,* July 23, 26, 29, 1868. The legislature in Florida did cast the state's three electoral votes for the Grant-Colfax ticket. The alternative was considered by Republican-dominated legislatures in Georgia and Louisiana. Abbott, *Republican Party in the South,* 88; Thomas Alexander, *Political Reconstruction in Tennessee* (Nashville: Vanderbilt University Press, 1950), 124–27, 131–32.

11. *Montgomery Daily Picayune,* July 24, 1868.

12. *Montgomery Daily Mail,* September 19, 1868. The *Mail* and the *Advertiser* routinely criticized the Alabama legislature. See *Montgomery Daily Mail,* July 16, 25, 28, and *Montgomery Advertiser,* July 31, 1868.

13. *Montgomery Daily Picayune,* August 7, 1868; *Montgomery Advertiser,* August 13, 1868; *Montgomery Daily Mail,* September 26, 1868.

14. Charles Hays to Gov. William Smith, August 21, 1868, Smith Papers, ADAH.

15. William Miller to Gov. William Smith, July 22, 1868, Smith Papers, ADAH; *Alabama Testimony,* I: John Jolly, 278; Meredith, "Reconstruction in Alabama," 5–6.

16. *Philadelphia Press,* quoted in *Tuscaloosa Independent Monitor,* September 1, 1868; William Miller to Gov. William Smith, July 22, 31, August 17, 1868, Smith Papers, ADAH; *Cincinnati Commercial,* October 10, 1868; Meredith, "Reconstruction in Alabama," 5–6.

17. *Demopolis Southern Republican,* September 29, 1869; *Alabama Testimony,* I: James Clarke, 257, John Jolly, 265–91, John Pierce, 297, 301.

18. William Jones to Gov. William Smith, August 17, 1868, Smith Papers, ADAH; *Mobile Daily Register,* August 12–13, 1868; *Montgomery Daily Mail,* July 28, 1868.

19. *Montgomery Advertiser,* September 12, 1868.

20. *Tuscaloosa Independent Monitor,* September 29, 1868.

21. *Alabama Testimony,* III: Francis Strother Lyon, 1411.

22. *Eutaw Whig and Observer,* quoted in *Montgomery Daily Mail,* September 29, 1868.

23. *Montgomery Daily Mail,* September 19, 1868.

24. *Washington Evening Star,* September 28, 1868; *Montgomery Alabama State Journal,* October 2, 1868; *Montgomery Daily Mail,* October 6, 1868; Trelease, *White*

Terror, 113, 118, 127, 137, 149, 154, 185; Abbott, *The Republican Party and the South*, 186–91.

25. *Montgomery Daily Mail*, October 2, 6, 1868.

26. Everette Swinney, "Suppressing the Ku Klux Klan: The Enforcement of the Reconstruction Amendments, 1870–1874" (Ph.D. dissertation, University of Texas, 1966), 191–93; for the role of the U.S. Army see James E. Sefton, *The United States Army and Reconstruction, 1865–1877* (Baton Rouge: Louisiana State University Press, 1967), 183, 213, 220–21.

27. *Alabama Testimony*, I: Turner Reavis, 338; Richard N. Current, *Those Terrible Carpetbaggers* (New York: Oxford University Press, 1988), 33–37, 153. See also for Warner, John Burkett Ryan, Jr., "Willard Warner: Soldier, Senator, and Southern Entrepreneur" (M.A. thesis, Auburn University, 1971).

28. *Alabama Testimony*, I: Willard Warner, 29–30; *Mobile Daily Register*, October 31, 1868; Current, *Those Terrible Carpetbaggers*, 154.

29. *Carrollton West Alabamian*, October 28, 1868.

30. *Tuscaloosa Independent Monitor*, November 3, 1868, July 29, 1869; *Alabama Testimony*, I: Willard Warner, 30. For Randolph see Nancy Anne Sindon, "The Career of Ryland Randolph: A Study in Reconstruction Journalism" (M.A. thesis, Florida State University, 1965), 1–3; Sarah Woolfolk Wiggins, "The Life of Ryland Randolph as Seen Through His Letters to John W. Dubose," *Alabama Historical Quarterly* 30 (Fall-Winter 1968), 146, 154, 164.

31. *Montgomery Alabama State Journal*, November 14, 1868; Foner, *Reconstruction*, 342–44. For a breakdown by county of votes see Louis V. Loveman, comp., "The Presidential Vote in Alabama, 1824–1980" (Gadsden, Ala., 1983), 5.

32. *Journal of the Senate, 1868*, 245–49; *Alabama Testimony*, III: E. Woolsey Peck, 1851–52, Simeon Brunson, 2002–03; *Montgomery Alabama State Journal*, November 18, 1868.

33. *Montgomery Advertiser*, December 17, 1868; *Acts of the Sessions of July, September and November, 1868, of the General Assembly of Alabama* (Montgomery: John G. Stokes, 1868), 443; *Journal of the Senate, 1868*, 457–59. Southern Republican legislatures considered but rarely passed common carrier bills: see Foner, *Reconstruction*, 369–71.

34. *Montgomery Advertiser*, November 29, 1868; *Montgomery Daily Mail*, December 2, 1868.

35. *Acts of the General Assembly, 1868*, 444–46, 452, 454.

36. *Demopolis Southern Republican*, July 11, 1869.

37. *Acts of the General Assembly, 1868*, 594–95.

38. *Demopolis Southern Republican*, September 29, 1869.

Chapter 4: A Southern Republican Goes to Washington

1. Charles Hays to Charles Dustan, January 2, 1869, in Charles W. Dustan Papers, Manuscript Division, ADAH.

2. *Montgomery Alabama State Weekly Journal*, January 9, 1869; William Warren Rogers, " 'Politics is Mighty Uncertain': Charles Hays Goes to Congress," *Alabama Review* 30 (July 1977), 164–65.

3. *Montgomery Advertiser*, May 7, 1867; *Alabama Testimony*, II: William Blackford, 1271–72; "Affairs in Alabama," James A. Abrahams, 763–65; Rogers, " 'Politics is Mighty Uncertain,' " 168.

4. William Jones to William E. Chandler, July 9, 1871, in William E. Chandler Papers, Library of Congress, Division of Manuscripts; *Montgomery Alabama State Weekly Journal*, October 21, 1870; Meredith, "Reconstruction in Alabama," 4, 15, 17; *U.S. Bureau of the Census, Ninth Census 1870* (Population), 11; Rogers, " 'Politics is Mighty Uncertain,' " 167–68; Fitzgerald, *The Union League*, 206. For allegations that Hays forces packed the convention with individuals whose bonds he had signed see *Marion Commonwealth*, July 29, 1869; *Selma Southern Argus*, July 14, 1869.

5. Claus to Charles Dustan, March 28, 1869, Dustan Papers, ADAH; *Demopolis Southern Republican*, May 5, 19, June 2, 9, 1869; Rogers, " 'Politics is Mighty Uncertain,' " 165–66.

6. Charles Hays to Charles Dustan, May 20, 1869, Dustan Papers, ADAH; Rogers, " 'Politics is Mighty Uncertain,' " 164–66.

7. *Demopolis Southern Republican*, June 23, 1869; Rogers, " 'Politics is Mighty Uncertain,' " 169–72.

8. *Montgomery Alabama State Journal*, quoted in *Demopolis Southern Republican*, June 23, 1869; *Montgomery Advertiser*, June 23, 1869.

9. *Marion Commonwealth*, June 10, 1869; *Montgomery Daily Mail*, May 5, 1869.

10. *Demopolis Southern Republican*, June 23, 9, 1869; Rogers, " 'Politics is Mighty Uncertain,' " 173–74.

11. *Demopolis Southern Republican*, June 23, 30, 1869; *Montgomery Daily Mail*, May 5, 1869.

12. James A. Moore to Charles Dustan, June 28, 1869, Dustan Papers, ADAH.

13. "To the Voters of Marengo County," circular in Dustan Papers, ADAH; Owen, *History of Alabama*, IV: 1079–80.

14. *Carrollton West Alabamian*, July 21, 1869.

15. *Tuscaloosa Independent Monitor*, July 10, 1869; *Gainesville News*, July 22, 1869; *Montgomery Advertiser*, July 14, 1869.

16. *Greensboro Alabama Beacon*, July 4, 1869; *Gainesville News*, July 22, 1869; *Demopolis Southern Republican*, July 21, 1869.

17. *Selma Southern Argus*, July 14, 1869; *Demopolis Southern Republican*, July 13, 1869.

18. *Tuscaloosa Independent Monitor*, July 24, 1869; *Greensboro Alabama Beacon*, July 31, 1869; Rogers, "'Politics is Mighty Uncertain,'" 185.

19. James W. Ceda to Charles Dustan, July 21, 1869, Dustan Papers, ADAH.

20. *Montgomery Alabama State Journal*, July 20, 1869.

21. *Demopolis Southern Republican*, July 28, 1869.

22. *Gainesville News*, July 15, 1869.

23. Connish to E. J. Dustan, July 8, 1869, Dustan Papers, ADAH.

24. *Greensboro Alabama Beacon*, July 31, 1869; *Demopolis Southern Republican*, August 4, 1869; P. M. Whetstone to Charles Dustan, July 16, 1869, Dustan Papers, ADAH.

25. *Marion Commonwealth*, July 29, 1869; *Tuscaloosa Independent Monitor*, June 24, 1869; Owens, *History of Alabama*, IV: 1419; Harwell H. Jones, "The History of Bibb County During Reconstruction (1865–1876)" (M.A. thesis, University of Alabama, 1932), 9–11.

26. *Montgomery Advertiser*, July 22, 1869.

27. *Tuscaloosa Independent Monitor*, July 20, 1869.

28. *Selma Southern Argus*, quoted in *Montgomery Advertiser*, July 3, 1869.

29. Charles Hays to Gov. William Smith, August 4, 7, 1869, Smith Papers, ADAH; Official Manuscript Returns, Congressional Election (1869), ADAH; *Greensboro Alabama Beacon*, August 7, 1869; *Tuscaloosa Independent Monitor*, August 17, 1869.

30. *Demopolis Southern Republican*, September 29, 1869.

31. Deed Book of Greene County (Office of Probate Judge, Eutaw, Ala.), W: 905, X: 232.

32. Ibid., Deed Book Y: 15–16; *Demopolis Southern Republican*, April 25, 1869; interview with Lowndes, May 24, 1986; Glass, *A Goodly Heritage*, 91–93.

33. Constance Mclaughlin Green, *Washington Village and Capital, 1800–1878* (Princeton: Princeton University Press, 1962), 13, 150–51; James Whyte, *The Uncivil War: Washington during the Reconstruction, 1865–1878* (New York: Twayne, 1958), 18; John B. Ellis, *The Sights and Secrets of the National Capital* (New York: United States Publishing Company, 1869), 400, 443, 450.

34. Ellis, *The Sights and Secrets of the National Capital*, 56; William H. Boyd, comp., *Boyd's Directory of Washington, Georgetown and Alexandria, 1870* (Washington, D.C.: Hudson Taylor Book Store, Pennsylvania Ave., 1870), 175.

35. *Washington National Republican*, October 12, 1874.

36. Ibid.

37. Ellis, *Sights and Secrets of the National Capital*, 141.

38. Joseph West Moore, *Picturesque Washington* (Providence, R.I.: J.A. & R.A. Kid, 1887), 131; Thomas J. Davis, "Alabama's Reconstruction Representatives in the United States Congress, 1868–1878," *Alabama Historical Quarterly* 44 (Spring-Summer 1982), 36.

39. Terry Lee Seip, *The South Returns to Congress: Men, Economic Measures, and*

Intersectional Relationships, 1868–1879 (Baton Rouge: Louisiana State University Press, 1983), 137, 146–47, 149–51, 171–72, 182–84; Walter T. K. Nugent, *The Money Question during Reconstruction* (New York: Norton, 1967); *Congressional Globe* (41st Congress, 2nd session), VI: 5303.

40. *Congressional Globe* (41st Congress, 2nd session), III: 2202–04, VI: 5522; Seip, "Southern Representatives and Economic Measures During Reconstruction: A Quantitative and Analytical Study" (Ph.D. dissertation, Louisiana State University, 1974), 155–58; William Horatio Barnes, *The History of the Congress of the United States, 1869–1871* (New York: W. H. Barnes & Co., 1822), 189.

41. Ibid.

42. *Congressional Globe* (41st Congress, 2nd session), III: 2202–04.

43. Charles Hays to Gen. Samuel W. Crawford, June 24, 1870, in *Alabama Testimony*, II: 1234; William Warren Rogers, "The Boyd Incident: Black Belt Violence During Reconstruction," *Civil War History* 30 (December 1975), 309–10, 324–26; Everette Swinney, "Suppressing the Ku Klux Klan: The Enforcement of the Reconstruction Amendments, 1870–1874" (Ph.D. dissertation, University of Texas, 1966), 57–58.

44. *Congressional Globe Appendix* (41st Congress, 2nd session), VII: 279.

45. Swinney, "Suppressing the Ku Klux Klan," 57–68; *Congressional Globe* (41st Congress, 2nd session), III: 2093–94, 2235, 2585, IV: 2962, V: 3668–69, 3884.

46. Charles Hays to Gov. William Smith, June 24, 1870, Smith Papers, ADAH.

47. Charles Hays to Gen. Samuel Crawford, June 24, 1870, in *Alabama Testimony*, II: 1234.

48. Gov. William Smith to Charles Hays, June 30, 1870, Letterbook of Gov. William Smith, 16, in Letterbooks of Governors of Alabama, ADAH.

Chapter 5: I Shall Die Game

1. Wiggins, *The Scalawag in Alabama Politics*, 61, 62; Perman, *Road to Redemption*, 58–61.

2. *Montgomery Advertiser*, September 3, 7; Owen, *History of Alabama*, IV: 1048–49.

3. *Montgomery Alabama State Journal*, August 19, 1870; *Demopolis Southern Republican*, June 15, August 24, 1870; Current, *Those Terrible Carpetbaggers*, 30–32, 157–62; Wiggins, *The Scalawag in Alabama Politics*, 57.

4. *Alabama Testimony*, III: Reuben A. Meredith, 1771–73, III: Charles Hays, 1835–36; Trelease, *White Terror*, 251.

5. Charles Hays to Gov. William Smith, August 13, 1870, Smith Papers, ADAH; *Alabama Testimony*, I: Turner Reavis, 327, 335, III: Charles Hays, 1835–36; *Demopolis Southern Republican*, August 24, 1870.

6. *Montgomery Alabama State Journal*, September 9, 1870; Loren Schweninger,

James T. Rapier and Reconstruction (Chicago: University of Chicago Press, 1978), 75–78; Current, *Those Terrible Carpetbaggers*, 161–62.

7. Henry Watson to A. C. Jones, August 14, 1870, in Henry Watson Papers, Special Collections Department, Duke University Library, Durham, North Carolina.

8. *Demopolis Southern Republican*, August 24, September 14, 21, 1870.

9. Charles Hays to Willard Warner, September 15, 1870, Smith Papers, ADAH.

10. *Alabama Testimony*, III: Charles Hays, 1836.

11. Anne Womack to Charles Hays, September 17, 1870, Smith Papers, ADAH.

12. Charles Hays to Willard Warner, September 18, 1870, Smith Papers, ADAH.

13. "To the Commanding Officers of Posts and Detachments in the State of Alabama," a circular in Samuel Wylie Crawford Papers, Special Collection Department, Duke University Library; *Montgomery Weekly Alabama State Journal*, April 22, May 27, July 22, August 5, 1874; Trelease, *White Terror*, 266–70, 273; Gene L. Howard, *Death at Cross Plains: An Alabama Reconstruction Tragedy* (Tuscaloosa: University of Alabama Press, 1984).

14. Gideon Harris to Robert McKee, April 13, 1872, Robert McKee Papers, ADAH; *Carrollton West Alabamian*, October 5, 1870; *Eutaw Whig and Observer*, April 28, 1864; John Gideon Harris Diary (1859); John Gideon Harris Papers, 6, 17, 21, 24, SHC.

15. *Greensboro Alabama Beacon*, September 10, 1870.

16. *Columbiana Shelby Guide*, October 4, 1870.

17. *Carrollton West Alabamian*, October 5, 1870.

18. Ibid., October 12, 1870; John Gideon Harris Diary (1859), 24, SHC.

19. *Montgomery Advertiser*, September 17, 1870.

20. *Carrollton West Alabamian*, September 28, 1870.

21. *Montgomery Weekly Alabama State Journal*, October 7, 1870; *Demopolis Southern Republican*, October 19, 26, 1870; *Alabama Testimony*, I: Charles Hays, 15–16; Willard Warner, 26.

22. *Montgomery Weekly Alabama State Journal*, November 14, 1870; *Alabama Testimony*, I: Charles Hays, 14, Willard Warner, 26–28, John Pierce, 301, 303.

23. *Alabama Testimony*, I: Charles Hays, 14–15, Willard Warner, 27–28, John Pierce, 302; *Mobile Daily Register*, October 29, 1870; for a full account of the Eutaw Riot see Melinda Meek Hennessey, "Political Terrorism in the Black Belt," *Alabama Review* 33 (Summer 1981).

24. *Eutaw Whig and Observer*, quoted in *Mobile Daily Register*, October 29, 1870; *Alabama Testimony*, I: Arthur A. Smith, 44–45; for comment see *Selma Weekly Times*, October 29, 1870; *Montgomery Daily Mail*, November 2, 1870.

25. *Alabama Testimony*, III: John G. Harris, 1602; *Carrollton West Alabamian*, October 12, 1870; *Montgomery Daily Mail*, October 29, 1870.

26. *Greensboro Alabama Beacon*, November 5, 1870.

27. *Selma Southern Argus*, quoted in *Greensboro Alabama Beacon*, November 5, 1870.

28. *Greensboro Alabama Beacon*, November 19, 1870; Official Manuscript Returns, Congressional Election (1870), ADAH; Wiggins, *The Scalawag in Alabama Politics*, 68–71.

29. Capt. W. G. Wedemeyer to Capt. W. F. Drum, November 12, 1870, in Records of Adjutant General Office, Record Group 94, Roll 715, Microcopy 619, NA (hereinafter cited as Adjutant General Records); *Alabama Testimony*, I: Arthur Smith, 49–60, III: John Harris, 1588.

30. Official Manuscript Returns, Congressional Election (1870), ADAH; *Alabama Testimony*, I: Charles Hays, 17–18.

31. Deed Book of Greene County (Office of Probate Judge, Eutaw, Ala.), Y: 314–16, 319; for evidence of Hays's debts see *Alabama Testimony*, I: F. M. Kirksey, 537.

32. *Congressional Globe* (41st Congress, 3rd session), I: 5–11; Trelease, *White Terror*, 216–19; Swinney, "Suppressing the Ku Klux Klan," 138–41.

33. *Congressional Globe Appendix* (42nd Congress, 1st session), II: 197, 268–69, I: 512, 522; Swinney, "Suppressing the Ku Klux Klan," 144–48, 158, 160–63; Davis, "Alabama's Reconstruction Representatives," 36.

34. Joseph Sloss to Robert Lindsay, April 12, 1871, in Gov. Robert Burns Lindsay Papers, ADAH.

35. *Tuscaloosa Independent Monitor*, April 11, 1871.

36. Your Friend to Charles Hays, April 8, 1871, Lindsay Papers, ADAH; *Alabama Testimony*, II: William Blackford, 1272–73, 1290–91.

37. *Alabama Testimony*, I: Charles Hays, 20; Swinney, "Suppressing the Ku Klux Klan," 143.

38. *Congressional Globe* (42nd Congress, 1st session), I: 562; Dorris, *Pardon and Amnesty Under Lincoln and Johnson*, 369–73; Abbott, *The Republican Party and the South*, 215–17.

39. *Alabama Testimony*, I: Charles Hays, 12–13, 19–20, Arthur Smith, 61.

40. Charles Hays to Secretary of Treasury George G. Boutwell, May 17, 1871, in Records of Collector of Customs, Record Group 56, NA (hereinafter cited as Collector of Customs Applications); Wiggins, *The Scalawag in Alabama Politics*, 78–79; Current, *Those Terrible Carpetbaggers*, 169–70.

41. Charles Hays to Thomas M. Peters, June 30, 1871, in Collector of Customs Applications, NA; Seip, *The South Returns to Congress*, 119.

42. Thomas Peters to Ulysses Grant, July 4, 1871, in Collector of Customs Applications, NA.

43. Charles Hays to George Boutwell, June 30, 1871, in Collector of Customs Applications, NA.

44. *Greensboro Alabama Beacon*, August 26, 1871; Charles Hays to President Ulysses Grant, July 22, 1871, in Collector of Customs Applications, NA; Current, *Those Terrible Carpetbaggers*, 170.

45. Anthony Dillard to Charles Hays, August 27, 1871, in Collector of Customs Applications, NA; Current, *Those Terrible Carpetbaggers*, 171.

46. *Alabama Testimony*, I: Charles Hays, 12–25; Swinney, "Suppressing the Ku Klux Klan," 299–300.

47. *Alabama Testimony*, I: Jolly, 265, 291, 295.

48. Ibid., Pierce, 304, 308.

Chapter 6: The Sacred and Inalienable Rights of Liberty

1. Briggs, *The Olivia Letters*, 256; Greene, *Washington*, 340–41, 344–45, 355, 374–76; Boyd, *Directory of the District of Columbia* (Washington, 1872), 229, (1873), 235; interview with Lowndes, May 24, 1986.

2. *Congressional Globe* (42nd Congress, 2nd session), I: 9–10, 634, III: 2447, V: 3652; Dorris, *Pardon and Amnesty*, 375–78; Seip, *The South Returns to Congress*, 223–24.

3. *Congressional Globe* (42nd Congress, 2nd session), I: 7, II: 1109, IV: 3253; Dorris, *Pardon and Amnesty*, 375–78; Seip, *The South Returns to Congress*, 163–65; Trelease, *White Terror*, 401–4.

4. *Congressional Globe* (42nd Congress, 2nd session), IV: 3077–78, 3579–86, V: 3931, 4026–28, 4030–31; *Alabama Testimony*, I: Charles Hays, 16; Gillette, *Retreat from Reconstruction*, 182.

5. *Tuscaloosa Times*, September 25, 1872; Hays's hotel bill, Fifth Avenue Hotel, New York, New York, June 18, 1872, in possession of Lowndes.

6. *Marion Commonwealth*, May 23, 1872.

7. McFeely, *Grant*, 380–81; Wiggins, *The Scalawag in Alabama Politics*, 79–81; *Alabama State Journal*, August 16, 1872.

8. Gideon Harris to Robert McKee, April 13, 1872, McKee Papers, ADAH.

9. *Marion Commonwealth*, May 9, 23, 1872.

10. *Livingston Journal*, May 17, 1872.

11. *Marion Commonwealth*, June 6, 1872.

12. Gideon Harris to Robert McKee, May 31, 1872, McKee Papers, ADAH.

13. Brewer, *Alabama: Her History and Resources*, 561–62; Owen, *History of Alabama*, IV: 1597–98. See also Robert H. McKenzie, "William Russell Smith: Forgotten President of the University of Alabama," *Alabama Review* 37 (July 1984).

14. *Eutaw Whig and Observer*, August 15, 1872; *Mobile Daily Register*, August 10, 1872; *Montgomery Advertiser*, August 9, 1872; *Montgomery Alabama State Journal*, September 4, 1872.

15. *Marion Commonwealth*, September 5, 26, 1872; "Affairs in Alabama," Duncan Dew, 539; Powell, "The Politics of Livelihood: Carpetbaggers in the Deep South," in *Region, Race and Reconstruction*, edited by Koussar and Morgan.

16. *Livingston Journal*, September 27, 1872.

17. *Greensboro Alabama Beacon*, October 5, 1872.

18. *Shelby County Guide*, October 3, 1872.

19. *Eutaw Whig and Observer*, October 10, 1872.

20. *Montgomery Alabama State Journal*, October 30, 31, 1872.

21. *Tuscaloosa Times*, October 16, 1872.

22. Ibid., October 2, 1872; *Marion Commonwealth*, October 3, 1872.

23. *Montgomery Advertiser*, October 26, 1872; *Northport Spectator*, September 28, October 5, 1872; *Marion Commonwealth*, September 26, 1872.

24. George Spencer to William Chandler, September 1872, Chandler Papers, NA; *Livingston Journal*, October 25, November 1, 8, 1872; *Eutaw Whig and Observer*, October 31, 1872.

25. *North Port Spectator*, September 14, 1872; Official Manuscript Election Returns, ADAH; Wiggins, *The Scalawag in Alabama Politics*, 82–83.

26. Joseph F. Johnston to Frederick Bromberg, November 9, 1872, Frederick G. Bromberg Papers, SHC.

27. *Eutaw Whig and Observer*, November 14, 1872; J. F. Johnston to Frederick G. Bromberg, November 9, 1872, Frederick Bromberg Papers, SHC.

28. President Ulysses Grant to Charles Hays, November 16, 1872, in possession of Lowndes.

29. Cornelia Hays to Charlie, March 28, 1872, in possession of Lowndes; Boyd, *Boyd's Directory of the District of Columbia* (Washington, D.C.: Richard B. Mohun, 1875), 601.

30. *Congressional Globe* (42nd Congress, 3rd session), III: 1659–60, II: 1425.

31. Charles Hays to John W. Douglas, November 28, 1872, Collector of Customs Applications, NA; Wiggins, *The Scalawag in Alabama Politics*, 89.

32. Anthony Dillard to Charles Hays, August 27, 1871, Collector of Customs Applications, NA.

33. Cash, "Republicans During Reconstruction in Alabama," 221; Charles Hays to Daniel D. Pratt, May 18, 1875, Collector of Customs Applications, NA.

34. Charles Hays to Daniel Pratt, May 18, 1875, Collector of Customs Applications, NA.; Cash, "Republicans in Alabama," 221.

35. *Eutaw Whig and Observer*, January 30, March 6, 1873.

36. Charles Hays to B. Perry, June 23, 1873, Military Records Division, ADAH.

37. Deed Book of Greene County (Office of Probate Judge, Eutaw, Alabama), Z: 400–401; "Affairs in Alabama," Duncan Dew, 542–43.

38. Irwin Unger, *The Greenback Era: A Social and Political History of American Finance, 1865–1879* (Princeton: Princeton University Press, 1964), 213, 235–36;

Seip, *The South Returns to Congress*, 190–94; *Congressional Record* (43rd Congress, 1st session), III: 2376–77, IV: 3073; Davis, "Alabama's Reconstruction Representatives," 36.

39. *Congressional Record* (43rd Congress, 1st session), I: 18, 555; Gillette, *Retreat from Reconstruction*, 196–99.

40. *Congressional Record* (43rd Congress, 1st session), II: 1096–97, V: 4242–43, 4782–86.

41. Gillette, *Retreat from Reconstruction*, 202, 205–10.

42. *Congressional Record* (43rd Congress, 1st session), I: 74, 83, 625, II: 1332.

43. Ibid., IV: 3358–59, I: 762, 765.

44. *Eutaw Whig and Observer*, February 26, 1872, April 23, 30, 1874.

45. *Congressional Record* (43rd Congress, 1st session), IV: 3991, V: 4702; *Eutaw Whig and Observer*, April 23, 30, May 14, 1874; *Washington Evening Star*, May 22, 1874.

46. *Eutaw Whig and Observer*, February 26, 1874.

47. *Demopolis Marengo News Journal*, quoted in *Tuscaloosa Times*, June 10, 1874.

48. *Eutaw Whig and Observer*, June 11, 1874.

49. *Congressional Globe* (42nd Congress, 2nd session), IV: 3077.

50. *Congressional Record* (43rd Congress, 1st session), II: 1096.

51. *Congressional Globe* (42nd Congress, 2nd session), II: 1552; William C. Harris, *The Day of the Carpetbagger: Republican Reconstruction in Mississippi* (Baton Rouge: Louisiana State University Press, 1979), xii–xiii.

Chapter 7: The Hays-Hawley Letter

1. *Washington National Republican*, September 16, 1874; Gillette, *Retreat from Reconstruction*, 211–16, 225–30; Rable, *But There Was No Peace*, 114.

2. "Affairs in Alabama," James K. Greene, 320.

3. Ibid., William Taylor, 745, James Abrahams, 766; *Montgomery Alabama State Journal*, August 1, 1874.

4. *Meridian Mercury*, quoted in *Carrollton West Alabamian*, August 19, 1874; *Montgomery Alabama State Journal*, August 5, 9, 1874; *Montgomery Advertiser*, August 8, 11, 1874; Rogers and Pruitt, *Alabama's Outlaw Sheriff*, 45–48.

5. *Montgomery Alabama State Journal*, August 13, 1874.

6. *Montgomery Advertiser*, August 4, 1874; *Montgomery Alabama State Journal*, August 23, 1874; Perman, *Road to Redemption*, 156; Wiggins, *Scalawag in Alabama Politics*, 91–94; Foner, *Reconstruction*, 552.

7. "Affairs in Alabama," George Williams, 1225, 1247–48. For Grant's policy in the South see Gillette, *Retreat from Reconstruction*, 166–79.

8. *Hartford Daily Courant*, September 15, 1874; "Affairs in Alabama," Emmanuel H. Saltiel, 1123–24; McFeely, *Grant*, 276; Rogers and Pruitt, *Alabama's Outlaw Sheriff*, 49–51. See also John Bard McNulty, *Older Than the Nation: The Story of the Hartford Courant* (Storington, Conn.: Pequot Printing Press, 1964).

9. *Hartford Courant*, September 15, 1874; Joseph Hawley to Charles Dana, September 20, 1874, in Joseph R. Hawley Papers, Library of Congress, Division of Manuscripts. See also William Warren Rogers, Jr., "Reconstruction Journalism: The Hays-Hawley Letter," *American Journalism* 7 (Fall 1989), 7–19.

10. *Indianapolis Sentinel*, quoted in *Mobile Daily Register*, October 9, 1874.

11. *Cincinnati Commercial*, October 1, 1874.

12. *New York Tribune*, October 7, 12, 1874.

13. *St. Louis Post-Dispatch*, September 22, 1874.

14. *Nashville Union and Telegram*, October 6, 1874.

15. *San Francisco Examiner*, October 2, 1874; *Richmond Dispatch*, October 14, 1874; *Charleston News and Courier*, October 23, 1874; *New York Times*, October 24, 1874; *Atlanta Constitution*, October 17, 1874.

16. *New York Sun*, September 28, 1874. See for Dana, Frank O'Brien, *The Story of the Sun* (New York: D. Appleton and Co., 1908), 148–50, 187, 189.

17. *Cincinnati Daily Gazette*, September 18, 1874.

18. *Washington New National Era*, August 27, September 24, October 8, 1874.

19. *Washington National Republican*, October 12, 1874; *Boston Globe*, September 16, 1874.

20. "Affairs in Alabama," Zebulon White, 1080–91; *New York Tribune*, October 12, 1874. For Reid's trip, see Reid, *After the War*.

21. *New York Tribune*, October 15, 1874.

22. "Affairs in Alabama," Zebulon White, 1083; *New York Tribune*, October 15, 17, 1874.

23. Joseph Hawley to Charles Dana, September 20, 1874, Hawley Papers, NA; *Hartford Daily Courant*, October 1, 1874.

24. Stephen Hubbard to Joseph Hawley, September 29, 1874, Hawley Papers, NA; *Hartford Daily Courant*, September 15, 1874; "Affairs in Alabama," Duncan Dew, 539.

25. *Demopolis Marengo News Journal*, September 26, 1874; *Montgomery Advertiser*, September 22, 1874; *Greensboro Alabama Beacon*, September 26, October 3, 1874; *Carrollton West Alabamian*, September 16, October 7, 1874; *Mobile Daily Register*, October 7, 1874.

26. *Hartford Daily Courant*, September 15, 1874.

27. Stephen Hubbard to Joseph Hawley, September 29, 1874, Hawley Papers, NA; "Affairs in Alabama," John Stokes, 1069–70, Josiah N. Beach, 1186–97, P. J. Glaser, 878; *Carrollton West Alabamian*, September 30, 1874.

28. *Cincinnati Commercial*, September 28, 30, 1874; "Affairs in Alabama," Duncan Dew, 539; *Congressional Record* (43rd Congress, 2nd session), III: 1851; Gillette, *Retreat from Reconstruction*, 217–19.

29. *Montgomery Alabama State Journal*, August 26, 1874; *Cincinnati Commercial*, September 28, 30, 1874; Wiggins, *The Scalawag in Alabama Politics*, 91–97.

30. *Carrollton West Alabamian*, August 19, 26, 1874.

31. *Montgomery Advertiser*, July 7, 1874.

32. Augustus Benners to Henry Watson, September 16, 1874, in Henry Watson Papers, SHC.

33. *Montgomery Advertiser*, October 4, 1874; *Demopolis Marengo News Journal*, October 3, 1874.

34. *Tuscaloosa Blade*, August 6, 1874.

35. *Montgomery Alabama State Journal*, October 28, 1874; *Marion Commonwealth*, October 15, 1874.

36. *Montgomery Alabama State Journal*, October 16, 1874.

37. *Marion Commonwealth*, October 15, 1874.

38. *Tuscaloosa Blade*, October 22, 1874.

39. *Birmingham Independent*, quoted in *Montgomery Advertiser*, August 12, 1874; *Marion Commonwealth*, August 13, 1874.

40. Perman, *Road to Redemption*, 156–57.

41. Official Manuscript Returns, Congressional Election (1874), ADAH; Wiggins, *The Scalawag in Alabama Politics*, 97–98; Gillette, *Retreat from Reconstruction*, 180, 238–52.

Chapter 8: We Shall Not Falter in the Struggle

1. Cornelia Hays to Charles Hays, March 29, 1872, in possession of Lowndes.

2. *Congressional Record* (43rd Congress, 2nd session), I: 171, 319; Seip, *The South Returns to Congress*, 202–3.

3. *Congressional Record* (43rd Congress, 1st session), II: 1096; *Congressional Record* (43rd Congress, 2nd session), II: 1011; Gillette, *Retreat from Reconstruction*, 260–63, 267–73.

4. James Garfield to Burke A. Hinsdale, February 13, 1875, in James Garfield Presidential Papers, Library of Congress, Division of Manuscripts; *Congressional Record* (43rd Congress, 2nd session), III: 1851–53, 1936, I: 73; "Affairs in Alabama," ii, xxxiv, xliv, xlviv; *Washington Evening Star*, February 6, 12, 17, 1875; Gillette, *Retreat from Reconstruction*, 285–89. See for bacon controversy U.S. Congress, Executive Document 14, "Suffering from the Overflow of Rivers in the South" (43rd Congress, 2nd session).

5. *Congressional Record* (43rd Congress, 2nd session), III: 1823–39, 1851–53, 1885; Gillette, *Retreat from Reconstruction*, 291.

6. U.S. Congress, House Miscellaneous Document No. 177, "The Beardslee Cadet Investigation" (43rd Congress, 1st session), 20, 32, 36, 37, 40; Greene, *Washington*, 345, 348, 359.

7. *Eutaw Whig and Observer*, February 18, 1875; "Beardslee Cadet Scandal," 20; Wiggins, *The Scalawag in Alabama Politics*, 104; Allen J. Going, *Bourbon Democracy in Alabama, 1874–1890* (Tuscaloosa: University of Alabama Press, 1951), 20–26.

8. *Congressional Record* (44th Congress, 1st session), IV: 1605; "Affairs in Alabama," Duncan Dew, 540; Seip, "Southern Representatives and Economic Measures," 270; *Boyd's Directory of the District of Columbia* (1876), 614; Francis Butler Simkins and Robert Hilliard Woody, *South Carolina During Reconstruction* (Chapel Hill: University of North Carolina Press, 1932), 118–19.

9. Burwell Lewis to Louisa Lewis, October 25, 1874, Burwell Boykin Lewis Papers, SHC. For Lewis see *Biographical Directory of the American Congress*, 1286; "Beardslee Cadet Investigation," 2, 12–14, 47–48.

10. "Beardslee Cadet Investigation," 14, 20, 47–53.

11. Ibid., 46–47.

12. *New York Times*, March 18, 1875; *Congressional Record* (44th Congress, 1st session), IV: 1515, 4855; Allen Weinstein, *Prelude to Populism: Origins of the Silver Issue, 1867–1878* (New Haven & London: Yale University Press, 1970), 100–102; Nugent, *The Money Question During Reconstruction*, 93–95; McFeely, *Grant*, 439–45.

13. *Talladega Our Mountain Home*, May 3, 1876; *Eutaw Whig and Observer*, July 13, 1876; *Cincinnati Weekly Star*, June 15, 1876; *New York Times*, June 3, 9, 16, 1876; Schweninger, *James Rapier*, 151–53; Wiggins, *The Scalawag in Alabama Politics*, 109–13; Keith Ian Polakoff, *The Politics of Inertia: The Election of 1876 and the End of Reconstruction* (Baton Rouge: Louisiana State University Press, 1973), 16–17, 20–21, 30, 59–60, 67–68.

14. *Washington Evening Star*, March 23, 1876; *New York Herald Tribune*, March 11, 14, 17, 1876; *New York Times*, March 17, April 30, 1866; *New Orleans Times*, quoted in *Montgomery Advertiser*, March 21, 1876.

15. Charles Hays to Rutherford B. Hayes, March 3, 1877, in Rutherford B. Hayes Presidential Papers, at Rutherford B. Hayes Presidential Center, Spiegel Gove, Fremont, Ohio; *Tuscaloosa Times*, May 24, 1876; *Eutaw Whig and Observer*, July 13, 1876; C. Van Woodward, *Reunion and Reaction: The Compromise of 1877 and the End of Reconstruction* (Boston: Little, Brown, 1951), 202–3; Wiggins, *The Scalawag in Alabama Politics*, 114–15.

16. Anne Miller Womack to Charles Hays, June 15, 1877, in possession of Lowndes.

17. *Eutaw Whig and Observer*, August 9, 1877.

18. "Address of Charles Hays," in "Proceedings of the Republican State Convention, held in Montgomery, Alabama, on July 4, 1878," in Lewis F. Parsons Pamphlet Collection, ADAH.

19. Charles Hays to Anne Miller Womack, March 11, 1879, in possession of Lowndes; Annual Premium, Office of Phoenix Mutual Life Insurance Company, March 7, 1878, in Hays Surname File, ADAH.

20. *Eutaw Whig and Observer*, quoted in *Montgomery Advertiser*, June 29, 1879. See also *Livingston Journal*, June 27, 1879; *Mobile Daily Register*, June 28, 1874; *Tuscaloosa Gazette*, July 3, 1874; *Carrollton West Alabamian*, July 2, 1879; *Eutaw Mirror*, June 24, 1879.

21. *Eutaw Whig and Observer*, quoted in *Montgomery Advertiser*, June 29, 1879.

Epilogue

1. *Congressional Globe* (42nd Congress, 2nd session), IV: 3077.

2. *Hartford Courant*, September 15, 1874.

3. *Congressional Record* (43rd Congress, 2nd session), III: 1852.

4. Seip, *The South Returns to Congress*, 37.

5. *Congressional Record* (43rd Congress, 2nd session), III: 1852; *Congressional Globe* (42nd Congress, 1st session), I: 436–41.

6. *Congressional Globe and Appendix* (42nd Congress, 2nd session), VI: 583.

7. *Hartford Courant*, September 15, 1874.

8. "Affairs in Alabama," P. J. Glover, 877.

9. *Congressional Record* (43rd Congress, 2nd session), III: 1852.

10. James G. Blaine, *Twenty Years of Congress, From Lincoln to Garfield* (Norwich, Conn.: Henry Bill Publishing Co., 1886), II: 448.

11. "Affairs in Alabama," Duncan Dew, 540.

12. Ibid., John P. Southworth, 1143–44.

13. *Congressional Record* (43rd Congress, 2nd session), III: 1852.

Bibliography

Primary Sources

Manuscripts

Alabama State Department of Archives and History, Montgomery
    Alabama Tract Book, Index, A, C, E.
    Civil Register County Officials, I (1819–1832).
    Dustan, Charles W. Papers.
    Gould, William Proctor. *Diary* (4 volumes).
    Hays Family Papers (in Surname File).
    Lewis, Governor David P. Papers.
    Lindsay, Governor Robert. Papers.
    McKee, Robert. Papers.
    Parsons, Governor Lewis. Papers.
    Patton, Governor Robert M. Papers.
    Secretary of the State of Alabama. Papers. Original Manuscript Returns for Presidential, Congressional, and State Elections in Alabama.
    Smith, Governor William Hugh. Letterbook, Nos. 15, 16.
    Smith, Governor William Hugh. Papers.
    Womack, John Warburton. Papers (Scrapbook).
Duke University Library, Special Collections Department
    Crawford, Samuel Wylie. Papers.
    Lewis, Burwell Boykin. Papers.
    Watson, Henry. Papers.
Rutherford B. Hayes Library, Fremont, Ohio
    Hayes, Rutherford B. Papers.

Library of Congress, Washington, D.C., Division of Manuscripts
  Chandler, William E. Papers.
  Garfield, James. Papers.
  Hawley, Joseph R. Papers.
  Johnson, Andrew. Papers.
  Sherman, John. Papers.
National Archives, Washington, D.C.
  Adjutant General's Office, Record Group 94.
  Bureau of Refugees, Freedmen, and Abandoned Lands, Record Group 105.
  Department of the Treasury, Applications for Collectors of Customs, Alabama,
    Record Group 56.
University of North Carolina, Southern Historical Collection
  Alcorn, James Lusk. Papers.
  Bromberg, Frederick G. Papers.
  Harris, John Gideon. Papers.
  Watson, Henry. Papers.
  Wright, Marcus Joseph. Papers.
Private Collection
  Meredith, E. C. "Reconstruction in Alabama." Estate of Roy Swayze, Eutaw,
    Alabama.

U.S. Government Publications

Biographical Directory of the American Congress, 1774–1971 (Washington, D.C.: U.S.
  Government Printing Office, 1971).
Congressional Globe, 40th, 41st, 42nd Congress.
Congressional Record, 43rd, 44th Congress.
List of Staff Officers of the Confederate States Army (Washington, D.C., 1891).
U. S. Bureau of the Census, Eighth Census of the United States: 1860.
——. Executive Documents, No. 14, "Suffering From the Overflow of Rivers in
  the South," 43rd Congress, 2nd session.
——. Executive Documents, No. 16, "Final Report of the Names of Persons
  Engaged in Rebellion who have been Pardoned," 39th Congress, 2nd session.
——. Miscellaneous Documents, No. 177, "The Beardslee Cadet Investigation,"
  44th Congress, 1st session.
——. Ninth Census of the United States: 1870.
——. Reports, No. 22, "Testimony Taken by the Joint Select Committee to In-
  quire Into the Condition of Affairs in the Late Insurrectionary States, Alabama,"
  42nd Congress, 2nd session.
——. Reports, No. 262, "Affairs in Alabama," 43rd Congress, 2nd session.
——. Reports, No. 704, "The Subcommittee of the Committee for Privileges and

Elections Report [on] Elections of 1874, 1875, and 1876," 44th Congress, 2nd session.
——— . Seventh Census of the United States: 1850.
——— . Statistical View of the United States . . . Compendium of the Seventh Census: 1850.
U.S. Congress, House. Executive Documents, No. 238, "Report of General George Meade," 39th Congress, 2nd session.

Official Alabama Documents

Acts of the Sessions of July, September, and November, 1868, of The General Assembly of Alabama. Montgomery: James Stokes & Co., 1868.
Alabama Manuscript Agricultural Census, 1850, II: DeKalb-Morgan.
Alabama Manuscript Slave Census, 1860, I: Autauga-Madison.
Alabama Reports 2 (1841). Tuscaloosa: Hale & Phelan, 1842.
Alabama Reports 19 (1851). Montgomery: J. H. & T. F. Martin, 1852.
Alabama Reports 25 (1854). Montgomery: Coward Martin, 1855.
Journal of the House of Representatives of the State of Alabama, 1829. Tuscaloosa: McGuire, Henry & Walker, 1830.
Journal of the Senate of the State of Alabama, 1868. Montgomery: James Stokes & Co., 1868.
Official Journal of the Constitutional Convention of the State of Alabama, 1867. Montgomery: Barrett & Brown, 1868.
"Report of [the] Joint Committee on Outrages." Montgomery: James Stokes & Co., 1868.

County Records

Chester County Courthouse, Chester, South Carolina. Probate Judge Office
Will Record Book, H.
Greene County Courthouse, Eutaw, Alabama. Probate Judge Office
Deed Record Book, A, B, C, G, H, X.
Will Record Book, B (1827–1841).

Newspapers

Atlanta Constitution, 1874.
Boston Daily Globe, 1874.
Butler Choctaw Herald, 1879.
Carrollton West Alabamian, 1868–1870, 1872, 1874, 1879.
Charleston News and Courier, 1874.

Cincinnati Commercial, 1868, 1874.

Cincinnati Daily Gazette, 1874.

Columbiana Shelby County Guide, 1870, 1872, 1874.

Demopolis Southern Republican, 1869, 1870.

Eutaw Mirror, 1879.

Eutaw Whig and Observer, 1863, 1864, 1872, 1874–1877.

Gainesville News, 1869.

Greensboro Alabama Beacon, 1843, 1848–1850, 1859, 1865, 1866, 1868–1872, 1874.

Hartford Daily Courant, 1874.

Indianapolis Sentinel, 1874.

Livingston Journal, 1872, 1874, 1876, 1879.

Louisville Courier-Journal, 1874.

Marengo (Demopolis) News Journal, 1873, 1874, 1876.

Marion Commonwealth, 1869, 1870, 1872, 1874.

Memphis Daily Avalanche, 1874.

Mobile Daily Register, 1868, 1870–1872, 1874, 1879.

Mobile Press Register, 1874.

Montgomery Advertiser, 1867–1870, 1872, 1874, 1878–1879.

Montgomery Alabama State Journal, 1868–1870, 1872, 1874.

Montgomery Daily Mail, 1868, 1870.

Montgomery Daily Picayune, 1868.

Montgomery Daily State Sentinel, 1867, 1868.

Montgomery Weekly Advertiser, 1867.

Montgomery Weekly Alabama State Journal, 1868–1870.

Montgomery Weekly Mail, 1869.

New Orleans Daily Republican, 1874.

New York Herald, 1867.

New York Sun, 1874.

New York Times, 1874, 1876.

New York Tribune, 1874, 1876.

North Port Spectator, 1872.

Richmond Dispatch, 1874.

St. Louis Post Dispatch, 1874.

San Francisco Examiner, 1874.

Selma Southern Argus, 1869, 1870.

Selma Times and Messenger, 1868.

Sumter County Guide, 1874.

Talladega Our Mountain Home, 1876.

Tuscaloosa Gazette, 1879.

Tuscaloosa Independent Monitor, 1867–1870.

Tuscaloosa Times, 1872, 1874, 1876.

Tuscaloosa Times Gazette, 1910.
Washington Evening Star, 1868, 1872, 1875, 1876.
Washington National Republican, 1874.
Washington New National Era, 1874.

Contemporary Articles, Books, Catalogues, Pamphlets,
and Speeches

A Catalogue of the Officers and Students of Franklin College, Athens, 1851–52. Athens: Christy & Lelsea, 1851.

A Catalogue of the Officers and Students of Franklin College, Athens, 1852–53. Athens: Christy & Lelsea, 1852.

Barnes, William H. *The History of the Congress of the United States, 1869–1871.* New York: W. H. Barnes & Co., 1872.

Blaine, James G. *Twenty Years of Congress, From Lincoln to Garfield*, 2 vols. Norwich, Conn.: Henry Bill Publishing Co., 1886.

Boyd, William, comp. *Boyd's Directory of the District of Columbia.* Washington, D.C.: Richard B. Mohun, 1875–1876.

――― . *Boyd's Directory of Washington, Georgetown, and Alexandria.* Washington, D.C.: Hudson Taylor Book Store, 1870.

Briggs, Emily Edison. *The Olivia Letters.* Washington, D.C.: Neale Publishing Co., 1906.

Catalogue of the Students of the Greene Springs for the Sixth Scholastic Year, Ending May 25, 1853. Tuscaloosa: M. D. M. Slade, 1853.

Catalogue of the Trustees, Officers, Alumni, and Matriculates of the University of Georgia, at Athens, Georgia from 1795 to 1906. Athens: E. F. Stone Press, 1901.

Catalogue of the University of Virginia Session of 1852–53. Richmond: H. K. Ellyson, 1853.

Clemenceau, George. *American Reconstruction, 1865–1870 and the Impeachment of President Johnson.* New York: Dial Press, 1928.

Deedes, Henry. *Sketches of the South and West.* Edinburgh: William Blackford & Sons, 1869.

Ellis, John B. *The Sights and Secrets of the National Capital: A Work Descriptive of Washington In All Its Various Phases.* New York: United States Publishing Co., 1869.

Hays, Charles. Address, in "Proceedings of the Republican State Convention, Held in Montgomery, Alabama on July 4, 1878," Lewis F. Parsons Pamphlet Collection.

Reid, Whitelaw. *After the War: A Southern Tour.* London: Moore, Wilstach & Baldwin, 1866.

Screws, Benjamin H. *The "Loil" Legislature of Alabama: Its Ridiculous Doings and Nonsensical Sayings.* Montgomery: R. W. Offutt & Co., 1868.

Snedecor, V. Gayle. *A Directory of Greene County For 1855–6.* Mobile: Strickland & Co., 1856.

Trowbridge, J. T. *The South: A Tour of Its Battlefields and Ruined Cities.* Hartford: L. Stebbins, 1866.

University of Virginia Matriculation Book, 2. N.p., n.d.

Secondary Sources

State Histories and General Works

Brewer, Willis. *Alabama: Her History, Resources, War Record, and Public Men from 1640 to 1872.* Montgomery: Barrett Brown Printers, 1872.

Garrett, William. *Reminiscences of Public Men in Alabama for Thirty Years.* Atlanta: Plantation Publishing Co., 1872.

Owen, Thomas McAdory. *History of Alabama and Dictionary of Alabama Biography*, 4 vols. Spartanburg, S.C.: Reprint Co., 1878.

Monographs

Abbott, Richard H. *The Republican Party and the South, 1855–1877: The First Southern Strategy.* Chapel Hill: University of North Carolina Press, 1986.

Alexander, Thomas B. *Political Reconstruction in Tennessee.* Nashville: Vanderbilt University Press, 1950.

Barney, William L. *The Secessionist Impulse: Alabama and Mississippi in 1860.* Princeton: Princeton University Press, 1974.

Benedict, Michael Les. *A Compromise of Principle: Congressional Republicans and Reconstruction, 1863–1869.* New York: Norton, 1974.

Bentley, George R. *A History of the Freedmen's Bureau.* Philadelphia: University of Pennsylvania, 1955.

Boatner, Mark Mayo. *The Civil War Dictionary.* New York: David McKay Co., 1959.

Cox, LaWanda, and John Cox. *Politics, Principle, and Prejudice, 1865–1866: Dilemma of Reconstruction America.* London: Free Press of Glenscoe, 1963.

Current, Richard. *Those Terrible Carpetbaggers.* New York: Oxford University Press, 1988.

Dorris, Jonathan Truman. *Pardon and Amnesty under Lincoln and Johnson: The Restoration of the Confederates to Their Rights and Privileges, 1861–1868.* Chapel Hill: University of North Carolina Press, 1953.

DuBose, John Witherspoon. *Alabama's Tragic Decade: Ten Years of Alabama, 1865–1874.* Birmingham: Webb Book Co., 1940.

Fitzgerald, Michael W. *The Union League Movement in the Deep South: Politics and Agricultural Change During Reconstruction.* Baton Rouge: Louisiana State University Press, 1989.

Fleming, Walter Lynwood. *Civil War and Reconstruction in Alabama.* New York: Columbia University Press, 1905.

Flynt, J. Wayne. *Montgomery: An Illustrated History.* Woodland Hills, Calif.: Windsor Publications, 1980.

Foner, Eric. *Reconstruction: America's Unfinished Revolution, 1863–1877.* New York: Harper & Row, 1988.

Gandrud, Pauline Jones, comp. *Marriage Records of Greene County, Alabama, 1823–1860.* Memphis: Milestone Press, 1969.

Gillette, William. *Retreat From Reconstruction, 1869–1879.* Baton Rouge: Louisiana State University Press, 1979.

Glass, Mary Morgan, ed. *A Goodly Heritage: Memories of Greene County.* Eutaw, Ala.: Greene County Historical Society, 1977.

Going, Allen Johnston. *Bourbon Democracy in Alabama, 1874–1890.* University: University of Alabama Press, 1951.

Green, Constance McLaughlin. *Washington: Village and Capital, 1800–1878.* Princeton: Princeton University Press, 1962.

Howard, Gene L. *Death at Cross Plains: An Alabama Reconstruction Tragedy.* Tuscaloosa: University of Alabama Press, 1984.

Kolchin, Peter. *First Freedom: The Responses of Alabama's Blacks to Emancipation and Reconstruction.* Westport, Conn.: Greenwood Press, 1972.

Koussar, J. Morgan and James M. McPherson, eds. *Religion, Race, and Reconstruction. Essays in Honor of C. Vann Woodward.* New York: Oxford University Press, 1982.

Lancaster, Clay. *Eutaw: The Builders and Architecture of an Ante-Bellum Southern Town.* Eutaw, Ala.: Greene County Historical Society, 1979.

Little, John Bucker. *The History of Butler County, Alabama, 1815 to 1885.* Cincinnati: Elm Street Printing Co., 1895.

McFeely, William S. *Grant: A Biography.* New York: Norton, 1981.

McMillan, Malcolm Cook. *Constitutional Development in Alabama, 1798–1901: A Study in Politics, the Negro, and Sectionalism.* Chapel Hill: University of North Carolina Press, 1955.

McNulty, John Bard. *Older Than the Nation: The Story of the Hartford Courant.* Storington, Conn.: Pequot Printing Press, 1964.

McPherson, James M. *Ordeal by Fire: The Civil War and Reconstruction.* New York: Alfred A. Knopf, 1982.

Nugent, Walter T. K. *The Money Question During Reconstruction.* New York: Norton, 1967.

O'Brien, Frank M. *The Story of the Sun, New York: 1833–1928.* New York: D. Appleton and Co., 1928.

Olson, Otto H., ed. *Reconstruction and Redemption in the South*. Baton Rouge: Louisiana State University Press, 1980.

Perman, Michael. *The Road to Redemption: Southern Politics, 1869–1879*. Chapel Hill: University of North Carolina Press, 1984.

——. *Reunion Without Compromise: The South and Reconstruction, 1865–1868*. New York: Cambridge University Press, 1973.

Polakoff, Keith Ian. *The Politics of Inertia: The Election of 1876 and the End of Reconstruction*. Baton Rouge: Louisiana State University Press, 1973.

Rable, George C. *But There Was No Peace: The Role of Violence in the Politics of Reconstruction*. Athens: University of Georgia Press, 1984.

Ransom, Roger, and Richard Sutch. *One Kind of Freedom: The Economic Consequences of Emancipation*. New York: Cambridge University Press, 1977.

Roark, James L. *Masters Without Slaves: Southern Planters in the Civil War and Reconstruction*. New York: Norton, 1977.

Rogers, William Warren. *The One-Gallused Rebellion: Agrarianism in Alabama, 1875–1896*. Baton Rouge: Louisiana State University Press, 1970.

Rogers, William Warren, and Ruth Pruitt. *Stephen S. Renfroe: Alabama's Outlaw Sheriff*. Tallahassee, Fla.: Sentry Press, 1972.

Rogers, William Warren, and Robert David Ward. *August Reckoning: Jack Turner and Racism in Post–Civil War Alabama*. Baton Rouge: Louisiana State University Press, 1973.

Schweninger, Loren. *James T. Rapier and Reconstruction*. Chicago: University of Chicago Press, 1978.

Sefton, James E. *The United States and Reconstruction, 1865–1877*. Baton Rouge: Louisiana State University Press, 1967.

Seip, Terry L. *The South Returns to Congress: Men, Economic Measures, and Intersectional Relationships, 1868–1879*. Baton Rouge: Louisiana State University Press, 1983.

Simkins, Francis B., and Robert Hilliard Woody. *South Carolina During Reconstruction*. Chapel Hill: University of North Carolina Press, 1932.

Stampp, Kenneth M. *The Era of Reconstruction, 1865–1877*. New York: Knopf, 1965.

Summers, Mark W. *Railroads, Reconstruction, and the Gospel of Prosperity: Aid Under the Radical Republicans, 1865–1877*. Princeton: Princeton University Press, 1984.

Thornton, J. Mills III. *Politics and Power in a Slave Society: Alabama, 1800–1860*. Baton Rouge: Louisiana State University Press, 1978.

Trelease, Allen W. *White Terror: The Ku Klux Klan Conspiracy and Southern Reconstruction*. New York: Harper & Row, 1971.

Unger, Irwin. *The Greenback Era: A Social and Political History of American Finance, 1865–1979*. Princeton: Princeton University Press, 1964.

Weinstein, Allen. *Prelude to Populism: Origins of the Silver Issue, 1867–1878*. New Haven & London: Yale University Press, 1970.

Whyte, James H. *The Uncivil War: Washington During the Reconstruction, 1865–1878*. New York: Twayne, 1958.

Wiener, Jonathan M. *Social Origins of the New South Alabama, 1865–1881*. University: University of Alabama Press, 1977.

Yerby, William Edward Wadsworth. *History of Greensboro, Alabama From its Earliest Settlement*. Montgomery, Ala.: Paragon Press, 1908.

Periodical Publications

Alexander, Thomas B. "Persistent Whiggery in Alabama and the Lower South, 1860–1867," *Alabama Review* 12 (January 1959).

Bethel, Elizabeth. "The Freedmen's Bureau in Alabama," *Journal of Southern History* 14 (February 1948).

Davis, Thomas J. "Alabama's Reconstruction Representatives in the U.S. Congress, 1868–1878: A Profile," *Alabama Historical Quarterly* 44 (Spring-Summer 1982).

Hennessey, Melinda Meek. "Political Terrorism in the Black Belt: The Eutaw Riot," *Alabama Review* 33 (January 1980).

McKenzie, Robert H. "William Russell Smith: Forgotten President of the University of Alabama," *Alabama Review* 37 (July 1984).

Rhodes, Robert S. "The Registration of Voters and the Election of Delegates to the Reconstruction Convention in Alabama," *Alabama Review* 8 (April 1955).

Rogers, William Warren. "'Politics is Mighty Uncertain': Charles Hays Goes to Congress," *Alabama Review* 30 (July 1977).

——. "The Boyd Incident: Black Belt Violence During Reconstruction," *Civil War History* 21 (December 1975).

Rogers, William Warren, Jr. "Reconstruction Journalism: The Hays-Hawley Letter," *American Journalism* 7 (Fall 1989).

——. "The Eutaw Prisoners: Federal Confrontation with Violence in Reconstruction Alabama," *Alabama Review* 43 (April 1990).

Schweninger, Loren. "Alabama Blacks and the Congressional Reconstruction Acts of 1867," *Alabama Review* 31 (July 1978).

Trelease, Allen W. "Who Were the Scalawags?," *Journal of Southern History* 29 (November 1963).

Wiggins, Sarah Woolfolk. "The Life of Ryland Randolph As Seen Through His Letters to John W. DuBose," *Alabama Historical Quarterly* 30 (Fall-Winter 1968).

Woolfolk, Sarah Van. "George E. Spencer: A Carpetbagger in Alabama," *Alabama Review* 19 (January 1966).

———. "Amnesty and Pardon and Republicanism in Alabama," *Alabama Historical Quarterly* 27 (Summer 1964).

———. "Five Men Called Scalawags," *Alabama Review* 17 (January 1964).

———. "Carpetbaggers in Alabama: Tradition Versus Truth," *Alabama Review* 15 (April 1962).

Theses and Dissertations

Bell, Robert K. "Reconstruction in Tuscaloosa County." M.A. thesis, University of Alabama, 1933.

Cash, William McKinley. "Alabama Republicans During Reconstruction: Personal Characteristics, Motivations, and Political Activity of Party Activists, 1867–1880." Ph.D. dissertation, University of Alabama, 1973.

Dudley, William Bell. "The Reconstruction Klan: A Survey of the Writings of the Klan With a Profile and Analysis of the Alabama Klan Episode, 1866–1874." Ph.D. dissertation, Louisiana State University, 1973.

Folmar, John Kent. "The Depletion of Republican Congressional Support for Enforcement of Reconstruction Measures: A Roll-Call Analysis, 1871–1877." Ph.D. dissertation, University of Alabama, 1968.

Gilmour, Richard A. "The Other Emancipation: Studies in the Society and Economy of Alabama Whites during Reconstruction." Ph.D. dissertation, Johns Hopkins University, 1972.

Hume, Richard. "The 'Black and Tan' Constitutional Conventions of 1867–1869 in Ten Former Confederate States: A Study of Their Membership." Ph.D. dissertation, University of Washington, 1969.

Jones, H. H. "The History of Bibb County During Reconstruction (1865–1876)." M.A. thesis, University of Alabama, 1933.

Parnell, Ralph Erskine. "The Administration of William Hugh Smith: Governor of Alabama, 1868–1870." M.A. thesis, Auburn University, 1958.

Ryan, John Burkett, Jr. "William Warner: Soldier, Senator, and Southern Entrepreneur." M.A. thesis, Auburn University, 1971.

Seip, Terry Lee. "Southern Representatives and Economic Measures During Reconstruction: A Quantitative and Analytical Study." Ph.D. dissertation, Louisiana State University, 1974.

Sindon, Nancy Anne. "The Career of Ryland Randolph: A Study in Reconstruction Journalism." M.A. thesis, Florida State University, 1965.

Swinney, Everette. "Suppressing the Ku Klux Klan: The Enforcement of the Reconstruction Amendments, 1870–1874." Ph.D. dissertation, University of Texas, 1966.

Taylor, James Leroy. "A History of the Ku Klux Klan in Alabama, 1865–1874." M.A. thesis, Auburn University, 1957.

Thomas, James D., Jr. "The Alabama Constitutional Convention of 1867." M.A. thesis, Auburn University, 1947.

Index